Whole-Scale Change:
Unleashing the Magic
in Organizations

Whole-Scale Change:
Unleashing the Magic in Organizations

Dannemiller Tyson Associates

BERRETT-KOEHLER PUBLISHERS, INC.
San Francisco

Berrett-Koehler Publishers, Inc.
450 Sansome Street, Suite 1200
San Francisco, CA 94111-3320
Tel: (415) 288-0260; Fax: (415) 362-2512; www.bkconnection.com

ORDERING INFORMATION

Quantity sales. Special discounts are available on quantity purchases by corporations,
associations, and others. For details contact the "Special Sales Department" at the
Berrett-Koehler address above.

Individual sales. Berrett-Koehler publications are available through most bookstores.
They can also be ordered direct from Berrett-Koehler:
Tel: (800) 929-2929; Fax: (802) 864-7626; www.bkconnection.com

Orders for college textbook/course adoption use.
Please contact Berrett-Koehler:
Tel: (800) 929-2929; Fax: (802) 864-7626

Orders by U.S. trade bookstores and wholesalers.
Please contact: Publishers Group West, 1700 Fourth Street, Berkeley, CA 94710
Tel: (510) 528-1444; Fax (510) 528-3444

Printed in the United States of America
Printed on acid-free and recycled paper that is composed of 85% recovered fiber,
including 15% post-consumer waste.

Library of Congress Cataloging-in-Publication Data
Whole-scale change : unleashing the magic in organizations /
    by Dannemiller Tyson Associates ... [et al.].
      p. cm.
    Includes bibliographical references and index.
    ISBN 1-57675-088-4 (pbk.)
    1. Organizational change. I. Dannemiller Tyson Associates. II. Title.
HD58.8 .W48 2000
658.4'06—dc21

00-010707

First Edition
05   04   03   02   10 9 8 7 6 5 4 3 2

The authors of this book are 15 consultants,
all partners of Dannemiller Tyson Associates in 1999
when we wrote this book together.
Using our own Whole-Scale processes,
we worked as a community,
one-brain and one-heart,
to bring our best wisdom to the
content of this book.

Kathleen D. Dannemiller, Paul D. Tolchinsky, Roland Loup, Sylvia James,
Jeff Belanger, Albert B. Blixt, Kathryn Church, Mary Eggers, Allen B. Gates,
Leigh M. Hennen, Henry Johnson, Lorri E. Johnson,
Stas' Kazmierski, Ron Koller, and Jim McNeil

Special thanks to Christine Valenza
for her creative graphic contributions.

Contents

C H A P T E R 3

Building Momentum:
Planning the Whole-Scale Project 45

C H A P T E R 4

Unleashing the Magic:
Strategic Direction 67

C H A P T E R 5

Co-Creating:
Designing Organizations 91

C H A P T E R 7

Sustaining the Momentum Systemically

D E E P D I V E B

Models and Processes
that Unleash the Magic 213

D E E P D I V E C

Strategic Planning
Models and Tools 235

D EEP D IVE D

Resources 253

Preface

What you hold in your hands is a very valuable map to the New World of organizational change. For many years, the brave folks at Dannemiller Tyson Associates have been pioneers and explorers. While many of us hovered at the edges of this New World, peering out across its dark and turbulent waters, wondering whether it was possible to change our methods and beliefs, they plunged into the unknown. Now, after many years of experimenting with radically new approaches to organizational change, they are sharing their hard-won maps with us. I'm grateful that they have been so courageous and that they kept such good records.

Dannemiller Tyson Associates set sail from the Old World that had taught us many restricting and pessimistic beliefs about ourselves as human beings. We were told that humans work well together only in small groups, that experts have our answers, that most people lack the ability to think creatively, and that people want to be told what to do by their leaders. These beliefs, and many more, are still discernible in most organizational change strategies. Most change techniques are variations on this basic process: A select few are assumed to know what is best for everyone. Vision, redesign, reward structures—each of these is the work of a few smart people. Small groups of the smart are sent off to do their work. Then they return to the organization and tell people what to do. All these others are eagerly waiting for the results. They gratefully accept the new set of directions and eagerly implement them. Everything works according to plan, and the organization is transformed.

Though this approach to change still predominates, we have a lot of firsthand experience with its failures. Research from several different sources (and, I assume, from your own experience) demonstrates that between 70% and 90% of change initiatives fail to achieve their objectives. The same is true for mergers and acquisitions. Not only do they fail to achieve promised results, they create many more problems with their unintended consequences.

From this abysmal record of failures, we can draw one of two conclusions: *Either it is impossible to change human organizations, or we're using the wrong approaches.* Because of our colleagues at Dannemiller Tyson Associates, we now know that *it is possible* to change, that it is our approaches that have been wrong, and that, with the right methods, true magic is possible.

All those engaged with whole system approaches are teaching us that when the entire organization or community is engaged in the work of planning its own future, or dealing with a difficult and meaningful issue, wondrous possibilities emerge. Using the term *magic* is absolutely appropriate. People who engage the whole of a system always use the word *miraculous* to describe the results. And after all the negative images we've carried for so many years—believing our colleagues were dull, self-serving, greedy, and disinterested—what we observe at a whole system event *is* miraculous. We quickly notice that our colleagues are engaged, creative, funny, compassionate, and forgiving. We discover one another in our full power, no longer held back by confining beliefs, stereotypes, or roles. We discover that we all care about the organization, that we all want to contribute, and that we're all surprisingly creative.

Now *that* is a miracle.

And this is a time that requires miracles. We can no longer solve the problems of organizations, communities, or nations by staying apart, leaving it to the experts, or depending on leaders to solve our difficulties. Yet at the very time when we most need to come together, we live with badly fractured relationships. Leaders don't trust workers; we don't trust one another; intractable problems refuse to be solved by piecemeal approaches. Everyone is exhausted by endless meetings, meaningless work, data overload, recurring conflicts, bad behaviors, heroic leaders, and problems that get larger rather than resolved.

I believe that, at its essence, our work is to reweave the world—to call together those we have kept apart, to understand problems in all their rich dimensions, to become sensitive to how systems move and change, to become aware of human potential rather than human problems. We are finding our way past the fragmenting and dehumanizing values of a worldview that told us we humans and the whole world could be understood by breaking things apart. As we free ourselves from this mechanistic worldview, we are invited to return to a more humane and traditional way of working together. Our species memory offers us the knowledge of how to work together for the common community— how to develop systems of relationships that sustain not only individuals, but the whole system. This memory and skillfulness is in us because it is in all life. We are remembering not how machines are put together, but how life organizes. It is this deep wisdom that needs to return to our organizational processes.

The wisdom is in each of us, and we are blessed that Dannemiller Tyson Associates has given us their maps. They lead us back to the rich and fertile land of human capacity and to a future where people know how to work together in relationships that give birth to new possibilities.

> Margaret J. Wheatley
> Author, *Leadership and the New Science*
> Co-author, *A Simpler Way*

Discovering the Magic:
What Is Whole-Scale?

Introduction

Our ever-changing environment combined with the warp speed of technology has placed unparalleled demands and expectations on each of us both where we work and where we live. These demands require leaders to uncover new approaches that harness the tumult, speed, and complexity of the new environment and use them to the organization's advantage. These demands are also requiring employees to adapt, change, and then change again, as they respond to the same challenges facing their leaders. As consultants, we believe there is an overwhelming need to change from the old structural organizational models of the twentieth century. We need commonsense ways to tap into and unleash the wisdom present in the entire workforce. We need processes to release the energy and combine that knowledge. That is the reason we believe that the Whole-Scale methodology makes important sense today. Whole-Scale enables the organization to quickly and effectively assess today's environment and map and implement a strategy to deal with it successfully now and in the future.

This writing is driven by the urgency we feel in bringing about change that empowers organizations and the people in those organizations to be truly successful in the future. We want to "open our hearts," share some of our experiences, and pass on ideas, theories, models, and processes that are robust in creating change.

The Richmond Savings Story—1995

We were approached by the President and CEO and the human resources director of the third largest credit union in Canada. They asked if we would go to Vancouver to work with their organization, using our Whole-Scale processes. These two men had been able to observe a Whole-Scale large-group event the month before and had a vision of what they could accomplish with their own organization.

Richmond is a suburb of Vancouver, changing culturally based on the influx of immigrating Hong Kong Chinese who are settling and building houses in Richmond. The president, Kirk Lawrie, had worked out a new Vision statement for the credit union in response to these changes. After seeing the Whole-Scale event with another company, he realized that he needed to involve all of his employees in setting direction toward that Vision for the year 2000.

Two Dannemiller Tyson Associates partners met with the Leadership Group of Richmond Savings and developed a draft Mission and Strategic Goals statements that could be articulated to and enriched by the entire organization in a series of large and small events. The first event was with a group that we call the Event Planning Team (EPT), which was a true microcosm of the whole credit union, including one of the leaders, a couple of middle management directors, and front line people of all types (tellers, loan officers, secretaries, technicians, and so forth). This group of twenty met with the consultants for two days to agree on a meaningful purpose and agenda for a large group event (250 participants). Together they answered the questions:

1. What will be different in our world as a result of these 250 meeting for three days (Purpose)?

2. Who needs to be in the meeting in order to achieve that Purpose?

3. What conversations need to take place among that group in order to achieve that Purpose?

The Purpose this group debated and finally consensed on was:

> To ensure the continuing success of Richmond Savings by
> capturing and focusing the energy toward shared direction,
> actions, and results, where each individual and group
> understands, passionately commits, and contributes to
> that collective success.

At that point, the group agreed there were some people missing from their own microcosm Event Planning Team, whose voices needed to be part of planning with the Purpose in mind. These people were invited and joined us. We then agreed on the following plan:

Days one and two would be a diagonal slice of people (another, and larger microcosm) representing all of the levels and functions of work geography (branches, central office). That group held discussions for two days, hearing from the various stakeholders, including customers, suppliers, each other, leadership, and competitors (role played by Richmond people), and would finish the second day with input from everyone in the room on the draft Strategy. Then that microcosm would return to work, freeing the other half to come together on days three and four to repeat the processes from the first two days, ending with input regarding the Strategy. The next day (day five), the leadership team returned to the meeting room, read and discussed the input they received from the entire organization, and rewrote the Strategy based on the wisdom the group had given to them.

Day six was a Sunday and the branches were closed, enabling every person in the organization to come to the meeting place to take the next steps. The Leadership Team described the work they had engaged in and the resulting rewrite of the Strategy, a copy of which was at each person's place when they arrived. When the leaders finished telling everyone what they had done, the President asked: "How did we do? Did we get it?" The room erupted into excitement and applause, even ending in a sustained standing ovation. The leaders were overwhelmed with the response.

Let us show you how the Strategy had changed:

Leadership First Draft Strategy	Enriched Rewritten Strategy
■ First choice for personal financial service	■ To build a superior sales and service culture
■ $2.8 billion in assets	■ To provide exceptional service support
■ Expenses are 1.2 percent of assets	■ To earn a reputation for outstanding advice and education
■ We have a 20 percent recognition of Richmond Savings in the lower mainland	■ To manage growth, productivity, and profitability

The rest of day six was spent developing systemwide action plans that would cause change in work processes and enable the group to achieve the new goal statements. After these plans had been developed and agreed upon, back-home groups developed committed action plans for their own office or branch. Follow-up continued by computer reports and by all-hands meetings to share what was happening.

Two years later, Kathie Dannemiller received a phone call from the President asking her if she would be willing to be interviewed for a Canadian news magazine that had noticed the amazing success of this group. Kathie, of course, agreed, and asked him what had been so surprising. He said, "We thought we were writing a strategy for the next five years, and the most surprising thing is that we have been successful on every measure in just two years. And what's been particularly amazing is that we have achieved the original goals, the draft first created by leadership, and we have achieved the rewritten goals. We are amazed. How do you account for us having achieved both sets?" Kathie said, "The goals, in fact, were the same. . . . The language of the rewritten goals spoke more clearly to the front-line person, and because people could viscerally understand what was needed, they made it happen!"

Although their leadership has changed, Richmond Savings thrives today, their strategy evolving appropriately because of the work they did together in 1995.

The Roots of the Term *Whole-Scale*

Our work with systemwide consulting has undergone significant change over the years. As the challenges of our clients have changed, our work has changed to support them. Each time our understanding of what is needed has undergone dramatic change. We have chosen to call what we do by different names as the work has evolved. Based on our work with Ford Motor Company in the early 1980s, the name we used was **Large-Group Interactive Processes.** During that time our clients told us that they needed to bring larger and larger groups of people together, in order to move quickly in the same direction. Later, from our work with Boeing on the challenges facing them in the early 1990s, they identified the work they needed to do as getting large groups of people connected around developing a common and accurate strategy. We then began to call our approach **Real Time Strategic Change.** During that time we discovered that when a microcosm of the organization had a common database and could identify what needed to be different in their work, at that very moment ("Real Time" in the meeting), change began. Several years ago, we realized how dramatically we had expanded our work and changed the focus. Ford taught us to "go big"; Boeing taught us to "get focused" with strategy; and now clients were asking us to continue doing those things and also find ways to go deeper by changing day-to-day behaviors and work processes in their organizations. By combining everything we knew about moving large groups fast in a focused direction, we realized that in these same types of microcosms the client could also develop new work structures and processes—large groups doing details in real time.

United Airlines, Indianapolis Maintenance Center, provided us our first real opportunity to combine and integrate the Socio-Technical Systems approach we had called **Real Time Work Design,** created by our partner Paul Tolchinsky with the Real Time Strategic Change. Both had been highlighted in Bunker and Alban, *Large Group Interventions* (Berrett Koehler, 1995). This new approach helped organizations meet their needs to move faster and deeper. We began to call our approach Whole-Scale because the power of the microcosm allowed them to see the whole system and work the whole system (the "whole" in Whole-Scale) regardless of the size of the microcosm (large or small—the "scale" in Whole-Scale).

What our clients helped us see is that the same robust change processes we had developed for Ford and Boeing could be applied to process issues, organization design problems, and the daily work issues of organizations. United forced us to develop a methodology that would not only move them faster, but would also take the conversations from the strategic to the day-to-day issues of whole systems. What we learned is that with any size group, when we work with a microcosm of the whole, we can help the system think "whole" about their present realities and future needs. Building a common database ignites action to begin in the moment. In that fashion we bring about significant change without having the whole system in one place at one time. Whole-Scale means that we are always operating as well as thinking of the whole organization as we work with true microcosms of that organization. Whether we are working with twenty people or 2,000 people, the principles of the microcosm and seeing "whole" are the same.

Large-group approaches to organizational change have become increasingly popular in the last few years because many leaders have learned that the style of management often referred to as "command and control" no longer works. Leaders are learning that they need to get real buy-in on strategy from their people. They need to find new ways to align and engage large numbers of people around a common, effective strategic focus and an organization structure that can be executed quickly!

The organizations we work with are typically being challenged by a quickly changing environment and experiencing a sense of urgency about operating in that environment. It is our goal to help leaders and organizations understand and believe that the change processes we call *Whole-Scale* are a viable way of responding to that urgency.

Unleashing the Power
of the Microcosm

If you want to shift the whole system at one time, you must be able to think the way the whole system thinks. Using microcosms—real subsets of the larger group that represent all the "voices" of the organization—in the overall change process is one of the features of the Whole-Scale approach that allows you—and the organization—to think and see "whole system." The microcosm contains the essential "DNA" of the whole organization. Working with groups that mirror the "whole" allows you to work with the "whole system" at a different level. The best way to change a system is to engage the whole system. Microcosms are the best windows through which to view the whole system in real time. They provide access to the whole system quickly and effectively. Having a critical mass of microcosms experiencing a paradigm shift helps the whole organization shift.

The underlying assumption in the use of microcosms is that the wisdom necessary for success is in all the people of the organization. The most effective change efforts include the voices of all key stakeholders, not just the voices of the top or the bottom or the middle. *All* of the people in the organization—plus those who are counting on the organization, such as customers, owners, or suppliers—must be able to speak and be heard. When you cannot get all—getting the "DNA" re-creates the whole, without having to have everyone. The decisions of any one representative microcosm should be exactly the same as those of any other "DNA" microcosm would be.

Why is this so important?

The traditional consulting approach has been to pull together the "experts" on a particular issue—often people who thought alike or had the same background or had the "right" status in the organization. This view is necessarily limited, often focusing on data of high-ranking, influential views. It's necessary to include those views; and, by themselves, they are not sufficient. Using the holistic view from a microcosm (or many microcosms) will illuminate the fact that people can contribute powerfully when they have enough information and when they are invited to do so.

In Whole-Scale, using microcosms means tapping into the wisdom of *every* area and *every* level of the organization—*all the way* throughout the process, not just the night before implementation. In Whole-Scale, involving people means engaging each person in a deep and meaningful way.

Whole-Scale processes evoke the system's wisdom without needing to direct or control the results. Thus, when the system is ready, the answers come. The job of leaders and the consultants who support them is to help the system get ready. The microcosm will have all the knowledge it needs once the organization has uncovered and combined the knowledge it possesses. Through the power of the microcosm, it is possible to create identity in the moment and to form new identities, without having to define every aspect of the system or get inside each person's head.

This moment, when new identities have formed within a microcosm, is the moment we call the "paradigm shift" moment. People (individually and as a whole) are seeing the world differently, are seeing themselves differently, and are connected around a common picture of their future and the actions they will need to take to get there. After the paradigm shift experience, participants are able (and indeed clamoring) to flex their newly uncovered wisdom and build toward the yearnings they have uncovered together.

Some of the small-group examples of microcosms that make the difference in Whole-Scale are Research Teams, cross-functional Task Teams, Core Teams as integrators, and Event Planning Teams. In Whole-Scale events, you can use microcosms in several ways. One of the most useful techniques is to use "max-mix" seating, which is simply a group of eight people at a table, representing basically the same mix of knowledge, yearnings, functions, levels, and attitudes that will be in the larger group. Each table in a Whole-Scale event is thus a microcosm of the room, and all those in the room together are a microcosm of the system.

Uniting Multiple Realities

The consultant must keep a continual focus on the simultaneous and sometimes conflicting realities that exist in the internal and external environments of the organization. In change processes, the real needs of participants in their back-home work should shape the content. Do not use simulations or role-plays. Rather, encourage participants to address real issues in real face-to-face dialogue.

Many organizations base their improvement efforts on the assumptions of problem solving. In fact, assuming that there is one "right" answer disempowers employees. If there is a "right" solution, it follows that there must also be a "wrong" solution. The right/wrong paradigm is a limiting and ineffective way to help organizations change.

You will have greater success if you operate under the belief that there is no "right" or "wrong" answer. An individual's answer is his or her "truth." "Each person's truth is truth" is the phrase you can use to help individuals listen to each other's perspectives. Helping people realize that all of the truths matter is equally important. Combining our truths gives us a much more robust view of the world and enlarges possibilities enormously!

What Is it? A Journey or a Process?

Whole-Scale processes also consist of a series of events: typically alternating small- and large-group interactions that enable the organization to undergo the necessary paradigm shift. The whole process is an Action Learning approach that uses Whole-Scale events as accelerators and works with microcosms of the organization. Whole-Scale is both a change journey and change processes.

Whole-Scale combines processes to help an organization change in order to meet the challenges of its environment. It takes the organization on an action-learning journey, unleashing the power of the microcosm, uniting multiple realities, and creating a paradigm shift . . . a change in the way the organization sees its future actions . . . that enables it to change in real time. As you help clients do these things using Whole-Scale methods, two models and a formula will guide you: the Converge/Diverge Model, the Action Learning Model, and the DVF Formula.

An important model to use is the Converge/Diverge Model, depicted in figure 1.1. The model shows the change journey in which an organization moves, over time, through a series of activities that create and sustain change in the organization. It represents a connected flow that integrates the individual, small groups, and the whole system to expand their database (diverge), combine their multiple realities (converge), explore possibilities (diverge), and make systemwide decisions (converge). The large ovals depict opportunities for a critical mass to "get whole" (converge). In the flow of convergence/divergence, large-group events accelerate the change journey; they bring together a critical mass that combines everything people have been learning from their individual and small-group efforts into a whole picture. In the larger group, they will make the decisions that will move them forward faster and deeper. The wisdom required is in knowing when to "go whole."

Our process for thinking about when to "go whole" comes from the work of Lawrence & Lorsch, in their book *Organization and Environment* (*Organization and Environment: Managing Differentiation and Integration* by Paul R. Lawrence

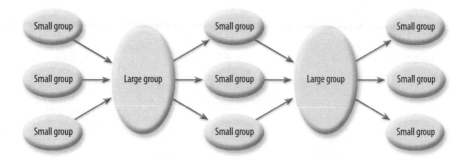

Figure 1.1 Converge/Diverge Model

and J. W. Lorsch). In this book the authors talk about the need for an organization to have both differentiation and integration. They define *differentiation* as "differences in attitudes and behaviors among functional organizations resulting from organizational segmentation with consequent development of specialized knowledge and mental processes." They see *integration* as "the quality of the state of collaboration that exists among departments that are required to achieve unity of effort by the demands of the environment." They also use the term *integration* as a process of achieving a state of integration. The moment to "get whole" is at the moment of maximum differentiation—to diverge one more inch might pull the organization apart, disconnecting us from each other. At the moment integration occurs, differentiation immediately begins again, and the whole cycle repeats itself!

In the Whole-Scale approach, the Converge/Diverge Model depicts how you can seek to help an organization unleash and combine its wisdom creating magic by ensuring that productive differentiation is brought "whole" by productive integration.

What Is Action Learning?

Another model that describes Whole-Scale processes is the Action Learning Model found in figure 1.2 (overleaf). The Action Learning Model is a picture of wholeness emerging—generating, releasing, and focusing individual and

The Action Learning Model pictures how we see incremental emergence of wholeness, generating, releasing, and focusing individual and organizational energy using the Whole-Scale approach:

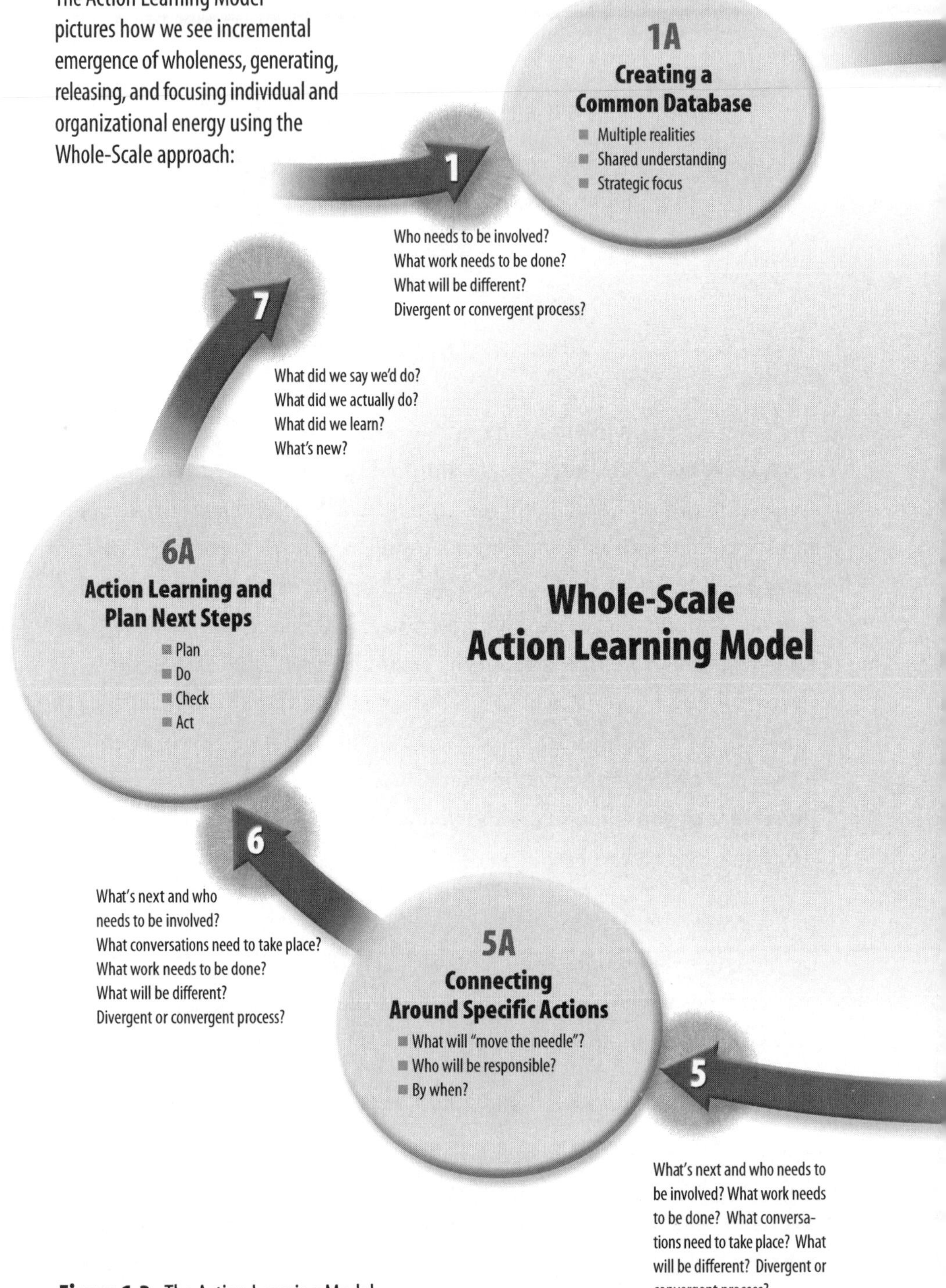

1A
Creating a Common Database
- Multiple realities
- Shared understanding
- Strategic focus

Who needs to be involved?
What work needs to be done?
What will be different?
Divergent or convergent process?

What did we say we'd do?
What did we actually do?
What did we learn?
What's new?

6A
Action Learning and Plan Next Steps
- Plan
- Do
- Check
- Act

Whole-Scale Action Learning Model

What's next and who needs to be involved?
What conversations need to take place?
What work needs to be done?
What will be different?
Divergent or convergent process?

5A
Connecting Around Specific Actions
- What will "move the needle"?
- Who will be responsible?
- By when?

What's next and who needs to be involved? What work needs to be done? What conversations need to take place? What will be different? Divergent or convergent process?

Figure 1.2 The Action Learning Model

2

What's next and who needs to be involved? What work needs to be done? What conversations need to take place? What will be different? Divergent or convergent process?

2A
Implications for Us
- How does this data impact us?
- Where are we right now?
- What are the possibilities?

3

What's next and who needs to be involved? What work needs to be done? What conversations need to take place? What will be different? Divergent or convergent process?

Dannemiller Tyson Associates

3A
Creating the Future We See
- Uncovering and combining our educated yearnings
- Picturing what we need to be
- Creating the shared image of where we need to be (e.g., new strategy, new culture, new structure)

4A
Agreeing on Change Strategy
- Bigger picture goals, based on the gap of where we are and our shared future
- Looking at possibilities for action

4

What's next and who needs to be involved? What work needs to be done? What conversations need to take place? What will be different? Divergent or convergent process?

1   This is a point where you might be beginning a systemwide change process and you would (as an Event Planning Team) be asking and acting on the issues.

2 – 7   The Event Planning Team, or some other group, needs to be asking these questions and acting on the answers to plan the next step.

organizational energy. It provides a continual "plan-do-check-act" set of Action Learning processes. Following the Action Learning path can facilitate a systems approach to engage all of the key stakeholders in the change journey. Based on Kurt Lewin's Action Research Model, the model is an application of systems thinking and action learning aimed at keeping the system whole at every step of the way.

The Action Learning Model is a commonsense way to look at how organizations get on the path to change. The Action Learning Model describes a powerful way to help a client system stay "whole" throughout the learning cycle. Organizations must continually re-examine the results they achieve at different points throughout a change process in order to inform the next step. This axiom is true for the next agenda items in a meeting, the next day of an event, and for the next step in the whole organization's journey.

Whether you are focusing on an event as an accelerator or the change journey as a whole, your best approach to helping the organization is to get the right people (a few or thousands) to have the right conversations that will enable them to achieve their purpose. Your interventions must be intentional at each step in the cycle. Design the work to engage the organization to provide its own answers to the questions noted beside each step in the model.

Throughout the flow of change, each oval in the model carries a different set of tasks and outcomes on the journey. The questions between the ovals ensure that the right people have the right conversations and thus ensure the wholeness of the system in the subsequent oval:

- What's next?

- Who needs to be involved?

- What conversations need to take place?

- What will be different because these conversations take place?

A key design issue at each oval and throughout the learning cycle is when the organization is answering the question "Who needs to be involved?" Is this the moment when the organization needs to engage a critical mass of the system to reunite around head and heart—to get a critical mass of the system whole again around its learnings?

Within each oval, the "who" is a microcosm or multiple microcosms (i.e., twenty people or 500 people). One of the initial activities of the microcosm is to build its own common database to inform its conversation and its work. Then, within each oval, the common database that the microcosm builds helps the organization uncover the right issues to address at that point. Once the issues are visible, the microcosm can address those issues and move the system toward the next level of the change process.

Shared information is the common thread that connects all the ovals in the learning cycle. The content of the information shifts as the system moves through that cycle. The focus is to create "wholeness" every step of the way.

In different parts of this model, different microcosms are involved. When a critical mass of the microcosms has gone through the Action Learning Model on the right issues, the whole system will change because it has in fact become an organization with a new paradigm . . . an organization that has a whole new picture of what it wants to be. We refer to this magical moment when the paradigm shift occurs as becoming "one-brain and one-heart[1]." Everyone in the organization sees the same things and cares passionately about creating this new picture.

The Action Learning Model serves as a general architecture for an overall Whole-Scale change process. Within a change process, the organization may go through many iterations of the learning cycle. For example, when

---

1. "One-brain and one-heart" means all people in the organization know the same things, all people in the organization *know* they know the same things, and they are all connected and committed to a common purpose and plan.

designing and conducting a critical mass/Whole-Scale meeting and follow-up, the organization goes through the whole Action Learning cycle. Each cycle takes the organizational learning deeper and helps the organization re-energize itself to sustain the change process and embed the new paradigm in its day-to-day workings.

Creating Paradigm Shifts: The DVF Formula

The DVF Formula, also called the D × V × F > R Model, depicted in figure 1.3 is a cornerstone of Whole-Scale work. We first developed this concept from the work of Richard Beckhard (*Organizational Transitions: Managing Complex Change* by Richard Beckhard and Reuben T. Harris, Addison-Wesley Publishing Company, 1987) at the National Training Laboratories. Dannemiller Tyson Associates' version of the model explains what it takes to bring about real change in an organization or in an individual.

Figure 1.3 The DVF Formula: A Model that Describes Conditions Necessary to Get a Real Paradigm Shift

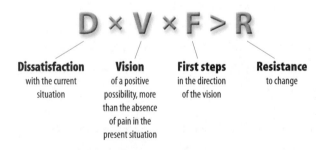

$$D \times V \times F > R$$

| **Dissatisfaction** | **Vision** | **First steps** | **Resistance** |
| with the current situation | of a positive possibility, more than the absence of pain in the present situation | in the direction of the vision | to change |

When all of the elements (**D** and **V** and **F**) are in place, in the individual and/or in the organization, the paradigm will have shifted and changes will be a given.

The first step in lasting organizational change is for each individual and the organization as a whole to share a common database of dissatisfaction "D" with things as they are right now. Everyone must be able to see and understand the view that others hold, and to understand, as previously described, that "each person's truth is truth." Everyone needs to see and value others' views and combine those views with their own perspective to create a common database from which the entire organization can move forward. "D" describes *why* we must change, the reasons for us to do anything any differently. In one organization, "D" might mean building a common understanding of the key drivers for change.

The second step is to establish a common vision "V" of what the organization yearns to be in the future. "V" describes the end point the organization seeks to achieve. Some define "V" as direction. Regardless, it paints the picture of the next stop on the horizon everyone in the organization is shooting for. Finally, the organization also needs agreement on significant, systemwide first steps, "F," to take to begin to move toward the vision. "F" describes the concrete actions that demonstrate progress toward the vision. If any of these three elements is zero, the drive for change cannot overcome the natural forces of resistance "R" that exist within any individual or organization.

In the mid-1980s, as we were facilitating the early stages of large-group work, we realized that the DVF Formula explained the results we began to see. The most startling result was that changes that had taken place in those earlier large-group meetings lasted at least six months to a year beyond what we expected. Equally startling was that even though some people believed that nothing had happened since the last meeting or series of meetings, six months later when we would bring people back together and ask them the Action Learning questions ("What did you say you'd do when you left the last session? What did you actually do? What did you do differently that you didn't expect to do? What did you learn from that?"), they would uncover, as a group, new meaningful results they had not noticed before. Things had changed; they themselves had changed—and yet the changes were not what they had expected when they left the meeting. Instead of doing what they had agreed to do, they did what needed doing. In the old way of working, they would have done what they had agreed to, whether or not it was right. As a result, they viewed themselves as failing because they weren't doing what they said they would do. Until they became "one-brain and one-heart" again, as an organization, they could not see that what they had been doing, individually, and as a group, was to invent altogether new ways to accomplish the results the participants were eager to achieve.

The D × V × F > R Model is a great deal more than simply a model for change. It is, in fact, an important model that enables the necessary paradigm shift to occur. When you help an organization to combine D, V, and F, when each of us sees the multiple realities in the room, the wisdom of the whole will be in place and a paradigm shift occurs. When the shift occurs, you can feel it in terms of a higher level of excitement and energy in the room. The paradigm shift lasts beyond the initial euphoria. It is literally impossible, once an organization has made a real shift, for it to go back to seeing the world in the old ways.

Summary

Pulling together a microcosm and/or a series of microcosms creates a critical mass of an organization—"one-brain and one-heart"—capable of building and living a new culture *in the moment.* As this same critical mass proceeds to model what the organization can be and how it will work, it becomes the vehicle by which powerful change occurs in the whole system.

Whole-Scale includes robust processes capable of quickly changing client systems and preparing them for further substantive change by:

- Clarifying and connecting multiple current realities

- Uniting multiple yearnings around a common picture of the future

- Reaching agreement on the action plans that move them toward that reality

- Building the processes, structures, and relationships that keep the organization moving forward

- Aligning the organization leaders and employees so that they can implement the changes together

When the microcosm has gone through this series of processes, it will produce a paradigm shift—a new way of seeing the world. Once the organization experiences the paradigm shift, people see the world differently. They are ready to take the actions that will begin to transform their shared vision into their shared reality.

The Star of Success Model

Pointing the Way to the Magic

How Whole-Scale Unleashes the Magic: The Systems Theory Perspective

The essence of Whole-Scale is concerned with how to cause profound, timely, and far-reaching change in *human* systems. We are often reminded of a quote attributed to Lewin, "Nothing is as practical as a good theory." The literature is currently active with various accounts of how systems theory and the new sciences bring new perspectives. Understanding how Whole-Scale change is grounded in open systems theory provides the connection between the magical results that can be achieved and the groundwater spring from which the magic flows. What we will do in this chapter is to bring to life our version of systems thinking and how we apply it to Whole-Scale change. For us the Star of Success provides the framework through which we look at the organization. As you will see, Strategic Direction (one of the Star Points) is our *True North* (or Southern Cross if we are in the southern hemisphere!). It guides everything we do.

Whole-Scale change is grounded in the elegant synthesis of more than 100 years of systems theory (as articulated by Fritjof Capra [*Web of Life*, 1996], Meg Wheatley [*Leadership and the New Science*, 1992], and Meg Wheatley and Myron Kellner-Rogers [*A Simpler Way*, 1996]). Systems theory addresses how the "brain" part of "one-brain and one-heart" guides the magical journey organizations experiencing Whole-Scale typically take. Whole-Scale Change evokes the self-organizing behaviors of living systems, using Action Learning as the journey and the Star of Success to guide the form and content of the organization's evolution to a more vibrant living system.

A Story of Systems Thinking in the Community:
The National Caucus and Center on Black Aged, Inc. (NCBA)

The Convening Issues

The National Caucus and Center on Black Aged, Inc. (NCBA) has strong roots in the civil and human rights movement of the 1960s and '70s. The convening issue for what started as an ad hoc organization was to give national visibility to economic, health, and social issues facing African-American elderly and to influence the 1971 White House Conference on Aging. Many of the original founders of NCBA have passed on; those who remain continue the struggle for a decent standard of living and quality of life, and they have fought to protect their legacy. To this end, they also recognized that it was important to plan for the future of the organization and to re-examine its mission in light of current social, economic, and political trends.

We received a call in the summer of 1999 to help the organization address these issues. The board had already established a Strategic Planning Committee to collect data using surveys and interviews with its members and chapter offices around the country. We met with the board of directors to understand what they hoped to create and what they perceived to be the most critical issues facing the organization as they looked to the future. Issues such as the lack of resources, the restructuring of federally funded social programs, and projected demographics for populations of color were foremost on their minds.

Following the Star: A Whole System Journey

An Event Planning Team was convened, which included representatives from the board, the Strategic Planning Committee, and the administrative staff of NCBA. They agreed that the purpose of their first event was "to garner the strengths and resources of all stakeholders in defining the mission and vision of NCBA and agree on our individual and collective roles and responsibilities in achieving them."

The team designed a two-day strategic planning retreat, which included the full board, staff, and representatives from various external stakeholder groups. Participants took a historical journey to build a shared understanding of how they arrived at the current state of the organization including obstacles faced and lessons learned from their struggle. Beneficiaries of NCBA services told stories about the role that NCBA had played in their lives and what NCBA meant to them. A trio of elderly women on the stakeholder panel described the feeling of security and the sense of community and family that living in one of the NCBA-sponsored housing projects afforded them. Another woman on the panel talked about having to re-enter the workforce at the age of seventy and the training and placement opportunities that she received through the NCBA employment program. The chief of the Racial Statistics Branch of the National Bureau of the Census shared current demographical data and projections for the next twenty years and the impact on political, economic, and social trends in the future.

Profound insights from these external stakeholders provided the impetus the organization needed to free itself from old assumptions about their constituency and the world in which they lived. Their work together at the event validated their identity, their mission, and the direction they were headed. For the first time, they had a shared commitment to their focus—how they would create and deliver value. Given that clear **"North Star,"** they wrestled to define *relationships*—their dual roles as advocate and service provider. Together, they let go of trying to be "another AARP" in order to focus on what they now saw together as their unique role. Once they had consensed on their image of NCBA's future and the role that the organization should play, everyone agreed to focus strategically on improving their marketing, increasing financial resources, developing human resources (including board development), and addressing health issues and the expansion of existing programs—processes and resources.

Outcomes

Now they are launched on a successful whole system journey. Several weeks after the event, the Strategic Planning Committee and the board members met to sustain the process by defining and agreeing on their desired results (objectives), developing action plans, and understanding their individual and collective roles in supporting the overall journey. With a clear understanding of the issues they face, the needs of their stakeholders, and a shared sense of the direction of the organization, NCBA prepares itself for the challenges of the new century.

An Exploration of Systems Thinking

The notion of *system* is essential to understanding how the magic of Whole-Scale Change works. In simple terms, a system is defined as:

- A collection of objects (for example, people, facilities, equipment) bound together to achieve some purpose

- The way in which the objects are bound together to form the organization's characteristics. For example, if the system is a car, it might be identified by:

  - Its purpose—exciting, safe transportation

  - Its features—stylish looks, high-performance ride

The elements of the system include the processes the system executes. For example, if the objects are engine, transmission, wheels, body, suspension, and vehicle controls, the processes would be:

- The engine converting gasoline energy to rotary motion of the crankshaft

- The transmission transmitting rotary motion from the engine to the wheels

- The wheels converting rotary motion to forward motion of the body

- The suspension providing stability

- The body providing a safe, comfortable, and functional environment for the occupants

- The vehicle controls converting driver foot and hand positions into engine speed and front wheel direction

Multiple kinds of relationships exist in systems:

- The way in which the elements in the system are positioned in relation to each other influences its dynamics. For example, in a car, the engine is under the body, the suspension system is between the wheels and the body, the wheels are under the four corners of the body, and the vehicle controls are inside the body.

- The functional relationships might be:
  - The engine provides power to propel the car
  - The transmission optimizes the power flow to the wheels
  - The wheels deliver power to the body
  - The suspension controls unwanted disturbance effects on the body

- The body provides power, protects, and provides comfort to the occupants

- The vehicle controls determine vehicle speed and direction

A particularly important property of a system is that no component or subsystem can do what the system itself can do.

Defining the system generates a boundary between what's in the system and what's not. What's *not* in the system is its environment. When data, energy, and material pass back and forth across the system's boundaries, the system is an open, dissipative system. Whole-Scale deals with open human systems.

Living systems are capable of self-organizing, developing new networks of structures and life processes. Given the free flow of information, they assume new structures and develop new life processes; that is, they adapt. How fast and how extensively living systems self-organize and the direction in which they self-organize depends upon the following:

- The dynamic interactions among the stages of development of the system's identity

- The building of relationships among the system's components (e.g., people, facilities, and equipment)

- The uncovering and flow of information within the system

To apply this knowledge to Whole-Scale Change, think of the organization as a living, self-organizing system as represented in figure 2.1. We see that the system's identity is derived from Strategic Direction because it defines what kind of organization is intended and how the system is intended to evolve. It drives the direction that the self-organizing system follows. The system's processes and systems evolve to determine what work is needed, how it is to be done, and what support is needed to do the work.

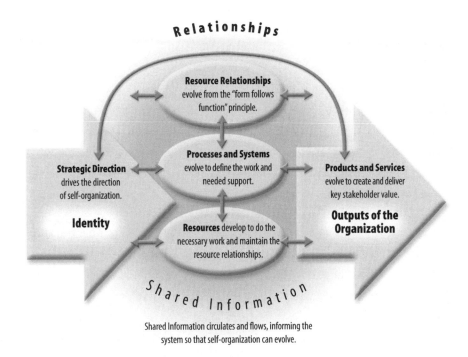

Figure 2.1 Whole-Scale Systems Thinking

The system's resource relationships follow the evolution of the system's processes and systems—form follows function. Relationships control and direct the flow of work. Resources do the system's work. Their capabilities evolve in response to Strategic Direction, processes and systems, and relationship demands. The shared information within the systems informs Strategic Direction, processes and systems, relationships, and resources creating feedback loops that enable evolutions and adaptations. A complex adaptation occurs as the information flow enables Strategic Direction, processes and systems, relationships, and resources to change and grow in insight, purpose, and capabilities. Finally, the net output is the set of products and services the system provides to its key stakeholders.

The phenomena of self-organization is driven by the dynamics of identity, relationships, and information [Wheatley, Kellnor-Rogers, Capra Self-Organizing Systems Seminar Notes, Sundance, UT 1996].

Finally, shared information is the life-blood of the organization. From it we create meaning and significance. It informs each of the other elements. Shared information is important because it energizes the resources, enables working through resource relationships, and assures that processes and systems operate whole and stay in balance.

Whole-Scale Change accelerates and focuses the direction of self-organization because it operates simultaneously on Strategic Direction, processes and systems, resource relationships, resources, and shared information. Using Whole-Scale processes, organizations are able to create new forms and functions. Each person, as a member of the system—and all of them as a microcosm of the system—simultaneously experience identity, establish relationships, and create shared information—resulting in a powerful shift in ways of believing and behaving.

The Star of Success—Six Keys to a Successful Journey

Because Whole-Scale is applied systems theory, the Star of Success provides an excellent organizational systems model. As a framework, the Star is a practical tool that helps organizations think through systemwide change. It causes the organization to ask itself six vital questions. Knowing the answers to these questions ensures focus for moving successfully into the future. The five Star points collectively correspond to a pattern, which if repeated, leads to repeated successes. Whole-Scale processes drive the evolution of the Star, allowing it to twinkle faster and brighter.

Strategic Direction—*True North*
- What's going on in our environment—now and in the future?
- What business are we in?
- Who are our stakeholders?
- What value do we choose to create for our stakeholders?
- How do we intend to create and deliver our value?
- What does success look like and how do we measure our performance?

Do we have the right Strategic Direction?

Do we have the right functions?

Shared Information—*Bringing forth a common world*
- What is the common context?
- What common data and information do we need?
- How are we going to create the data and information?

Do we have the right Pattern of Success?

Processes and Systems—*Ways and means*
- What work is needed?
- How will we do the work?
- What systems are needed?

Do we have the right information?

Do we have the right form?

Resources—*Capabilities Needed*
- People?
  - Committed to *True North*?
  - Committed to each other?
- Right skills and knowledge?
- Facilities/equipment/software?
- Financial?

Do we have the right resources?

Relationships—*Building connectivity between people*
- Reporting relationships?
- Functional relationships?
- Distribution of power—the ability to make *and* keep decisions?
- External relationships?
- Internal relationships?

Figure 2.2 The Star of Success—Framing the key questions critical to a successful whole system journey.

The Star of Success Model provides an objective way for members of the organization to focus their time, money, and energy. Action Learning provides the processes for asking and answering the questions in ways that make sense for the whole organization. Whole-Scale organizational change requires the combination of both Action Learning and "Star power"—you can't have one without the other.

Do We Have the Right Pattern of Success?

The first and most fundamental question, *Do we have the right pattern of success?* asks the organization to examine what it does and why, as well as why it is, or is not, achieving results. Organizations understand that key stakeholders are people who have a vested interest in the organization's success and have the ability to influence that success. Organizations also understand that their reality has two dominant elements:

- They will be successful, and in fact continue to exist, only to the degree they create key stakeholder value—shaping and meeting key stakeholder hopes, aspirations, yearnings, and longings.

- They must compete for key stakeholder time, energy, and money.

Because stakeholder hopes, aspirations, and yearnings change over time, patterns of success become outdated over time, no longer creating and delivering stakeholder value. Thus, the same critical question, *Do we have the right pattern of success?* invites the organization to examine the likelihood of its future success and existence and to provide answers that will make its continued success and existence more likely.

Five other critical questions, each with related subquestions, assist the organization in creating a pattern of success. As always, the answers come through Action Learning processes.

Do We Have the Right Strategic Direction?

The second fundamental question, *Do we have the right Strategic Direction?* asks the organization if it has a clear direction and pathway to the future. Various internal stakeholders may answer this question differently. Whole-Scale provides a way to create the shared information that allows a common answer to emerge. The result, Strategic Direction—*True North*—provides the constant bearing to point toward the organization's destination and the light to illuminate the pathway to its future. The organization must answer six subquestions to determine its *True North.* In determining *True North,* the organization must also answer other important questions. These are in the model.

When we answer the questions "Who are our stakeholders?" and "What value do we choose to create for them?" we are creating:

- **Purpose**—its *fundamental reason for being* considering all stakeholders' hopes and aspirations. Purpose identifies stakeholders and connects the organization with what the stakeholders really desire from the organization, phrased in terms of deeply held wants and needs.

- **Mission**—its focus for action. It is a clear and short, compelling statement of the focus of all action to satisfy purpose.

When we answer the question, *How do we intend to create and deliver value?* we are expressing the organization's:

- **Guiding Principles**—the core behavioral principles governing behavior and action in pursuit of purpose, particularly when the "going gets tough."

- **Strategic Thrust**—the strategy for how the organization will compete for stakeholder time, energy, and money. Strategic thrust defines the *basis of competition* in pursuit of purpose—marketing strategy, product and service strategy, process and system strategy, resource relationships strategy, resource strategy, and shared information strategy.

Finally, when we answer the question, *What does success look like and how do we measure performance?* we are really beginning to articulate the organization's:

- **Strategic Goals**—a statement of the Preferred Future the organization intends to create. They are the compelling description of the Preferred Future.

- **Strategic Objectives**—the time-phase, measurable results of the strategic thrust. They are the milestones along the path to *True North* and measure progress toward the strategic goals.

Do We Have the Right Functions?

The third element of the Star asks, *Do we have the right functions?* This question addresses work processes. Processes and systems provide the definition of what work gets done, how it gets done, and what systems and infrastructures (e.g., technology, information, rewards, attraction and retention systems, etc.) the organization needs to create to support the pursuit of *True North*. This Star point also raises additional questions for the organization to answer:

- What kind of work do we need? How will we do the work?

- What core, or primary, processes enable us to create value in pursuit of *True North?*

- What secondary but important processes support the core processes in pursuit of *True North?*

- What systems does the organization need?
  - The accountability systems to match authority, responsibility, and accountability in pursuit of *True North*
  - The system to manage the organization's finances in pursuit of *True North*
  - The reward and recognition systems to compensate and value contributions in pursuit of *True North*
  - The information systems to provide common data needed to pursue *True North*

Do We Have the Right Form?

The fourth fundamental question and Star point is *Do we have the right form?*
The relationships point of the Star defines how the resources (people, facilities,
equipment, and software) relate to and interact with each other and with
external stakeholders to pursue *True North*. The questions we often ask at this
point are:

- What kind of reporting relationships do we need?

- What kind of functional relationships do we need?

- How do we want to distribute the ability to make and keep decisions?

- What kind of external relationships are needed?

In this element we are working with the organization to determine the (1) right
jobs, (2) right organizational work groups, and (3) right mechanisms to assure
that what we create is integrated and coordinated in powerful ways. In addition,
we can look at how to physically arrange employees and work groups to
successfully achieve Strategic Direction.

Do We Have the Right Resources?

Given the answers to the previous Star point questions, we can then ask, *Do we
have the right resources?* The resources point of the star defines the characteristics
of the people, facilities, and equipment the organization needs to pursue *True
North*. It raises these additional questions:

- What kinds of people, with what kinds of attitudes, belief systems,
  skills, and knowledge does the organization need?

- What facilities and equipment does the organization need?

- What financial resources are needed?

As a result of asking and answering these questions involving the whole system or a critical mass microcosm we:

- Achieve commitment to *True North*. Substantial collective belief in and commitment to *True North* are essential for pursuit of Purpose

- Develop commitment to each other. Substantial commitment among people is essential for pursuit of Purpose

- Determine the appropriate skills and capabilities required to execute the Strategic Direction

- Determine the facilities, equipment, and software (the brick and mortar) required to enable Strategic Direction

Do We Have the Right Shared Information?

The final question, *Do we have the right information?* takes the organization full circle. Shared information provides the foundation and Strategic Direction provides the context for interpreting the data that creates shared information. This question raises three additional questions:

- What is the context?

- What kind of common data and information do we need?

- How are we going to create the data and information?

As with the other Star points, Action Learning processes provide the answers by determining:

- Who needs data? What data do they need?

- How is the data to be processed and interpreted?

- How will we communicate the resulting information?

A Whole Systems Perspective:
The Shining Star

Looking from a systems perspective, consider how Whole-Scale unleashes the magic. Magic results when individuals uncover their own hopes, aspirations, and yearnings and combine them to create collective hopes, aspirations, yearnings, and longings—the organization's Preferred Future. Then, they uncover and combine individual wisdom to determine and follow the path to the Preferred Future.

Whole-Scale makes all the Star points "twinkle" so the entire Star of Success shines brightly. Table 2.1 illustrates how various applications of Whole-Scale cause the Star to shine.

Table 2.1 Whole-Scale and the Star of Success

	Star of Success Point				
Whole-Scale Application	**Strategic Direction**	**Processes and Systems**	**Relationship**	**Resources**	**Shared Information**
Strategic Direction Development	X	O	X	O	X
Work and Organization Design	O	X	X	X	X
Mergers and Acquisitions Support	X	X	X	X	X
Leadership Development	X		X	X	X

Legend: **X** = Primary focus   **O** = By-product

Whole-Scale unleashes the magic by aiding and abetting a self-organizing system. Whole-Scale enables the organization to create and realize its own Preferred Future, driven by the critical need to create and deliver key stakeholder value. It defines the direction and accelerates the rate at which the system molds its identity, evolves its work processes and systems, forms its relationships, develops its resources, and shares its information. To the people in the system, the Whole-Scale Change approach seems magical because it involves and engages them in determining their individual and collective future. It connects them with each other in human ways that evoke deep and personal meaning.

Implications of the Star as a Diagnostic and Planning Tool

The Star of Success is a systems model that can be used to diagnose and address issues that organizations are facing. Usually there is an "ouch!" somewhere. If the issue is lack of training, the Star will help put that hot issue in context as a resource or a process question. It will force us to look at the other points of the Star, especially the strategy, to see what the root cause is.

When planning, the Star guides the conversation to make sure that the strategy adequately addresses all the aspects of success. The achievement of the strategic Preferred Future for the organization requires that we do the right work, with the right form and resources, and that we do what is necessary to keep the system whole.

Because Whole-Scale is applied systems theory, the Star is a practical tool that helps organizations think through systemwide change. As a framework, it causes the organization to ask itself vital questions. Knowing the answers to these questions ensures focus for moving successfully into the future. The five Star points collectively correspond to a pattern, which if repeated, leads to repeated success. Whole-Scale processes drive the evolution of the Star, allowing it to twinkle faster and brighter.

The Star of Success Model provides an objective way for members of the organization to focus their time, money, and energy. Action Learning provides the processes for asking and answering the questions in ways that make sense for the whole organization. Whole-Scale organizational change requires the combination of both Action Learning and "Star power"—you can't have one without the other.

A Story About Using the Star of Success to Point to the Magic:
The SSO Story

The Business Situation

The Sensor Systems Operation (SSO) in the mid-1980s was part of SSO Division, Missiles and Sensors Division, Defense and Aerospace Corporation. SSO developed and manufactured complex airborne electro-optical systems for defense applications. SSO Division was the flagship of Defense and Aerospace Corporation and generated the majority of Defense and Aerospace profits and cash. SSO formed the Defense and Aerospace nucleus when its parent company entered the defense business in the late 1950s. SSO, led by entrepreneurial leadership, was born in the conservative management style and environment of the late 1970s.

By the mid-1980s, the command-and-control management style was no longer working. Poor teamwork was also a concern. Additionally, the development programs that were the basis of SSO's formation had been converted to production programs. For a variety of reasons, SSO was losing $5 million per year. The combination of unsatisfactory financial performance and poor teamwork image resulted in a change of leadership. Missiles and Sensors Division general manager gave the new leader a simple charge, "Turn it around."

Because the new leader had formerly been a member of SSO, he understood its management style and the environment in which SSO lived. The new leader asked himself the following central question, *Does SSO have the right pattern of success? e.g.,* is what we're about appropriate and are we going about it in the best way we can? While answering this central question, he answered several other key questions:

- Do we have the right Strategic Direction?

- Do we have the right functions, *e.g.,* are we doing the right work in the right ways and is the work supported by the right systems?

- Do we have the right relationships, *e.g.,* do we have the right human, functional, and spatial relationships among our people, facilities, and equipment and stakeholders?

- Do we have the right resources, *e.g.,* do we have the right people, facilities, and equipment?

- Are we operating with the right information, and is it available to all when needed?

The leader's answers to these questions led him to believe that he had problems across the board! To be successful, he had to begin at the beginning, with a clear Strategic Direction.

A Whole-Scale Intervention from the Star of Success Point of View

The new leader's arrival was a clear signal that change was in the air. He had been exposed to large-scale interactive change. It was clear that SSO needed a large-scale change. Consequently, when given the turnaround challenge, he enlisted Dannemiller Tyson Associates to help SSO ask itself the previous questions and provide its own answers.

The intervention followed the Action Learning process, informed and guided by the Star of Success. The Dannemiller Tyson Associates consulting team spent some time scoping the project. They interviewed key managers and individual contributors. Soon they began to understand the organization's multiple realities and shape the intervention.

What emerged as the intervention was the following:

- First, to build a leadership community of the fifty managers and key individual contributors to agree on the desired change

- To convene a large-scale meeting of a critical mass, those individuals who were necessary to effect the desired change

- To help the organization put action plans in place

- To hold a series of reunions (or checkpoint meetings over the next six to nine months) to learn from what SSO had done and make new plans as necessary

The new leader recognized the value of involvement and engagement of the critical mass in shaping SSO's future. He also recognized that, because of the organization's history, people needed to see the Leadership Team as providing the overall guidance. He also understood the change task had to focus on creating a new pattern of success. Therefore, he sponsored a Leadership Team effort that created a draft Strategic Direction. He then sponsored an organizational alignment event to obtain feedback from the critical mass and enrich the Strategic Direction. The focus of the Strategic Direction was to be the supplier of choice for airborne electro-optic systems to be known for high performance, high quality and reliability, teamwork, and superior customer relations.

Once the Strategic Direction was clear and the leader had obtained commitment, he, with the help of the consultants, turned the organization's attention to the other points of the Star of Success. Table 2.2 shows what the various points of the Star revealed and the interventions that seemed most likely to help the organization get on the path to *True North*.

Table 2.2 Points Revealed by SSO's Application of the Star of Success

Point of the Star	What It Revealed	Interventions Put in Place
Processes and Systems	Deficiencies in design and production processes existed Designers did not fully understand design requirements	Put first-time yield teams in place to identify production problems preventing quality production the first time, and to determine root cause and take corrective action Implement quality function and Taguchi methods to ensure complete and thorough understanding of customer requirements, to translate the voice of the customer into technical language, and to make appropriate design trade-offs
Relationships	Interpersonal and external relationship deficiencies existed	Begin team building and development. Involve customers, division managers, and stakeholders to help identify and resolve issues
Resources	Deficiencies in skills and knowledge existed	Implement training in root cause problem solving, quality function deployment, Taguchi design of experiments, and statistical process control
Shared Information		Ensure vertical and horizontal communications—generating a common database on where SSO was going and why, how it was going to get there, and status on where it was. (The Strategic Direction provided a context for interpreting the common data and bringing forth a common world-view among SSO stakeholders)

The Action Learning Model provided a continual plan-do-check-act set of learning processes, allowing the organization to assess and learn, plan and learn, check and learn, and act and learn. Each Whole-Scale event played through the Action Learning Model. In addition, day-to-day, week-to-week, and month-to-month, normal management activities played through the Action Learning Model. The Model provided the processes and the Star of Success provided the desired endstate and then pointed the way. Together, they achieved the following results, transitioning the organization through a breakpoint (a point at which the rules of the game change by 180 degrees) and replacing an outmoded pattern of success with a new pattern of success.

Event Outcomes

The events had significant impact on the participants, individually and collectively. Participants saw their own worlds and SSO's world differently in significant ways. They saw the possibilities of a new and different world and a path to creating it. This new world revealed a different level of performance and way of being. Participants heard how customers and Division management saw their strengths and weaknesses. They performed a self-diagnosis, revealing for themselves what was working and what was *not* working. They used the results of the diagnosis and the inputs from customers and Division management to create shared information regarding what needed to change and how it could change. They created a shared vision of a Preferred Future and developed action plans intended to bring the Preferred Future into reality. During the event, they experienced significant shifts in relationships. Participants were able to relate to each other in deeper, more fundamental ways and experience community among themselves and with other division stakeholders outside of SSO.

Results After One Year

Production work was planned and executed in significantly different ways. Financial performance went from a $5 million annual loss to a profit of $1 million. The image of poor teamwork became an image of superior teamwork, and SSO became a valued contributor to the Division.

Summary

The Star of Success Model causes the organization to ask itself questions in five major areas:

- Strategic Direction

- Functions

- Relationships

- Resources

- Information

Taken together, with the organization's own right answers in each, these areas form a pattern—the right pattern of success.

Whole-Scale unleashes the magic that realizes the potential of organizations by simultaneously causing all points of the Star of Success to twinkle brightly and harmoniously. It enables the organization to continuously self-organize by:

- Uncovering and combining the hopes, aspirations, and yearnings of the people in the organization and applying their wisdom to define ways to create and deliver value to *all* key stakeholders

- Developing new work processes and systems that produce the products and services that convey value

- Forming and shaping resource relationships that control the flow of work and allow the system to operate with balance and harmony

- Developing resources that do the work and maintain the integrity of the resource relationships

■ Creating shared information based on common data and common context that enables the system to know how it is relating to its environment and how it is performing

Whole-Scale dramatically and profoundly impacts the direction and the rate at which the system self-organizes by involving and engaging the key stakeholders in the self-organizing process, thereby gaining the commitment and releasing the energy required for the organization to realize its potential.

The Project Planning Journey

Building Momentum:
Planning the
Whole-Scale Project

Building a Solid Foundation by Thinking "Whole" Every Step of the Way

Introduction

Leaders report that they are frustrated with the pace of change ("Too slow!"), while employees describe the latest change effort as "the flavor of the month" ("The last bunch of outsiders thought they knew too!"). With Whole-Scale processes, we are working with the organization to help everyone get the results they want: managers discovering new ways of leading that result in faster change, and employees having the information they need and the power to do something with it. A project plan that integrates all change efforts is a necessity.

Everything in this chapter is just good consulting, not new news. Any change journey needs to start with the end in mind, make a plan, involve stakeholders, have leadership commitment. . . . Not new news. Our purpose in writing this chapter is to build on that good consulting by describing what we are discovering about getting started on a change project using the Whole-Scale approach. All of the aforementioned steps are necessary and do not always occur sequentially. Sometimes a step does not require any attention at all. The needs of the client system at the time will dictate what is needed at that time.

Leaders want to know *What can you do for us?* or *What would you suggest from here?* We believe that the answers to those questions lie in the organization itself. Therefore, it is sometimes wise to begin the start-up or scoping phase of a Whole-Scale intervention by involving a microcosm of the organization. The microcosm is typically a cross-functional leadership group including labor and management, or it could be a diagonal slice of the organization, representing the various levels and functions within. That representative slice of the organization becomes a window through which everyone builds a common picture of where the organization is in the change process. This microcosm group also articulates what needs to happen in the future in order to move from where the organization is to where it wants to be. What needs to happen for the change effort to be successful?

Although a microcosm or representative slice of the organization provides a window, it is important to begin as quickly as possible to involve larger numbers of employees. Throughout the change process, large group events further accelerate the pace of change. Microcosms can both plan and participate in the large-group events. Whole-Scale continually involves microcosms of the whole system in both small- and large-group work, ever expanding the involvement of more front-line workers.

Scoping the Project

How do you know the right plan for a change effort if you truly believe that the wisdom emerges along the way? How is a Whole-Scale approach to scoping different? A traditional way of diagnosing the organization, of scoping the project, is to interview stakeholders and feed back to "someone" a summary of themes with recommendations or ideas for the project. In Whole-Scale we work with a microcosm group to build a common database and think through the change journey, adjusting as we go based on new data.

The Initial Meeting

The primary purpose of this first meeting is to uncover and combine the yearnings of those people charged with making change happen. Together with the client system, we are building a holistic picture of what can happen in the change processes and how the Whole-Scale process can help. As is true in so much of whole system work, many layers of action and conversation happen all at once inside a single simple process—the initial meeting. Some of those conversations include:

- Combining the individual views into a system view of where the organization is at the current time

- Painting a picture of the Whole-Scale process so that the client understands it well enough to see the possibilities and to see how Whole-Scale might enable the journey they need to take

- Differentiating roles and responsibilities of the leaders and consultants

- Building a relationship with the client (it is not just all task work!)

- Helping the client be realistic about the responsibility they are about to undertake and what they can accomplish

- Emphasizing the importance of "joint" whole system diagnosis

If the initial meeting does not involve leadership, and there is an initial decision to move forward, usually the next step in the contracting phase is to meet with the leader of the organization or the Leadership Team.

Engaging Leadership

Helping leaders explore Whole-Scale, how it could be used within their organization, and thinking through their own involvement in this process is a major part of scoping a Whole-Scale effort. The definition of the appropriate leadership will vary from organization to organization. The leaders may include union and management leaders, a steering committee for the project, an informal group who work as leaders of the change process, or a traditional Leadership Team.

Some of the ways that can help leaders determine whether Whole-Scale is the right approach and, if so, what that process will require of them, include the following:

- Talk with leaders in terms of their strategy and their desired results. Leaders will be most interested in change if they are comfortable that the change will help them achieve their own goals. Explore with the leaders what they yearn to achieve in the organization and describe how Whole-Scale can help them achieve these desired results.

- Understand the journey they believe the organization must go on to achieve its goals, then listen to see where Whole-Scale might enable or enhance that journey!

- Describe the $D \times V \times F > R$ Model. Leaders often connect with this model because of its simplicity and its appeal to common sense. Leaders often link the model to change efforts in their organization. You may be able to structure a conversation with leaders around their dissatisfaction, their vision, and possible first steps for change.

- Use the $D \times V \times F > R$ Model as a framework for conversations. Listen for the business case, the real *why* we must change. Determine the extent to which the leader believes everyone understands and accepts the *why*, as well as understands and is committed to the vision and direction of the organization. Finally, determine the degree to which everyone is acting in a concerted way to achieve that vision.

- Have a common sense discussion about the North Star–Six Keys to Success to develop a framework for whole system thinking. Perhaps a gut-level assessment using some assessment tool will help uncover initial gaps between *current* and *preferred* realities.

- Consider using videos showing the work to make the process real to the client. Videos allow leaders to see what a Whole-Scale event can accomplish with a large group in the room. One of Dannemiller Tyson Associates's clients, Richmond Savings Credit Union of Canada, produced a video to document the Whole-Scale process Dannemiller Tyson Associates used with them to involve the entire organization in developing and implementing a five-year strategic plan. PECO Energy Company in Philadelphia made another helpful video that depicts their organization using Whole-Scale processes for work design. Other videos illustrate the breadth of Whole-Scale applications. Videos provide a visual image of what the organization can do, but more importantly, they bring large-group meetings to life.

- Have the leaders talk to other leaders who have used Whole-Scale in their organizations. Talking to others who have been down similar paths is one of the most powerful ways for leaders to understand the journey of the organization, their role as leaders, and some of the things to expect.

- Arrange for leaders to observe a Whole-Scale event, if possible, to get the full picture of the process, the impact on the participants, and the roles of leaders.

- If they are willing to consider something different, have them play a part in a Whole-Scale event.

- Help them understand that as leaders they will also change. Whole-Scale does not "fix" others in the organization. If leaders are exhibiting old, unproductive behaviors and doing work in the same old way, six months into a change effort, systemwide change will not have occurred because leaders are a critical part of that system. System change is often really individual change, and such change begins with the leader.

Assessing Readiness

Readiness is helping engage the organization in a process of deciding what the organization can realistically do in a potential change effort. We do not see ourselves in the business of assessing, but we are in the business of helping our clients to assess *current* reality. Our job is to help them decide what is the appropriate amount of change they need to make at that moment in time.

In Whole-Scale, we are working from our belief that organizations are always ready to begin the journey of change. There is never a good time in an organization's life to change, yet change they must. We have discovered that even when they are "not ready," they really are! and the change just needs uncovering. Often what emerges is not what they thought the changes would look like.

As a result, we find it unnecessary to perform a formal readiness assessment. During the time it takes for an assessment, the client is losing precious weeks and months. Instead, we engage with the client where they are in their journey; engaging the whole system wherever it is allows us to bring all the readiness issues, chaos, and uncertainty into the process simultaneously.

One critical question consultants often ask is *Should we invest our time, energy, and finances with this client?* Based on our experiences, there are a few questions we ask to determine whether to engage with a client. These questions can be broken down by category, and are:

Timing

Is the organization at a moment in time where they can commit to a change effort? Other projects in progress, heavy vacation times, and budget cycles are just a few things that affect our decisions regarding when to engage an organization.

DVF Formula

Are enough people with power and influence sufficiently dissatisfied with the status quo that they want to engage in a change process? Is there a compelling business reason for the change effort? Is the leadership willing and able to step up and articulate a clear vision that guides the organization? Are there enough people and resources to carry out the next steps required to implement any decisions that come out of the process?

Willingness to Work Participatively with Their Organizations

Does leadership support an approach that engages people within the organization? Can they accept a collaborative relationship with the consulting team? Will the leadership team do their part in outlining a vision the entire organization can work with? Will the leadership team listen and yield to the wisdom of the microcosm?

Contracting

Contracting includes formal and informal agreements related to the project. Many of the topics to cover in this phase are generic contracting issues for any consulting process.

Some of the key issues to cover include:

- Scope of the project including how the Whole-Scale project fits with other change initiatives within the organization

- Role of leadership in the change effort—agreement as to support needed from leadership if the project is to be successful

- Partnership with other external consulting teams

- Role of the internal consulting team as partners and learners with external consultants

- Time investment of internal consulting team, Leadership Team, and whole organization

- Project deliverables—description of and agreement on mutually desired outcomes

- Project costs—consultant fees and expenses, as well as description of total cost

Proposals can be verbal and informal or written and very formal. Ours have been as short as two pages and as long as a book! Our proposals and ultimately the contracts themselves are word pictures of the journey we will take together with the organization; they are the expression of the clients wants and needs. Looking through the Action Learning framework, the challenge in writing proposals is to describe what we and the client believe, in that moment, will be the work that will need to take place. At the same time, the proposal must be flexible enough to allow for adaptation as we learn from each successive step.

At Ford Milan, Dannemiller Tyson Associates's proposal was two pages long and described a journey that would take place over a six-month period. The ultimate contract described the journey correctly, but the timing was off by three months. The client system actually moved faster than it had envisioned and asked Dannemiller Tyson Associates to pick up the pace!

In a number of situations the proposal becomes a living document, changing as the right path becomes clear or informed by a previous step. At NASA John H. Glenn Research Center, the proposal began as a flowchart. Over the course of the change effort, consultants and clients worked together to revise and update the flowchart as they learned more about how to engage the system and complete the work.

As we write a proposal, we work to capture the yearnings of the organization and its leadership. We listen closely to what we are learning about the organization and incorporate that information into the outcomes and process in our proposals. For both written and verbal agreements, we discuss the roles for ourselves and the organization and how we'll work together.

Developing the Project Plan

Proposals will often include some or all of the following in the project plan or statement of work:

Purpose　Based on the initial discussions and agreements, document the project Purpose. Do not fall into the trap of creating a Purpose that is just an activity. These are boring and speak only to a minority of the organization. Remember, a good Purpose is a statement that unites what different groups in the organization want.

Vision of Success　Build on the Purpose and define what success looks like when the project is complete. Include the desired results from the Whole-Scale perspective. Project forward in time and assume the project has been successful. From this future perspective, create an image of success.

- What results have been achieved?

- What are key stakeholders saying and doing?

- What deliverables are expected from the project?

- What are the desired results?

Statement of Work

Describe the overall work to be done during the project. Include all phases of work from start-up through project completion. Use the roadmaps of chapters 5, 6, and 7 for guidance.

Project Structure

Describe the project structure in a way that shows how the Project Team(s) relates to other teams involved in the change effort. Describe what tasks various Project Team members will do. What are the reporting relationships? What are the roles and responsibilities of each team member? How will the team make decisions? Who will have the power to keep *and* make what decisions? Who must the Project Team(s) inform or consult before making decisions?

Schedule and Key Milestones

Develop a chart of the tasks the project will entail. Start with the end date and work backward. Include the relationships among the tasks for start and stop dates. Identify the key milestones that show when the team can determine critical measurable progress.

Project Resources

Identify the people (skills, knowledge, numbers), facilities, equipment, software, and financial resources needed to perform the work within the planned schedule.

Aligning and Developing Leadership

Having the Leadership Team involved, prepared, and able to "sing out of the same hymnal," thus sending a clear message to their people, is crucial because people yearn for real leadership. A Whole-Scale process makes leaders very visible and effective. When leaders describe the world they see, others know enough to become appropriately involved. Coach them to stay out of the activity-focused language trap and to speak in purpose-and-results language. This kind of language sends a clear message to the organization that the time for real change is at hand.

In any Whole-Scale project, leaders change and share their knowledge with the whole system. In addition, people learn from each other and from their leaders. Leadership development starts with the first conversation and lasts throughout the project. Sometimes training is involved, but much of the development occurs as leaders work together and with a critical mass of their people on real, strategic issues important to the success of the organization.

Leadership development includes the leaders as individuals and/or the leadership team as a whole. There are, of course, many ways to help leaders develop the new skills they need to lead in a less "command and control" world. You can help with, for example, coaching, team-building, facilitating strategic analysis and planning retreats, and conducting training and leading feedback sessions. Helping leaders to be at their best in the Whole-Scale sessions excites and comforts participants, and it gives them a sense of confidence in the process and in the leadership, further enhancing the prospect for positive and sustainable change.

One of the skills that leaders need at their disposal is the ability to lead and manage change. In healthy organizations, the primary role of leadership is to manage change. We believe that Whole-Scale brings out the best in managers by helping them to model the behaviors required for transformational and effective leadership. This means helping the leaders understand that it is they who will often change the most in the way they work on a day to day basis. It can be difficult for a leader who has come up through the ranks to let go of the idea that they "know it all." When leaders move from a "knowing" stance to one of "inquiring," employees begin to feel comfortable enough to give quality input.

Some of the goals of leadership development within Whole-Scale include:

- Leaders function comfortably in a "new" organization paradigm.

- Leaders understand the Star of Success Model or other systems models and how these models can help define a whole system change effort.

- Leaders have confidence in the overall draft change plan.

- A Leadership Team becomes "one-brain and one-heart" about the organization's strategy and the new culture it needs to achieve the strategy.

- Leaders are clear on their roles throughout the change process as a team and as individuals.

- Leaders have clear contracts with each other and with the consulting team.

- Leaders have developed a draft whole system roadmap for the change process.

- Leaders are open to changing the way they lead/manage.

At the Veterans Administration/Human Resources organization, the model of leadership is not a traditional hierarchical model. The VA/HR has political appointees, central HR staff and leadership, and field HR staff and leadership. This distributed and non-centralized approach meant that Dannemiller Tyson Associates was not able to assure leadership alignment and development prior to the event itself. Instead, consultants convened an ad hoc leadership group at the event itself. This was the first time they ever met as a group. The strategy worked! Mike Walker, staff specialist, described it this way, "After ten years, the leadership finally gave me the space to do my job in the organization. In the last year, I was able to build coalitions to get things done that we have needed to do for years. I was able to do more work in the last year than I did in the previous nine years."

Doing "Discovery" Work

If you've outlined with the leadership what needs to happen and decided it is appropriate to proceed, gathering stakeholder data and input is the beginning of the organization "working the plan." Start by helping broaden the perspectives of the people in the organization so they get a picture of the possibilities for the future. The reason to do this is because people cannot create what they do not envision, and often that vision is limited simply by what people know in the moment.

There are three areas of discovery to have an organization consider:

1. What other organizations have done or are doing in certain areas

2. What world class organizations are doing in certain processes

3. What is going on outside the organization that could impact its future

Visits to other organizations by a research group have major impact on expanding innovation and creativity as the group thinks about their future possibilities. These visits can help break the old paradigms for the organization. Some examples illustrate this point.

In the early days at Ford, the research team became known as the "Wow! Wow! Group" because it would visit Motorola or Dana Corporation or another cutting-edge company and come back and say, "Wow! You won't believe what these companies are doing! Wow!"

NASA John H. Glenn Research Center created a group called the "working group." Their job was to gather as much data about the future as they possibly could. The team interviewed scientists and science-fiction writers and searched the Internet avidly for information about the future. Those who were creating future scenarios for the year 2020 used this information as a precursor to strategic planning.

Within one government organization that was becoming a free-standing, for-profit organization, a cross-functional team of employees benchmarked private sector organizations with similar products and processes to understand what *world class* meant and to bring this data to the rest of the organization.

Building an Infrastructure to Enable Whole Systems Change

Working with the internal/external consulting team, two groups are typically active throughout the change process: the Leadership Team or Steering Committee and a Core Team. Each of these is a representative mix of people who are a part of the affected organization (by our earlier definition, typically a microcosm). They typically exist for the duration of the project and facilitate, oversee, and guide the efforts of the system.

The Leadership Team or Steering Committee

This group is made up of leaders from the organization. Often, if there are unions involved, the wisdom is to include them! This group's function is to provide guidance, support (in the form of people, money, and time), and give direction to the efforts. This group sanctions, champions, and charters the work of teams and the organization as a whole; ultimately it is this group that approves and assures the implementation of the decisions made. Its role is often the following:

- Lead and guide the change effort

- Oversee, monitor, and guide employee participation in the effort

- Identify and attack underlying organization issues preventing increased performance and participation

- Charter the Core and Task Team's activities and act as the sponsor of their efforts

- Provide the Strategic Direction for the business, as well as the business case for the changes they are pursuing

- Educate themselves, and others, regarding possibilities for change

- Approve and enable the implementation of the recommendations made for change

- Define business case for change

- Define outcomes, boundaries, and measurement for the change process

- Decide on structure for the change process

- Review progress toward the outcomes

- Model the new behaviors of the new culture

- Set the values and accompanying behaviors that shape the culture

- Approve and oversee the project plan for the change process

- Coordinate all major activities across change initiatives

- Ensure that all change initiatives support the strategy

Other Team Structures

The Core Team   This Team is a microcosm of the organization. Its lifespan is usually the life of the project. Membership mix may vary at different phases of the project.

The Core Team is not a decision-making body, it is a decision support group. This group functions to (1) collect and provide the information people will need to make informed, high-quality decisions, (2) support the Leadership Team or Steering Committee in analysis of information, (3) create possibilities for systemwide consideration, and (4) sponsor the forums in which the organization members can make those decisions. The Core Team takes the decisions the organization's representatives have made and make sure that there is follow-through. Finally, this group acts as the communication conduit to the rest of the organization; they design and facilitate town hall meetings and other communication sessions to get the word out about the results of the large-group meetings. In different locations, this team has been called the "Change Team," the "Pioneers," and the "BPE Team" (for business process reengineering).

The Core Team ensures that the work of the various "small" groups (whether fifteen or 500 people) informs and impacts the whole system.

The job description of the Core Team includes:

- Bring options and models to others (critical mass of the organization) to educate and make decisions together

- Document the current state processes just enough to educate others

- Identify opportunities and propose focus (push back to the Steering Committee, if necessary)

- Conduct and document benchmarking visits

- Educate the organization (and session attendees) on the possibilities

- Communicate to those not involved directly in the change effort

- Solicit inputs from the broader organization to be included in the thinking and decision-making process at each event

- Develop cost benefit analyses for the new solutions

- Determine implementation plan scenarios

- Recommend process opportunities and priorities

- Develop "straw models" and "out-of-the-box-thinking" ideas for the session participants to consider

- Organize and participate in the whole systems sessions of the new organization

Task Teams   Throughout the change process, a variety of Task Teams may be chartered for specific products (*e.g.,* Process Design Teams, Structure Design Teams, Research Teams . . .). Often at these large-group meetings, people volunteer to do specific task work. Task Teams may work simultaneously, particularly if they are launched together and later brought back together for any integration required. In addition, Task Teams also may work in conjunction with the Core Team. As you read farther in the book, Task Teams have been called just that, Task Teams, or occasionally "Working Groups," or "SWAT Teams." Regardless of the name you give them, their job is short-term, very focused and project-results driven.

For the large-group meetings, Whole-Scale Events, we convene two other types of teams. We convene an Event Planning Team (a microcosm of the meeting participants) to define the meeting's purpose and detail the meeting agenda. We also bring together a Logistics Team (not meeting participants), who makes sure all the behind-the-scenes activities are "staged" to ensure a seamless meeting for the participants. Typically the lifespan of each of these teams is the life of the meeting itself (approximately four to six weeks). Each of these teams and its function is described in much more detail in the *Whole-Sale Change Toolkit*. For now, some of their characteristics are described following:

Event Planning Teams   Event Planning Teams vary in size from six to thirty or more participants—whatever size it takes to be a true microcosm of the participants in the event they are planning. They are a short-term team that usually disbands after the event they plan.

They are a microcosm—a diagonal slice of the participants in the event/meeting—a mixture of:

- Levels of management, a cross-section of the functions within the organization represented as stakeholders within the project, which could include executive leadership, experts within the organization with data and answers, stakeholders impacted by and implementing the changes (people who can test the reality of the work being done)

- Attitudes toward change

- Demographics: gender, length of service with organization, and so forth

Each Event Planning Team is a source of data about the organization. They provide reality tests of the organization, help educate facilitators and other consultants, and develop the purpose and agenda for the event. In addition, they act as a sounding board for leaders, coaching leadership. Often they become ambassadors for the event, recruit and coach presenters, and help make agenda changes during the event itself, based on feedback from participants.

Logistics Team for an Event/Meeting   Logistics Teams are responsible for all the behind-the-scenes support that makes these large-group meetings a seamless experience for participants. Logistics Team members are *not* participants in the meeting. Internal consultants, trainers, and people interested in learning more about Whole-Scale may staff Logistics Teams. Also, volunteers from other companies who are interested in learning more about Whole-Scale design process may staff Logistics Teams.

The Logistics Team:

- Ensures that the session flows smoothly, that everything and everybody is where they need to be at the right time

- Has responsibility for all materials, room set-up, registration, escorting subgroups to breakout rooms during sessions, typing, distributing handouts, moving microphones—in short, all the arrangements and activities that help create successful events

A logistics "czar" acts as the stage manager for the session, building and managing the Logistics Team. The Logistics Team, with the facilitators/consultants, hold a staging day, the day before the event/meeting.

The Consultant

The consultant has several roles and responsibilities:

- Serve as an "out-of-the-box" thinking resource by being current in the literature of organizational consulting and maintaining a strong network of thought leaders

- Counsel, coach, and advise the Leadership Team and Steering Committee on roles, responsibilities, and strategic planning issues

- Be an expert in designing and facilitating whole system strategic planning processes

- Counsel, coach, and advise the Core Team

- Together with an Event Planning Team, design and facilitate:
  - Leadership alignment events
  - Process and organization design events
  - Strategic Direction organization alignment events
  - Reunions and checkpoint sessions

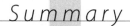

Summary

The Need for a Strong Foundation

The change initiative is a whole system change effort. It consists of a sequence of small- and large-group planning and execution activities. It is much more than an event. It is a window to new possibilities that needs to stay open. This approach goes beyond the notion of telling people what to do and resenting them for not doing it fast enough. Rather, it taps the hopes, aspirations, yearnings, longings, and wisdom of the critical mass of people in the organization. It respects each individual's brain and heart. It unleashes real human power . . . and with that power comes responsibility. To unleash this power without harnessing the energy that fuels it in a focused manner is irresponsible.

The fact is that when a critical mass has become connected around the brain and heart, continuation is not difficult, but it is essential to plan for symbolic actions that will keep hope alive and growing. Thus, the need for things such as a solid infrastructure for change and a solid commitment to see change implemented are essential to make sure that this opportunity for individuals to make a difference works. Because large Whole-Scale events are so dramatic a step in the life of an organization, they tend to grab attention in profound ways. Be careful at the start of the Whole-Scale processes to paint a picture of Whole-Scale that shows these large events as part of a bigger comprehensive change process, not as ends in themselves.

Insights

- Ground all change work in the master plan of Strategic Direction.

- Use the Star of Success as a guide to whole system change planning.

- Always begin Whole-Scale events with a microcosm Event Planning Team, and use this team and other teams appropriately as windows on the system.

- Recognize, and continually help others to recognize, that Whole-Scale events are powerful, but not all-powerful. They are accelerators to the change process.

- Help leadership understand the importance of living with the decisions an Event Planning Team makes. In truth, they will be open to data from the leaders, and they are able (as a true microcosm) to "see" the needs of the people who will be in the room more clearly than the leaders can. If the leaders want the Event Planning Team to make changes, a dialogue with them will undoubtedly get the desired result.

- Be careful to notice the flow of the Whole-Scale processes. If you want to change a module or replace it with another, notice the effect on the flow of learning and energy.

- Taking modules out of context will usually not be helpful, either.

- Above all else, do your clients a true favor: Never work alone! Ron Lippitt (a treasured early teacher in the behavioral science field) used to say: "If you work alone, you cheat your client. You need a team to watch both process and content." For a large event, you will typically need two external consultants and at least two internal trainers/consultants.

Strategic Direction—*True North*

- What's going on in our environment—now and in the future?
- What business are we in?
- Who are our stakeholders?
- What value do we choose to create for our stakeholders?
- How do we intend to create and deliver our value?
- What does success look like and how do we measure our performance?

Do we have the right Strategic Direction?

Do we have the right functions?

Shared Information—*Bringing forth a common world*

- What is the common context?
- What common data and information do we need?
- How are we going to create the data and information?

Processes and Systems—*Ways and means*

- What work is needed?
- How will we do the work?
- What systems are needed?

Do we have the right Pattern of Success?

Do we have the right information?

Do we have the right form?

Resources—*Capabilities Needed*

- People?
  - Committed to *True North*?
  - Committed to each other?
- Right skills and knowledge?
- Facilities/equipment/software?
- Financial?

Do we have the right resources?

Relationships—*Building connectivity between people*

- Reporting relationships?
- Functional relationships?
- Distribution of power—the ability to make *and* keep decisions?
- External relationships?
- Internal relationships?

Figure 4.1 The Star of Success points to True North, helping to define an organization's Strategic Direction.

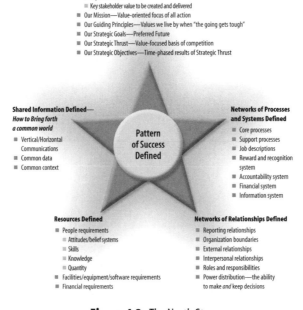

Strategic Direction Defined—*True North*

- Our Purpose—Fundamental Reason for Being
  - Business we're in
  - Key stakeholders
  - Key stakeholder value to be created and delivered
- Our Mission—Value-oriented focus of all action
- Our Guiding Principles—Values we live by when "the going gets tough"
- Our Strategic Goals—Preferred Future
- Our Strategic Thrust—Value-focused basis of competition
- Our Strategic Objectives—Time-phased results of Strategic Thrust

Shared Information Defined—*How to Bring forth a common world*

- Vertical/Horizontal Communications
- Common data
- Common context

Pattern of Success Defined

Networks of Processes and Systems Defined

- Core processes
- Support processes
- Job descriptions
- Reward and recognition system
- Accountability system
- Financial system
- Information system

Resources Defined

- People requirements
  - Attitudes/belief systems
  - Skills
  - Knowledge
  - Quantity
- Facilities/equipment/software requirements
- Financial requirements

Networks of Relationships Defined

- Reporting relationships
- Organization boundaries
- External relationships
- Interpersonal relationships
- Roles and responsibilities
- Power distribution—the ability to make *and* keep decisions

Figure 4.2 The North Star

Unleashing the Magic:
Strategic Direction

Introduction

The traditional approach to strategic planning relegated the planning and deployment to a group of internal or external "experts" who produced lengthy documents that quickly gathered dust on the shelf. Often the strategic plan was a closely guarded secret held by the leaders whose decisions seemed mysterious and arbitrary because no one had seen the whole plan, much less had input to it.

In the new millennium, it is increasingly clear that rapid, responsive, and effective planning and implementing of change has become a necessary organizational survival trait. More than that, organizations and communities need to build the capacity to continuously revamp themselves in response to environmental changes. The very heart of our work in organizations has been and continues to be strategy development and deployment. In fact, today our work in rapid, strategic alignment and deployment seems even more critical. We need to include in our "way of doing business" processes for both continuous and discontinuous change. This way of doing business periodically involves and engages small and large groups, including key stakeholders, in building a shared common picture of reality from their multiple realities. Organizational stakeholders go on to design a compelling course of action that springs from

Figure 4.3 The Strategic Planning Model

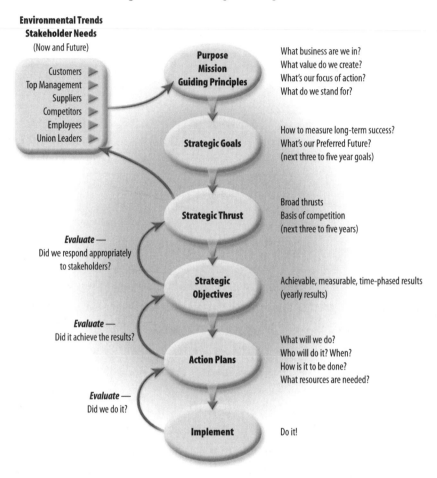

Environmental Trends
Stakeholder Needs
(Now and Future)

Customers
Top Management
Suppliers
Competitors
Employees
Union Leaders

**Purpose
Mission
Guiding Principles**

What business are we in?
What value do we create?
What's our focus of action?
What do we stand for?

Strategic Goals

How to measure long-term success?
What's our Preferred Future?
(next three to five year goals)

Strategic Thrust

Broad thrusts
Basis of competition
(next three to five years)

Evaluate —
Did we respond appropriately
to stakeholders?

**Strategic
Objectives**

Achievable, measurable, time-phased results
(yearly results)

Evaluate —
Did it achieve the results?

Action Plans

What will we do?
Who will do it? When?
How is it to be done?
What resources are needed?

Evaluate —
Did we do it?

Implement

Do it!

✓ their shared yearnings. This alignment means that everyone is managing the business from the same perspective and striving for the same outcomes, thus releasing enormously effective energies.

In traditional methods, the wisdom of the people within organizations was largely left untapped. In addition, the leaders missed the opportunity to align each person's day-to-day behavior in support of achieving the strategy. In contrast, the Whole-Scale approach creates "one-brain and one-heart." It encourages people to think and act strategically as a whole. When everyone,

Strategic Terms and the Questions They Evoke

Stakeholders　Who are the people who are counting on the organization? Who can influence and impact the direction of the business? Who has important interests in the business and the efforts of the organization? Who has the power of the "no," meaning their voices could derail the effort? Who has the power of "yes," meaning their voices are needed to ensure success?

Purpose　What business is the organization in? What are the boundaries of its activities? What are the hopes, aspirations, and yearnings of the stakeholders? What do we mean by value—the deeply seated reactions and responses to our activities? What possibilities can be envisioned for creating stakeholder value? What is the fundamental reason for the organization to exist—expressed in terms of value to be created for each set of key stakeholders?

Mission　What is the focus of all value creating action? What is the short, clear, compelling statement that captures everyone's heart and mind, serving to focus everyone's daily activities on actions that achieve the Purpose?

Guiding Principles　What are the vital few rules and tenets that govern behavior when "the going gets tough"? What are the core values that define what we stand for? What really defines us behaviorally? What are our sacred core beliefs about behavior—if we violate them, are we not suitable to belong?

Strategic Goals　What will success look like for this organization at the end of the planning period? What does the organization aspire to become? What is its Preferred Future? What are the broad focus areas that the organization needs to address? What is the desired end state in the next three to five years?

Strategic Thrust　What is the basis of competition (the strategy) for capturing stakeholder time, energy, and money? How will value be created? What are the threats and opportunities? Who are the target customers? What products and services will be offered? What are the focusing guidelines for developing work processes and systems, organizational relationships, external relationships, resources and capabilities, and sharing information needed to achieve the Purpose?

Strategic Objectives　What are the time-phased results of our strategic thrust? What specific results will the organization accomplish over the planning period? What are the milestones that will tell us we are making progress on our goals as we head toward the organization's Preferred Future? How will we measure success along the path to our Preferred Future?

from the top to the bottom of the organization, recognizes the same business reality and connects to the actions that deal with this reality, they shift their myopic self-interest to an enlightened organizational perspective (what Peter Block calls "enlighted self-interest").

This chapter focuses on sharing what we've been learning about the Whole-Scale approach to crafting and implementing strategy, engaging the wisdom and spirit of organizations and communities. Then, if your interests take you broader into a short history of strategic planning and deeper into models, see "Deep Dive C: Strategic Planning Models and Tools." This Deep Dive includes specific data gathering and analyses models, which we are creating and using with some of our clients, when these tools fit their needs, culture, and situation.

The Whole-Scale Approach
to Crafting Strategic Direction

The Whole-Scale approach to developing and implementing Strategic Direction is based on engaging the entire organization in thinking and acting strategically. Having people aligned on strategy means that each person in the organization knows the answer to the question, *What do we need to do to be successful?* that is, *What value can we create for our key stakeholders and how will we create and measure it?* Having people aligned in this way ensures that the organization creates extraordinary value for its key stakeholders by:

- Developing an understanding of and commitment to its Strategic Direction—*True North*

- Understanding the strengths and weaknesses of, opportunities for, and threats to the organization

- Executing an implementation plan and gaining the commitment to execution, which achieves the Strategic Direction

Whole-Scale processes unleash the magic that happens when organizations work together to craft Strategic Direction, their master plan for whole system change.

Alignment on Strategic Direction results from engaging everyone in the organization together in conversations about the business. Whole-Scale processes enable a critical mass, if not the whole organization, to have these conversations occur at organizationwide events, typically two- to three-day meetings. Organizational leadership, supported by small-group work done before such meetings, provides the guidance and analyses for these alignment meetings. In the meetings, participants work together to gain a shared understanding of current realities of the environment, go on to create a shared vision of the future, and begin planning the actions they will take to realize their shared vision. After the alignment event, back at work, their shared understanding and vision continue to guide and align individual actions.

There are two key components to strategic alignment and execution: leadership alignment and organization alignment. Leadership alignment is making sure ✓ the Leadership Team is aligned in their thinking and actions to create success in the future. It is critical in the change process that the Leadership Team members are predictable to each other and to the organization so a consistent message of support and direction is present throughout the organization. Without clear sponsorship and direct participation by leadership, change efforts seldom succeed. The second component, organization alignment, is engaging at least the critical mass of the organization in developing and implementing the strategic plan.

For Whole-Scale change to be successful, leaders need to be aligned in the following areas. These include:

- A Purpose, Mission, Strategic Goals, and Objectives, as well as a Strategic Thrust that reflects their best thinking. They then share this Vision and Strategy with members of the entire organization, who enrich it by bringing forth fresh thinking and different views from every level and function

- The guiding principles that inform the new culture. Leaders must begin "walking the talk" of that culture by modeling behaviors reflecting those values

- A strategic action plan that drives the Whole-Scale change process

- Ways to lead and manage the change process—providing needed resources, monitoring results, removing barriers, and adjusting the strategy based on what they learn

In the Whole-Scale approach, organization alignment and effective implementation occur by inviting the entire organization to participate in the finalization of strategy in a meaningful way rather than selling them on a "done deal." The conditions necessary for that alignment are rooted in the $D \times V \times F > R$ Model (chapter 1), which includes:

- Everyone has access to the same information—the same picture of the world—that the leaders have, and vice versa.

- Everyone has an opportunity to hear directly from their leaders about both the vision for the future and the draft strategy for getting there as well as what's in and out of bounds and why.

- People provide meaningful input on the strategy to combine their wisdom and knowledge with that of the leaders.

- The leaders practice transformational leadership by listening to what people have told them (for example, they process the input) and incorporating it into a revised strategy that everyone can support.

- First steps are identified that will allow each person to understand and participate in moving toward the future.

If you look at the process of understanding and making decisions about developing Strategic Direction as a journey, the pathway is a process of convergent and divergent thinking and action that involves the whole

Strategic Direction

= True North

 organization. Figure 1.1, our Converge/Diverge Model, describes this journey. This approach to developing Strategic Direction involves both small-group work and large-group work, centered on each of the system elements (see figures 4.1 and 4.2).

Throughout the journey, the Leadership Team's role is to lead by guiding and supporting the process. It involves and engages both small and large groups, and helps them uncover shared hopes, aspirations, and longings. It then ensures that achievable plans are put in place and executed to achieve the hopes and aspirations.

Initial small-group work involves engaging the Leadership Team in discussions on Strategic Direction to look at the overall strategy development process and Strategic Direction content. Frequently, the Leadership Team establishes a Steering Committee to guide the development of the Strategic Direction and a Core Team to do the Strategic Direction homework for the Leadership Team. We briefly described the work of both the Steering Committee and the Core Team in chapter 3. In the case of strategy development and deployment, the Core Team often will conduct the environmental scanning required. In addition, they might craft a draft Strategy for the Leadership Team's review and finalization. As a microcosm of the organization, the Core Team is thus providing the Leadership Team with a window on the organization's wisdom and knowledge and to the external environment.

With new insights, the Leadership Team can then blend its wisdom and knowledge with that of the Core Team to lead and manage more effectively. Its work product is a draft Strategic Direction document of which they have a shared understanding and ownership.

As soon as the Leadership Team is clear and energized about a strategy that they all they believe will create success in the future, they are ready to share it with a critical mass of the organization in the two- or three-day meeting. One of the important things we have learned in our work is the power of a process we now call "the turnaround." The magical ingredient of the turnaround, we have discovered, is that people first get educated, playing on the same playing field, seeing the same things. Then they give input on the Strategy. We have found that if you ask people for input when they aren't properly informed, they won't give wise answers and they won't feel smart.

The reason we believe people need to meet for two to three days is that our experience tells us it takes time to build a shared, expanded view—to see the world through others' eyes. Prior to the meeting, an Event Planning Team, a microcosm of the meeting participants, has identified who they want to hear from and what information they need in the meeting in order to accomplish the meeting Purpose. This usually involves hearing from each other, leadership, stakeholders both outside and inside the organization, as well as industry experts about what's going on in their environment now and the challenges they see in the future. During the first day or more of the meeting, each view is explored through presentation and open forum, a process we created in the 1980s to enable large groups to listen to and then dialogue with presenter(s) to probe for deeper understanding and clarity. The magic of the open forum process is that participants, working as a microcosm, ask wiser questions and feel smarter. In open forum, participants in table groups or clusters share with each other what they hear (because they each listen through a different filter), their individual reactions to what they heard, and agree on questions of understanding and clarity.

The Leadership Team is living transformational leadership. They are bringing their "best thinking" to the organization, listening to people's specific recommendations to enrich the strategy, and agreeing to what they believe needs to be in the final Strategic Direction. An important part of that process, we find, is that the Leadership Team has had to consense on the turnaround. The next morning in the meeting, they present what they heard, what they changed and why, and what they didn't change and why. We call this process "the turnaround" because at that moment everyone's thinking shifts to a new, collective picture of the future they can create together. Everyone feels wise, powerful, energized, and connected. Together, they identify and commit to individual and collective actions to leap forward with strategic intent.

After the large-group meeting, more small groups, often comprising volunteers from the meeting(s), then work on implementation. Implementation could include work and organization design, product and service development, or resource development. Reunions and checkpoints ensure that everyone continues their focus with a continuing check back on the changing environment.

Every Whole-Scale change effort must emerge from and be driven by Strategic Direction. Once the organization is aligned around Strategic Direction, it can achieve alignment around the changes it needs to make to implement the strategy. These changes may involve work redesign or a shift in the culture. Those organizations with a robust strategy that they are comfortable with and for which there is full alignment are ready to go on to another phase in the change process. In the sense of Action Research, the outcomes of the strategy phase drive the next step. In either case, Whole-Scale changes are a key part of the implementation of strategy.

Strategic Direction Development and Implementation Roadmap

The interactive journey of developing and implementing Strategic Direction is illustrated in figure 4.3, the Strategic Direction Development and Implementation Roadmap. The map follows the Converge/Diverge Model (see figure 1.1).

When the Roadmap is well executed, the *True North* point of the Star of Success (figure 4.1) shines brightly. The organization is energized, action is focused, and key stakeholder value is the ultimate aim. It has clearly articulated a shared Preferred Future, and people are committed to pursuing it. The pathway to the Preferred Future is clearly illuminated, with measurable milestones to mark progress along the way.

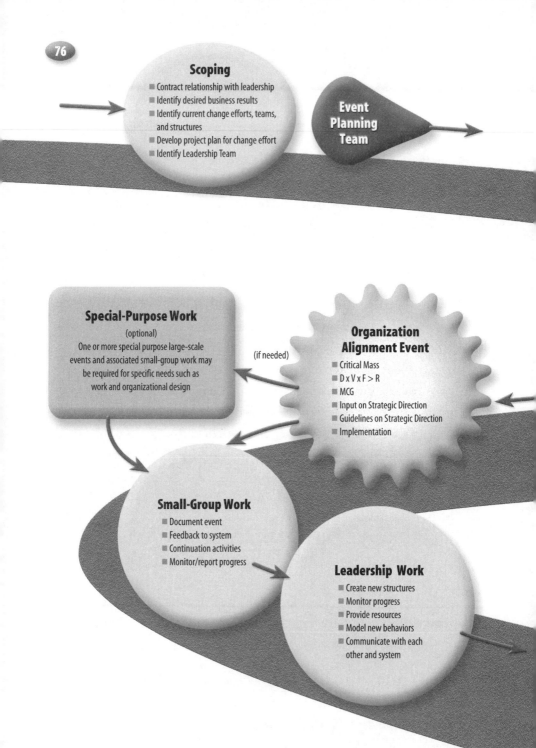

Scoping
- Contract relationship with leadership
- Identify desired business results
- Identify current change efforts, teams, and structures
- Develop project plan for change effort
- Identify Leadership Team

Event Planning Team

Special-Purpose Work
(optional)
One or more special purpose large-scale events and associated small-group work may be required for specific needs such as work and organizational design

(if needed)

Organization Alignment Event
- Critical Mass
- $D \times V \times F > R$
- MCG
- Input on Strategic Direction
- Guidelines on Strategic Direction
- Implementation

Small-Group Work
- Document event
- Feedback to system
- Continuation activities
- Monitor/report progress

Leadership Work
- Create new structures
- Monitor progress
- Provide resources
- Model new behaviors
- Communicate with each other and system

Figure 4.3 Strategic Direction Development and Implementation Roadmap

Leadership Team Alignment Event

Alignment on relationships, roles, and
responsibilities and consensus on
Mission/Vision/Values/Goals
prepare draft Strategy
continuation thinking

Small-Group Work

- Core Team chartering
- Data gathering and analysis
- Research of possible site visits
- Prepare draft Strategic Direction
- Begin communication with
  organization
- Select Event Planning Team

Event Planning Team

Small-Group Work

- Logistics planning
- Facility
- Invitations
- Speakers
- Logistics team
- Finalize design

Event Planning Team

Reunion/Checkpoint

- Review commitments
- Assess progress
- Learn from what has happened
- Celebrate success
- Decide what needs to happen next
- Metrics (team/organization)

Small Group and Leadership Work

Continuous monitoring,
communication,
and improvement

A Story About Developing Strategic Direction—
The Vision Systems Company

The Business Situation

The Vision Systems Company was the flagship of its privately held parent holding company. It developed and produced heads-up, heads-down, and head-mounted displays for high-performance and rotary-wing military aircraft. In the view of its leaders, the management style in the early 1990s was fairly autocratic and top-down driven. People were not empowered and, consequently, there was little management depth.

Vision Systems had sole source positions with several major customers, large military aircraft prime contractors, on several critical tactical aircraft. Because the cost of switching suppliers was quite high, the prime contractors tolerated Vision System's relatively poor delivery and quality performance—however, "The times they were a'changin'."

One of Vision Systems' major customers, Major Aircraft Prime, decided its future survival and, yes, even future success, required significant change in the performance of its supplier base. As was typical in the aerospace industry, Aircraft Prime's value-added costs amount to only 30 percent of total cost. Suppliers accounted for the other 70 percent of costs. Consequently, Major Aircraft Prime realized that if it wanted to become a world-class, high-performance aircraft prime contractor, suppliers would have to focus on improving quality, on-time delivery, and themselves become world class. Major Aircraft Prime, therefore, instituted a preferred supplier program. Some key features of the preferred supplier program were:

- Numerical measures of quality and delivery performance

- Qualitative measure of responsiveness

■ Business process assessment based on a modified Malcolm Baldrige Quality Award Criteria

Just before Major Aircraft Prime announced its preferred supplier program, a new president of Vision Systems came onboard. He noted that Major Aircraft Prime–related revenue accounted for approximately 50 percent of Vision Systems' revenue and a significantly higher percentage of Vision Systems' profits. Then, he looked at Vision Systems' performance compared to Major Aircraft Prime's standards for a preferred supplier and decided to take complete stock of Vision Systems' strategy and operating style.

The Intervention

The new President had been a Dannemiller Tyson Associates client in previous executive positions and was well aware of the potential that Whole-Scale could bring to improved organizational effectiveness. Prior to engaging Dannemiller Tyson Associates, he did a personal strategic gap analysis. Although the Star of Success (and the strategic gap analyzer described in "Deep Dive C: Strategic Planning Models and Tools") did not exist at that time to provide him a gap analysis framework, the new President intuitively followed the Star of Success in his analysis.

His assessment was based on his observations and the data from the Major Aircraft Prime preferred supplier program. If you weren't a preferred supplier you couldn't do business with them, and the leader's gap analysis made it clear that the current quality and delivery ratings were abominable! When Vision Systems' quality performance was first measured, it was 65 percent. When its delivery performance was first measured, it was 40 percent. Goals were based on the understanding that moving more than one performance level per year was extraordinarily difficult and that achieving world-class performance was a significant challenge. And they had to pull it off; it had to be accomplished! (The gaps are detailed in Gap Analysis Results, Deep Dive C: Strategic Planning, figure C.7.)

Because the strategic gaps were large and extremely important in Strategic Direction and the processes and systems to get there, the new President focused on closing these gaps. He realized that as a by-product of a Whole-Scale approach to strategy a significant reduction would happen in relationships, resources, and shared information gaps because Whole-Scale works simultaneously at a whole system level.

Based on his understanding, he worked with the Vision Systems' Leadership Team, a group of twelve, to develop the Strategic Direction that would focus on world-class performance. Early in this Strategic Direction development process, the leader felt he was the only one who thought getting to world-class levels was an important goal that the organization could attain within two years. Given his compelling need to move fast and leap to world class levels, he asked Dannemiller Tyson Associates to help deploy the strategy throughout the company using a Whole-Scale process, generally following the Strategic Direction Development and Implementation Roadmap.

Immediately this involved a deployment event with all 150 of Vision Systems' managers and key individual contributors. Then, over the next two years, they continued to maintain their focus and go deeper by having a series of bi-monthly, four-hour reunion events. These events followed the Action Learning cycle: "What did we say we'd do, what did we actually do, what did we learn, and what do we need to do differently now?" In addition, each year a different microcosm of vision managers gathered as a planning team to design the all managers' and key contributors' two-day reunion. The purpose of this annual meeting was to anticipate and respond to the changes in the environment as they moved to a world-class manufacturing organization.

A critical element for achieving world-class performance involved discarding the traditional approach to manufacturing in favor of a version of the Toyota production system. The process for implementing this new workflow generally followed the Whole-Scale Organization Design Roadmap in chapter 5. A new Vision Systems Core Team handled the implementation.

The Results

Within eighteen months, the quality and delivery levels had improved to 100 percent. Responsiveness ratings improved markedly. At the last checkpoint, Dannemiller Tyson Associates learned that the organization had maintained 100 percent quality and delivery assessments for eighteen quarters. As impressive and important as the numerical improvements were, equally as impressive and important was the impact on customer relationships, internal interpersonal relationships, and attitudes. Where people had previously accepted poor performance as normal, world-class performance became the norm. If performance threatened to deteriorate, people took immediate corrective action. People were proud! Additionally, significant improvement in skills and knowledge was observed. People learned how to build units one at a time, high quality, and on time. Vision Systems had the best improvement record of any Major Aircraft Prime supplier!

A Story About Applying
Whole-Scale Approach to Strategic Thinking:

Scenario Building

The Business Situation

The leader of a space division was trying to get the leadership and key engineers thinking longer term and bigger picture. Many of them had projects they were working on that took five to ten years to complete. Even though that sounds like a long time, their knowledge was very narrow about the specific program they were involved in and narrow scope around the overall program. No one was thinking the big picture.

He wanted to "blow the walls out" on the thinking of the space program. As we discussed possibilities for how to achieve this, the idea of twenty-year scenario planning emerged.

The Intervention

The leader created a Steering Committee for this strategic thinking effort. It was made up of leaders within and outside the Division and other key staff members. Their main role was to define the playing field for the scenarios—how many years into the future they would be, what the elements to consider in writing the scenarios would be (technology, politics, international cooperation in space, and so forth). The Committee also served as the overall project steering group. They were in charge of making sure the project moved along and that the outcomes could be integrated site wide and implemented easily.

They found it challenging to keep the project moving! We were working with an excellent internal consulting team along with the Steering Committee. Together, we developed a project plan that we revised probably four or five times. People were curious to participate and prepare scenarios; at the same time, they were hesitant in case it didn't work! Because we were essentially doing Action Research, we were continually flexing our process to make it work. (See figure 4.4, Scenario Building.)

In addition to the Steering Committee and the internal consulting team, there was a Data Team. This group, called the "Working Group," had the responsibility, over a six-week timeframe, to gather data on all the elements that the Steering Committee identified. Their charge was to discover the future! They were to conduct "discovery" work about the possible futures confronting space exploration and space technology. In addition, they were to look at trends in education, population movement, industrial innovation, and so forth.

What was fascinating was that once they got into doing the research, they found tons and tons of data. They were able to get on the Web, go in person, and find tremendous amounts of information. They then created a format for displaying the data so it was useful in the scenario planning process.

We held two large-group sessions. One was a half-day session to introduce all the "Working Group" data to those who were going to be involved in developing

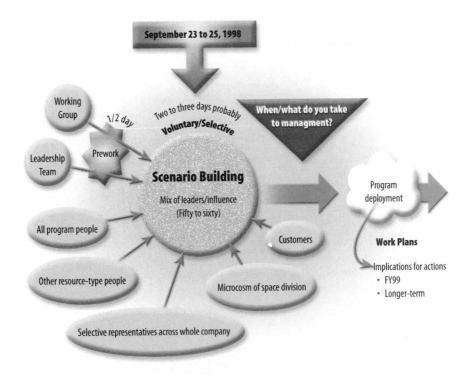

Figure 4.4 Scenario Building

scenarios (sixty to eighty participants, a cross-section of management, engineers, and planning and program people). Each category of data was presented by one person from the "Working Group" who had performed research. In the second large-group session, the sixty to eighty participants developed the scenarios, pulling on all the specific data that had been gathered about the elements. At the session, participants developed four or five different scenarios for the world of space in the year 2020. Each scenario was based on a different set of situation assumptions (what if we had conservative estimates for budget/low international cooperation/high political visibility; another would have different elements to vary).

An Event Planning Team designed the agenda for the scenario building session. They made sure that participants heard from outside speakers who had a vision of space in the future and from the customer in order to expand their thinking even further. They had time to really understand the data. Then they wrote the scenarios. In addition to the scenarios created by the whole group, individuals were given the opportunity to bring in their own scenarios. Once the scenarios were pulled together, we looked for common elements among all the scenarios. These common elements would define part of a path for strategic planning. The intent was to ensure that no matter which scenario came true, the organization would be positioned to respond.

After the session, the scenarios were made available to those in planning to guide the strategic planning.

The Results

At the session, two to three things jumped out that they needed to get going on right away. One was that they needed to become more visible and have more of a marketing approach. Overall, a critical mass shifted to thinking long range and whole program, all sharing a deep, common database that they had thought through together.

Systems Approach
to Strategic Thinking

Powerful organizational change results when appropriate resources, relationships, processes and systems, and shared information reflect and support the organization's sense of identity (Strategic Direction). These elements work together to form an interactive and interdependent system.

Without a firm grounding in Strategic Direction (the "why" and "how" of change), the "what"(changes in processes and system, resource relationships, and resources) will seem like arbitrary, flavor-of-the-month tactics. As a result people are much less likely to support them. Also, without the *True North* of Strategic Direction, people cannot adjust their actions appropriately when conditions change even if they want to.

The success of changes to any one of these elements will be limited and perhaps canceled if the organization ignores the others. One of the primary tasks of leading and managing the change effort is to pay attention to constraints caused by gaps, contradictions, and conflicts between what the organization says its direction is, how people do their work, and how they behave with one another. Successful implementation of strategy includes welcoming and acting on continuous feedback on how people are doing at keeping these elements in balance. Regardless of what the presenting issue is, when you enter an organization, always ask if there is a compelling reason, articulated in *True North,* to do what is being suggested.

When seeking to foster change, the first place to look is Strategic Direction, regardless of where the organization is feeling "pain." Begin by asking, *Is there a clear Strategic Direction?* If speed, agility, and quality decision-making top to bottom are important for an organization, then aligning everyone to Strategy is required.

In some cases the key driver for Whole-Scale Change may address only a part of the Strategy. For example, in the past the need for the culture to shift to a more customer-focused stance often drove the normal Total Quality Management efforts. A response to re-create work to meet changing organizational needs may drive work redesign efforts. Culture change may stem from the need to be able to respond more quickly to the marketplace with products and services and to move with the accelerating speed of technology. Each of these efforts may come from a portion of the Strategy and impact parts of the whole Strategy. The key message is that part or all of the Strategy must drive any Whole-Scale Change.

Unique Features of Roles and Responsibilities for Strategic Direction Development

Building on the infrastructures discussion in chapter 3, two groups are typically active throughout the strategy development process: the Leadership Team or Steering Committee and the Core Team. Each of these is a representative mix of people who are a part of the affected organization. They typically exist for the duration of the project and facilitate, oversee, and guide the efforts of the system. In each of the stories we described, both operated in different ways.

The Leadership Team or Steering Committee

Following we build on our description in chapter 3 of the Leadership Team or Steering Committee role. Ultimately it is the Leadership Team or Steering Committee that approves and assures the implementation of the decisions made. As they lead and guide the Strategy development, they focus on the following:

- Frequently, the group may prepare the first draft of the Purpose, Mission, and Guiding Principles, then pass the first draft to the Core Team. Alternatively, they may give the Core Team broad guidance and have the Core Team develop a draft for concurrence

- Oversee, monitor, and guide employee participation in the Strategic Direction development

- Identify and attack underlying organization issues preventing increased performance and participation

- Charter the Core Team's activities and act as the sponsor of their efforts

- Provide the Strategic Direction, using the Core Team as a homework group, for the business, and the business case for the Strategic Direction

■ Educate self, and others, regarding possibilities for change

■ Approve and implement the recommendations of any large-group Strategic Direction enrichment and enhancement sessions

The Core Team in Strategy Work

This Core Team functions to (1) collect and provide the information people will need to make informed, high-quality Strategic Direction decisions, (2) support the Leadership Team or Steering Committee in analysis of information, (3) suggest options for strategic decisions, and (4) help provide the forums in which the organization can make those decisions; they then take the decisions the organizations' representatives have made and make sure that there is follow-through. Finally, this group acts as the communication conduit to the rest of the organization; they design and facilitate town hall meetings and other communication sessions to get the word out about the results of the large-group meetings.

The Core Team is not a decision-making body; it is a decision support group. The job description of the Core Team is:

■ Be the homework resource for the Leadership Team or Steering Committee, bringing the organization's wisdom to Strategic Direction development through the microcosm

■ Do the environmental scan homework for the Leadership Team or Steering Committee

■ Enrich the Purpose, Mission, Guiding Principles, and Strategic Goals developed by the Leadership Team or Steering Committee *or* develop a draft Purpose, Mission, Guiding Principles, and Strategic Goals if requested

■ Perform strength, weakness, opportunity, and threat analyses

- Develop strategic thrust and strategic objectives alternatives

- Support organization alignment activities

- Communicate with those not involved in the Strategic Direction alignment sessions

The Consultant

The consultant has several roles and responsibilities:

- Serve as an "out-of-the-box" thinking resource by being current in the strategic planning literature and maintaining a network of leading strategic planning thinkers

- Counsel, coach, and advise the Leadership Team and Steering Committee on roles, responsibilities, and strategic planning issues

- Provide expertise in designing and facilitating whole system strategic planning processes

- Counsel, coach, and advice the Core Team

- Together with the Event Planning Team, design and facilitate:
    - Leadership alignment events
    - Core Team charter events
    - Core Team working sessions
    - Strategic Direction organization alignment events

Summary

In each of the stories in this chapter, the reason the Whole-Scale approach "worked" is that it allowed the leaders and the people to uncover and combine their common longing for an organization of their own choosing.

Strategic Direction defines the master pattern of success, bringing the organization's focus to creating and delivering key stakeholder value. The Whole-Scale approach to strategy development keeps all elements of the organization focused and balanced in the value exchange process:

- The organization provides products and services to key stakeholders and builds desired relationships with key stakeholders.

- In return, key stakeholders provide time, money, or energy to the organization.

The organization answers the questions in the Strategic Direction point of the Star of Success by "filling in the blanks" in the Star's *True North* point. These include the following:

- The organization's Purpose—its Fundamental Reason for Being

- The business the organization is in

- The organization's key stakeholders and the value the organization will create and deliver

- The organization's Mission, Guiding Principles, Strategic Goals, and Objectives

- The Strategic Thrust or "way of doing business"

Whole-Scale strategy development is an interactive process that involves and engages the entire organization in uncovering its hopes, aspirations, yearnings, and longings, then matching them with its perceptions of key stakeholder hopes, aspirations, yearnings, and longings.

Strategic Direction—*True North*
- What's going on in our environment—now and in the future?
- What business are we in?
- Who are our stakeholders?
- What value do we choose to create for our stakeholders?
- How do we intend to create and deliver our value?
- What does success look like and how do we measure our performance?

Do we have the right Strategic Direction?

Do we have the right functions?

Shared Information—*Bringing forth a common world*
- What is the common context?
- What common data and information do we need?
- How are we going to create the data and information?

Do we have the right Pattern of Success?

Processes and Systems—*Ways and means*
- What work is needed?
- How will we do the work?
- What systems are needed?

Do we have the right information?

Do we have the right form?

Resources—*Capabilities Needed*
- People?
  - Committed to *True North*?
  - Committed to each other?
- Right skills and knowledge?
- Facilities/equipment/software?
- Financial?

Do we have the right resources?

Relationships—*Building connectivity between people*
- Reporting relationships?
- Functional relationships?
- Distribution of power—the ability to make *and* keep decisions?
- External relationships?
- Internal relationships?

Figure 5.1 The Star of Success points that address Processes, Relationships, and Resources enable an organization to quickly align the whole system to support change.

Co-Creating:
Designing Organizations

Introduction

This chapter describes a fast and deep approach to crafting and aligning a whole system by focusing on the four points of the Star of Success that address processes, structures, information, and resources. In the process of designing/ redesigning the ways people do work in an organization to support desired business results (a way aligned with the Strategy, within a culture that supports the way people yearn to work together to get those results) organizations seek to answer the following questions:

- Have we optimized our processes?

- Have we created a level of self-sufficiency in the workplace that unleashes human spirit and creates flexibility?

- Do we have the processes (core and/or support) we need?

- Does our structure enable us to achieve the results we need?

- Do we have the information we need, when we need it?

- Do we have the jobs, roles, and relationships we need?

Whole-Scale: The Organization Design Application

Whole-Scale Change represents the journey organizations take as they invent or re-invent themselves. Whole-Scale Organization Design involves large numbers of people to participate in a change effort and designs/redesigns the organization to accommodate and support the changes. A model describing the integration of these two processes is shown in figure 1.1 in chapter 1, the Converge/Diverge Model.

Whole-Scale has thus become *a process that allows the simultaneous creation and implementation of new organizations with whole system involvement.*

Whole-Scale Organization Design builds on the roots of the Socio-Technical Systems Model. The essence of the STS (Socio-Technical Systems) approach is the integration of three elements in the creation of organizations: the social or people element, the technical or process element, and finally, the systems and infrastructures element:

■ The social system incorporates all of the needs and wishes of people and includes the structure of jobs and the understanding of what

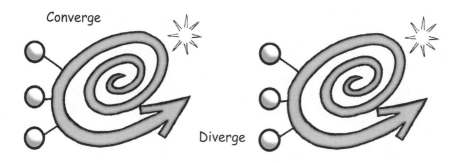

Converge

Diverge

The Converge/Diverge Model

motivates people at work. In the social system, the manifestation of structure was typically a hierarchy.

- The technical system refers to the processes and procedures the organization needs to accomplish its work. Processes and procedures define the tasks that make up the work of people. The technical system includes the operations that create value for the customer or end user.

- Systems refers to the information systems and infrastructures (for example, recognition and rewards, training, compensation, performance feedback, and so on) that support the social and technical aspects of the organization.

The principles that underlie this STS Model are:

- The elements of any organization are too interdependent to be looked at independently

- Powerful solutions come from looking at and integrating all three STS elements

- The right design for any organization depends on the best fit among the three elements

- The answers are everywhere and in everyone

For more information check out the model in figure 1.1.

Whole-Scale Approach to Organization Design

If the process of understanding and making decisions about the social, technical, and systems elements of an organization is a journey; it is a journey of convergent and divergent thinking and action that involves the whole organization. Thus Whole-Scale Organization Design involves small-group work alternating with large-group work, all centered on each of the three elements (social, technical, systems) described previously.

Whole-Scale Organization Design begins with small groups working on various aspects of understanding the organization's current situation. This often involves a number of task teams (indicated by the small circles on the Roadmap) working on various issues or assignments in support of the organization's change effort. They work on everything from understanding the current process to benchmarking how other companies are dealing with the same types of issues.

These task groups and other representatives of the system (sometimes the whole system) then come together in a Whole-Scale session to compare notes and agree on next steps in the change process. These large-group meetings (depicted by the larger circles, in the Converge/Diverge Model, see figure 1.1) often spawn new initiatives and new small-group work. Small-group work enables large groups to do better work. Large groups in turn enable small groups by ensuring alignment and providing opportunities to tap the wisdom of everyone in the organization. The power of this converge, diverge, converge cycle enables organizations to move much faster and deeper in implementing change.

The Whole-Scale Organization Design Implementation Roadmap

What follows is the evolving Roadmap for moving organizations faster and deeper. Because roadmaps have a linear aspect to them, it is a good idea to view the Roadmap with entrance/exit ramps at any point, depending on where the organization needs to focus. The Roadmap assumes that leaders are aligned around a business strategy. To begin the journey of the Whole-Scale Organization Design Implementation Roadmap (see figure 5.2 on next two pages), one of the first actions is to link the design effort to the organization's Strategy. When linkage is clear, organizational alignment can occur through the launch phase of the Roadmap.

Unique Features of Infrastructures for Whole-Scale Organization Design Implementation Roadmap

In organization design, three groups are typically active throughout the organization design process: the Leadership Team or Steering Committee, the Core Team, and a group known as the Research Team or the Implementation Planning Team. Each of these is a representative mix of people from the organization. The groups typically exist for the duration of the project and facilitate, oversee, and guide the efforts of the system.

The Leadership Team or Steering Committee

The Leadership Team or Steering Committee (see chapter 3) champions, sets boundaries, and charters the work of teams and the organization as a whole. Ultimately, it is this group that approves and ensures the implementation of design decisions.

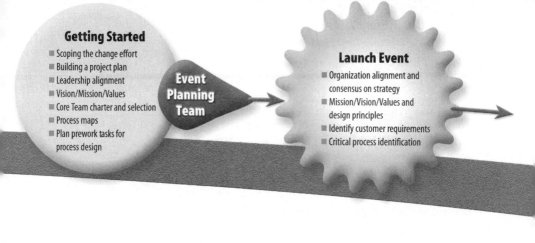

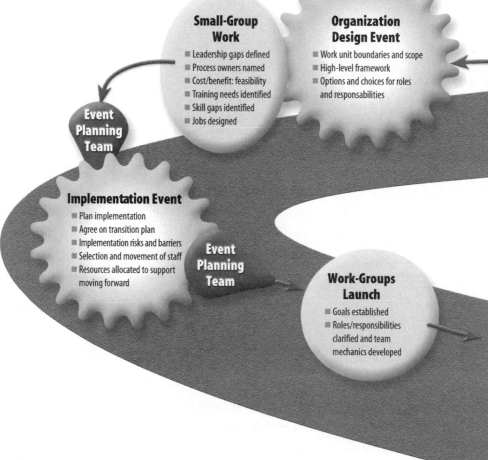

Figure 5.2 Whole-Scale Organization Design Implementation Roadmap

Small-Group Work

- Process mapping (as is)
- Process models developed for new processes
- Communication to rest of system
- Plan for prework for organization design

Event Planning Team

Process Design Event

- To-be models created
- Customer requirements revisited
- Process analysis
- Process principles agreed upon
- High-level inputs and outputs

Small-Group Work

- Organization models and options
- Identify process owner candidates
- Begin to identify transition team members and leaders
- Complete detailing of new process solutions
- Communicate to rest of system

Event Planning Team

Event Planning Team

Deep Dives on Focused Topics

- Rewards and recognition
- Goals established
- Metrics (team/organization)
- Skill-based pay
- Supervisory issues

Event Planning Team

Reunion Event(s)

- Stabilize
- Continuously improve

The Core Team

The Core Team (also known as the "Work Design Team," the "Reengineering Team," or the "Change Champions") oversees the change project. It is not a decision-making body. Rather it functions to (1) collect and provide the information people will need to make informed, high-quality organization design decisions, (2) provide the forums in which to make those decisions, (3) make sure that there is follow-through on the decisions, and (4) act as the communication conduit to the rest of the organization. They design and facilitate town hall meetings and other communication sessions to get the word out about the results of the large-group meetings.

The job description of the Core Team is as follows:

- Document the current state processes sufficiently to educate others

- Identify opportunities and propose focus (push back to the Leadership Team, if necessary)

- Conduct and document benchmarking visits

- Educate the organization (and session attendees) on "possibilities" related to:

  - Process

  - Organization designs

  - Implementation barriers and hurdles

- Communicate with those not involved in the design sessions:

  - The case for change

  - The vision and the first steps

  - What has happened

  - The organization's current state

  - Next steps

■ Solicit inputs from the broader organization to be included in the thinking and decision making at each event

■ Develop cost benefit analyses for the new solutions

■ Determine implementation plan scenarios:

    ■ Phases

    ■ Stages

    ■ Gaps and priorities

■ Identify process opportunities and priorities

■ Develop "straw models" and "out-of-the-box" ideas for the session participants to consider

■ Organize and participate in the detailed design of the new organization

The Research or Implementation Planning Team

Often the organization finds additional representative microcosms useful to support the change efforts in different ways. Two examples are the Research Team and the Implementation Planning Team. Both these examples support the Core Team and may be comprised of a subset of members from the Core Team or all new members.

At Ford Milan a group of sixteen employees from across the organization visited six sites and brought their insights and understanding back for others to see. Throughout the process this group kept bringing forth new ideas and even representatives from some of the sites to educate and enlighten the rest of the staff.

The Steering Committee typically charters the Research Team at the outset of the change process. This team supports the Core Team and researches and benchmarks the environment to determine applicable best practices and options for the organization to consider, because people can more easily create what they can envision or see. The team's job is to seek and collect "out-of-the-box" ideas and possibilities to stimulate the creativity of those who need to decide.

On the other hand, the Steering Committee often charters the Implementation Planning Team after it has made design decisions. This team's focus is on the follow-through required to ensure the planned changes take place and are anchored in the new workplace, both behaviorally and culturally.

The Road to Organization Design

The Roadmap depicts the components of work design and the balance between large-scale and small-scale work. Although much of the focus is on the large-group activities, it is actually what happens in the small groups that brings about the new organization. The question becomes, *What do you do in small groups, and what work must be accomplished in the large-group format?* The answers seem to be as follows:

- Convergence is necessary when the whole system must be committed in order for the solutions to work. Alignment and commitment will move the process of change faster and deeper, and being whole will enable the system to be smarter than it might be with just a few opinions and ideas available.

- Divergence works well when multiple pieces can be looked at independently then brought back together.

The marriage of Whole-Scale methodology and work design provides an opportunity for everyone to be involved in creating the organization of their choosing by answering the questions: *What is meaningful work? How can we create jobs that are consistent with the answer to that question?*

In addition to preparing the leaders for this initiative, there are several critical components to the Whole-Scale process that involve both large and small groups at different points. Setting up various infrastructures is necessary to oversee and manage the process of re-creating the work, inventing processes that don't exist, re-creating other processes that aren't working properly, and so forth.

Getting Started

Getting started in organization design is not much different than getting started in strategic development and implementation. Much of the activity is the same. What is critical, beyond those same elements of the strategy process, is the chartering activity that is embedded in getting started.

The Leadership Team or Steering Committee does chartering. There are two important inputs the Steering Committee must make to the overall organization design effort. These are boundary conditions and design criteria—both serve as reference points for design. Boundary conditions set the overall parameters for the design; they describe the conditions that must be adhered to during design. Design criteria establish the qualities and characteristics to which the design must conform. Design criteria may derive from boundary conditions, but usually not the other way around.

Boundary Conditions

Boundary conditions typically take three—sometimes four—forms:

Givens—those items that you must take for granted. They are hard as nails and cannot be overcome or changed. The organization design effort must develop design alternatives that are within the context of the Givens. Examples of Givens include:

- Headcount must neither increase nor decrease as a result of the redesign.

- There will be no replacement or purchase of capital equipment during the next three years.

- The new organization must have no more than two levels.

Constraints—conditions that are generally inflexible. They may be candidates for change if you (and the organization) can make a strong enough case for change. Examples of Constraints include:

- Budgets for the next year will increase by 2 percent (and special allocations are possible).

- Current space allocations are fixed (and negotiation with other departments for additional space is possible).

- The design must adhere to the terms and conditions of the current union contract (and side agreements may be negotiated).

Opportunities—elements and features to examine for positive change. These might be phrased by the leadership as follows: "We want you to consider the following items in the redesign." Examples of Opportunies include:

- Self-regulating groups as a basic structure of the organization.

- Reconfiguring space to increase efficiency and promote an environment for the effective design of peoples' work.

- Pay for skill and knowledge.

- Methods for increasing everyone's technical skill and knowledge.

Guarantees—elements that the organization must make as a matter of political expediency. Guarantees remove a roadblock that would otherwise prevent a redesign effort from moving forward. For example:

- No one will involuntarily lose employment as a result of the redesign.

Design Criteria

Design criteria usually derive from the information discovered in the analysis phase of the project. They typically take the form of a prioritized list of requirements that establish the qualities and characteristics the new organization should embody. A typical design criterion begins with the phrase "The organization should be designed to . . .) followed by an action verb and a specific description of an organizational characteristic or quality. There is no "right" number of design criteria. Too many criteria will complicate the design task. On the other hand, designers need a clear sense of direction. Anywhere between eight and fifteen criteria is a workable number.

For example, the design criteria might state that:

The organization should be designed to:

- Drive customer centricity.

- Reduce hierarchy and push decisions to the lowest level possible.

- Simplify work processes.

- Minimize organizational boundaries.

- Reduce the time required to make decisions and act.

- Allow flexibility for changes in outcome demand requirements.

- Assemble whole pieces of work in order to minimize process hand-offs.

Leadership Alignment

Getting the leadership onboard is critical to the success of any change initiative, particularly one of this magnitude! It is important that leaders have a shared Vision of where the organization is heading, how they will implement solutions, and most importantly, their own role in this process. The workforce will look to the leaders to see if they are truly "walking the talk" in the spirit of the new culture and the organization that they want to create. If leaders are not aligned regarding end results, the problems the initiative is attempting to solve, or the boundaries and constraints of the effort, then the process is at risk.

Consultants need to take the time with leaders, in off-sites and other activities, to enable them to test their alignment with each other. The results of this alignment include project plans, organization design charters, and often the role/job descriptions of the various teams and actors in the process.

The Launch Event

The purpose of the Launch is to create the understanding of, and momentum for, the changes the organization is making. This session sends a wake-up call to the organization and signals that maintaining the status quo is no longer an option. By bringing together a critical mass of the organization and various stakeholder groups—employees, customers, providers, leadership—you begin to create alignment around the need for change and the Vision of the change.

If Strategy is not in place, then the Launch Event becomes a Strategy planning and deployment session. If Strategy is in place, the Launch becomes the Opportunity to demonstrate how this work design initiative supports the Strategy and to build the business case for the effort. Bringing people together at the outset of the change enables them to move more quickly through the process itself. Aligning people early and involving them in what will unfold provides them with the information they need to let go of some of their fears and concerns, thus speeding up the change process.

Small-Group Activity: Task Teams

Often, the Launch meeting creates teams to work on specific challenges, such as social issues or business process improvements. Task Teams do divergent work that moves the design/redesign process forward. They gather data, offer possibilities, make recommendations, and so on. In some cases these Task Teams have performed the work of the Core Team.

The makeup and charter of these small groups needs to ensure a diverse range of resources and perspectives to keep the group focused on their designated task. Finally, you will need to encourage multiple teams to agree on a process for staying connected with each other as they work through their respective issues. The process works much better when everyone is connected to what everyone else is doing!

Design Events: Process and Organization

As an organization begins to move through the design process, it will become increasingly important to convene the employees from time to time to collect/ disseminate information (for example, input from employees on new organizational processes, job/role design, and organization structures) and focus on specific issues as needed. Depending on the timeframe of the whole change effort, these events can take place every four to six weeks. Design events provide an opportunity to increase involvement within the organization by involving participants in the decision-making process. Design events (whether process design or organization design) are the converging moments for the organization. Process design sessions may need to occur prior to organization design sessions because the work arrangements and jobs/structures that are created flow from the processes themselves. Process activity defines work activity and scope.

New Brunswick Telephone, in St. John New Brunswick, used Whole-Scale to tackle two to four overall business processes simultaneously. They took on processes in each session that had interdependency with the others people were working on in that session. Employees working on one process were therefore able to act as a "second set of eyes" for the others to ensure that they addressed overlaps and interdependencies in each.

During process design sessions the organization may create as few as one new business process and as many as five new business processes. These sessions may last two to three days, with an end result of a high-level new way of creating the product or activity.

Organization design sessions have also lasted two to three days. The end result is a high-level organization design that describes the overall architecture of the organization, defines how the work will be divided, and describes the composition of the organization units created.

Between these events small-group activities occur. The activity may be detailing the decisions that have come from the sessions themselves or communication with those not in attendance at the session to get their inputs and suggestions.

Small-Group Activity: Transitioning and Training

Once the organization has made decisions and is ready to put the new system in place, it must address many details—including such issues as the job selection process, the physical layout requirements, and the human side of the system. Anxiety is a natural response for many people in organizations planning change. Many people are uncomfortable if they have to change not only their *jobs* but also *the ways in which* they work (for example, going from a "command and control" environment to self-directed teams).

The new system doesn't automatically begin with the "flip of a switch." Everyone needs training and resources to prepare for living in the new organization and making a transition in their work so that nothing falls between the cracks during any process changeover. These support activities are "micro-design" activities because people are fleshing out their work and their relationships with a high degree of detail. This micro-design process helps build foundations for change and anchors both the new work and the new culture firmly in that foundation.

Implementation Events

Once the game plan for transition is complete, it's time for an Implementation Launch Event. Although all of the Whole-Scale meetings are critical, the initial Launch and this meeting are the two most important to ensure success. During the Implementation session people see where and how they fit in and learn about the transition plan for the next six months to a year.

The Implementation session aligns the whole organization on the implementation approach. This alignment and common database help sustain momentum and provide the energy necessary to speed implementation.

Reunion Events

Reunion events may be fairly short (one-half day or less) meetings with the workforce every four to six weeks to check the progress they are making. (Their frequency enables the agenda to be shorter than other reunions described for other Whole-Scale applications.) These meetings are instrumental in maintaining the focus and sustaining the momentum for change. Employees have an opportunity to share what they are learning about the new organization, identify issues that must be addressed, and provide feedback on the progress of the transition.

Deep Dives

As the new processes and supporting organizational structure begin to take shape, specific issues for implementation emerge. These are opportunities for "Deep Dives," handled one by one in a series of smaller meetings or handled simultaneously in a large group. Deep Dives resemble work-out-type sessions. They have a very specific focus (problem to solve or process, policy to create, and so forth), and provide only a limited time in which to create the solutions.

The principles used to design Deep Dive meeting(s) are the same as any small- or large-group interactive meeting:

- What's the purpose?

- What conversations need to take place?

- What work needs to be done?

- Who are the right people?

The Whole-Scale Organization Design Implementation Roadmap (figure 5.2) describes the generic process of organization design. Figure 5.3, Dannemiller Tyson Whole-Scale Work Design Projects and Phases of Work, represents the reality of this approach. The organization design process rarely happens the same way twice!

Figure 5.3 Dannemiller Tyson Whole-Scale Work Design Projects and Phases of Work

| | *Phase of Work* | | | | | | |
Company	Startup/ Leadership	Launch	Process Design	Org. Design	Implement	Deep Dives	Reunion
Ford Milan (280)	X	X				X	
United AirLines I (350)		X		X		X	X
United AirLines II (350)		X	X				X
Monsanto (130)		X	X	X		X¹	
World Bank (150)		X	X				
Bank of America (350)		X	X	X			
Dowty-Montreal (160)	X	X	X	X			
Revere (550)	X	X	X		X		
PECO Energy (800)	X	X	X	X			
Armstrong (320)					X		
U.S. Government I (150)	X	X	X	X	X	X	X
U.S. Government II (500+)	X	X	X	X	X	X	
U.S. Gov't III (OTE) (350+)	X	X	X	X	X	X	★
Quantum (small-scale) (ongoing)	X	X	X	X	X	X	X

1 Deep Dives conducted in Work Units   ★ Conducted by client consultants without Dannemiller Tyson Associates support

Applying Whole-Scale to Organization Design at a Government Education and Training Organization

Overview

What Happened	Comments
The company's change journey involved more than 450 people and transformed the organization over a ten-month period. Figure 5.4 depicts the journey.	After completing this work the entire organization met again for one day to clarify expectations and negotiate needs with each other. The plan is for a reunion at the 90-day period.
It began with Getting Started (in this case with the Managers and internal consulting team), moved through the Launch Event and then through a series of large-group and small-group activities.	The journey that this organization took represents most of the steps in the Roadmap and fine-tunes the concept of convergence-divergence thinking.
The end result of the Whole Office Workshops (WOWs as this client called its Whole-Scale sessions) was a new organization design, down to the work group level. Transitioning occurred over a two-month period (at which time staff rebid on jobs, including management positions). A series of Implementation Events called Micro-Design Meetings launched the new organization.	Large-group sessions included the entire organization. Small-group activities involved as many as 150 people at a time in Task Teams to complete and report out work results to the larger whole. Task Team templates enable small groups to focus their conversations.
	These sessions, one for each new Division, launched the implementation activity required for that Division. At these sessions new work groups began the process of becoming teams, clarifying roles, goals, and team procedures, and beginning to coordinate and integrate with other teams.

GETTING STARTED: OCTOBER/NOVEMBER 1997

Scoping the Change Effort and Building a Project Plan

Background and Convening Issue   In the 1990s, Congress cut budgets and pressed government organizations to downsize and consolidate resources. "Change is not a choice" was the mandate. The government wanted organizations to move to a more businesslike approach—to think and behave like a business, to become more efficient and focused on customers' needs. This training and education organization had to turn budgeted funds over to customers—other government entities—to then market and sell services. The organization had to submit "an integrated business plan, demonstrating likelihood of maintaining solvency over the long term." They needed a radical, new way of looking at how they operated.

Budget cuts required drastic reductions in some courses and eliminated many others. Customers complained that this training organization was unresponsive, inflexible, and lacked relevance. More and more frequently, they turned to other training alternatives. At the same time, most courses earned at least an average of four on a five-point rating scale, with five as the highest mark students could give a class. Employees were generally proud of the programs they had built over the years and pointed to the frequent good evaluations their courses got. Few employees recognized the danger of becoming irrelevant and did not embrace the need for change.

By the fall of 1997, a small team from the organization was working with consultants to write the business plan. As they worked, it became clear to some team members that, if it was to survive as a business, the "whole system" needed to change. They began to champion the idea of re-creating the organization as a business, not just to make the existing organization work in a business environment. They felt that the entire organization, not just a small group, needed to engage in preparing for this new way of doing business.

■ A dream in the backyard, Columbus Day 1997—several internal staff had heard of and seen some Whole-Scale work applied to strategy deployment and they called Dannemiller Tyson Associates. Their question was, *Can you apply your methods to transforming the office, not simply preparing it for a business environment?* We met for a day at the home of one of the internal consultants on a government holiday. Over the course of the day we laid out the issues, defined the critical paths, and put together a Roadmap for transformation that would take the next twelve months.

- The organizational leader agreed to use a whole systems approach to change. At an all-hands meeting (their term for a meeting of the entire workforce) in October '97, the leader said, "Change must come from the bottom up as well as the top down." At the same time she announced that the organization's leadership would serve as sustaining sponsors or leaders of change on subjects that the business plan would address.

- The proposal that Dannemiller Tyson Associates created, together with the backyard group and organizational leaders, was to apply the Whole-Scale approach to building organization alignment. The effort would engage the whole organization in small-group work and large-group work (they called the large-group work Whole Office Workshops or WOWs) to create a shared case for change; criteria for designing the new office; a new macro structure that supports customer mission; a micro design of each new team; and a transition plan to "go live" October '98. In addition, leadership alignment and development would take place throughout the year, focusing on specific needs at critical moments of challenge. In fact, the project plan concept the organization's leaders originally discussed in the backyard on Columbus Day played itself out over its twelve-month period, even though changes emerged along the way—including a change in top leadership.

Building on the Infrastructure

Because the organization had already begun business planning, an infrastructure of sustaining sponsors—data collection groups, each one headed by a member of the corporate board—already existed. The issues were to do the following:

- Accelerate and integrate the sustaining sponsor groups

- Develop the leadership

- Engage the whole system

- Create office momentum to change processes and structures

The transformation plan integrated the organization where it was in the business planning process, the sustaining sponsors, and the data collection teams that were already structured and functioning. In addition, it created a Change Team consisting of the internal consulting team and key managers who were heavily involved in the change process. Later the leadership rechartered this team as the Transformational Change Team. The team was aligned with the corporate board and attended their meetings.

Leadership Alignment: Why Change?

Earlier the leader had expressed concerns that this organization had a history of going through the motions and would not break out of the box or stretch. Currently the organization was performing its work processes in stovepipes. We worked with the Change Team to design and facilitate a change management orientation and alignment meeting to charter the Steering Committee to lead change.

The work of the one-day leadership alignment meeting was three clear products:

1. Make the case for change

   ■ Does this organization want radical change or incremental change? (This became input to WOW I)

   ■ What is the scope? What are the Givens? What are the opportunities for exploration?

   ■ What is in-bounds, and what is out-of-bounds?

2. Clarify expectations for the Steering Committee

   ■ Determine what the committee and the employees see it doing to lead, sponsor the redesign, and be champions

   ■ Get clarity about sustaining sponsors: role and clear charters for each Task Team (what's needed, when)

3. Determine next steps, then plan the project

   ▪ Integrate business planning with work redesign

      ▪ What's the logical flow?

      ▪ What's the work that needs to happen to inform decisions at each phase?

   ▪ Think about rewards, hiring/selection, training, new skills, and staffing

   ▪ Prepare for next week's meeting (all management off-site), engaging all managers in leading the change

Leadership Alignment: All Managers Off-site November '97

During the backyard meeting in October, the internal consulting team had identified the concern regarding middle managers. This group had a long tradition of resisting change, and in government they were seen as a real obstacle to change. The game plan structured a series of one-day off-sites for the entire seventy-five-member management team. The purpose of these sessions was to explore with and prepare these managers for the coming changes. Basically the outcomes were to get aligned on: (1) their role as the management system, (2) the case for change, and (3) preparation for WOW I. The purpose of this first session was: to become a mutually supportive Leadership Team with clear goals and decide what comes next.

THE JOURNEY

WOW (Whole Office Workshop) I: "Ensuring Our Future in a Competitive Business Environment"

For three days, more than two hundred and fifty participants (employees, customers, stakeholders, and strategic partners) met to bring together all Office of Training and Education officers to determine their professional future in a competitive business environment by:

- Clarifying the environment

- Defining the office's future

- Creating a unified effort

After presentations from managers, customers, and leaders, WOW participants developed a list of attributes that they believed would be important for the organization as a business. The WOW created energy for change, with people walking away feeling that they had to transform. Prior to the WOW, the organizational leader accepted a promotional opportunity, and no one had come to replace him. After the WOW, a few felt cynical, saying, "This is all great, but a new director will come in and all our efforts will be cast aside!"

Transformational Change
Project start—
in a backyard, Columbus Day, 1997

Corporation Board Meets
- Build case for change
- Charter to lead transformational change
- Continue to write business plan

Why Change?
Input to WOW

November 3, 1997

Managers Off-site
75 Managers
- Alignment
- Prep to lead WOW

Figure 5.4 One Organization's Journey with Whole-Scale Change

November 17, 1997

Small-Group Activity: Starting the Process

After the WOW, sustaining sponsor groups started to meet again. Informed by input from WOW I, teams began to work on process design, marketing, benchmarking, and measurements for the new business and the human resource issues that emerged. The challenge of creating a new organizational framework is to break out of traditional ways of thinking and envision something new. We often say that "we cannot create what we cannot imagine." To prepare for the organization design and bring possibilities of what the new organization could become, a team of managers visited three corporations.

In early February 1998, the new director came onboard. Not only did he have experience leading organizations through major change, but getting participation from people was key to how he had led change in the past. He also had experience applying a Whole-Scale Change approach.

Knowing that the organization was teetering on his definition of whether this was to be "incremental or transformational change," the new leader pulled all managers and workforce together for a couple of hours to dialogue about his Vision of the change. At that meeting and thereafter, his recurring theme to managers and the workforce was "The best way to guarantee your future is to create it yourself." He explained the methodology as a way to "gain participation and involvement of people in the office and draw on the ideas and commitment of everyone in bringing about the change. And it presumes that the wisdom is

Change Team Created

WOW I
Launch
More than 250 participants

- Building the case for change
- Alignment on strategy/direction
- Inputs to Task Teams

December 1997

in the people, in the organization, and not merely in the director or the managers." At that meeting, he was clear, "I am not here to write a business plan; I am here to align the organization closer to the government's mission."

Small-Group Activity: Customer Conversations

The goal was to make the organization more flexible and increasingly capable of adapting as the demands of customers dictated. The director explained that the transformation would help people learn how to focus on the customers' interests and be more flexible. "To align what we do with the government's mission," he explained, "it is critical to know as much as possible about what the managers want from us. Therefore, our number one job is to determine immediately what our customers' training needs really are."

To get this information, the Marketing Task Team carried out what they called "customer conversations"—interviews with people who controlled the money for training. About fifty employees, working in pairs, carried out discussions with some eighty high-level customers. Two interviewers conducted each structured discussion; one served as the primary interviewer and the other as the primary note-taker. Each interviewer's personal challenge was to truly hear the voice of the customer rather than just gather data that justified the office's current way of doing things and personal beliefs about what the customer needed.

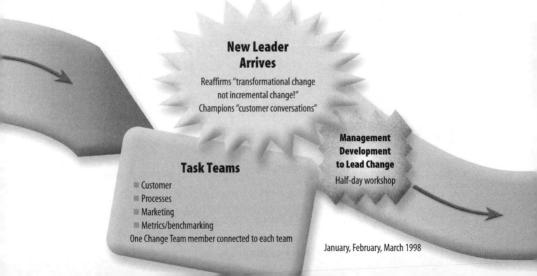

New Leader Arrives

Reaffirms "transformational change not incremental change!"
Champions "customer conversations"

Task Teams

- Customer
- Processes
- Marketing
- Metrics/benchmarking

One Change Team member connected to each team

Management Development to Lead Change

Half-day workshop

January, February, March 1998

The leader felt that by starting with these customer conversations, he was encouraging people to develop and practice the skills they would need to survive as a business, because they would need to listen to customers every day in the new organization. "We are behaving our way into the future," he said.

The end result of this small-group activity was a two-day off-site, at which managers and interviewers analyzed the data collected in the customer conversations. A picture began to emerge of the challenges that customers saw themselves facing and the qualities of the training they would most want. The participants at the off-site called this picture the customer story. It painted a vivid image of what the new office was going to have to do to truly win the customers' loyalty. In addition, participants more deeply understood that the old organization was not resilient or responsive enough to give customers what they said they wanted.

WOW II: Listening to Customers

At a one-day whole office workshop "Listening to our Customers," the interviewers described to about two hundred and fifty employees how they had conducted the customer conversations and analyzed the data. Participants then developed advice for designing an office to meet the customers' needs,

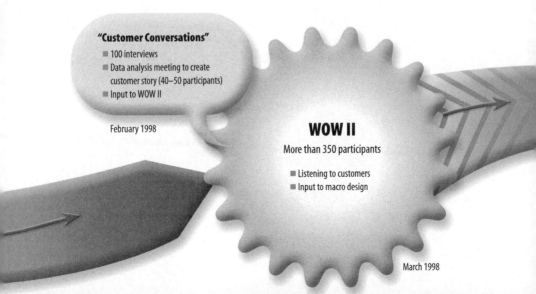

"Customer Conversations"
- 100 interviews
- Data analysis meeting to create customer story (40–50 participants)
- Input to WOW II

February 1998

WOW II
More than 350 participants
- Listening to customers
- Input to macro design

March 1998

thus preparing managers and a few others for another off-site to develop new design options for an Office of Training and Education that would be better able to give its customers what they said they wanted.

The end result of this WOW was a clear set of customer requirements, inputs to macro design, and a new set of Task Teams to work on the next set of transformation issues.

Small-Group Activity: Creating High-Level Organization Models

Immediately following WOW II, fifty senior employees got together at a four-day off-site. Their job was to develop three or four high-level organization designs, based on the customers' story and the advice they received from participants at WOW II. Their goal was to create options that participants were 70 percent comfortable with and 100 percent committed to making work. Their job was to bring these back to the whole organization for a final decision.

Site Visits:
- HP
- PG&E
- Buckman Labs
- FAA

Management Off-site—
Creating:
- Vision and Values
- New organization framework options

April 14–20, 1998

Managers engaged in three rounds of small- and large-group discussions and boiled eight proposed models down to three designs for the entire organization to consider. During this off-site, managers also created a shared Vision, defined a set of organizational values, and determined one unifying set of design criteria, against which the organization would make the final decision. Less than a week after the Managers' off-site, all employees attended WOW III "Designing the New Office." Their mandate was, "Think about what we could be, and not what we are."

WOW III: Designing the New Office

WOW III was probably the most significant emotional event of the entire process. During this two-day whole office workshop three hundred employees reviewed the three designs, debated the relative merits of each, and talked about their future. Many were fearful that the design that most resembled current reality would be selected. Still others worried about their jobs in any of the new structures. On the morning of the second day, all staff voted on the design

WOW III

More than 300 participants

- Designing the new office
- Macro framework for new organization structure
- Launch Organization Design Teams

April 1998

choice they believed best-positioned OTE for the twenty-first century. The clear winner was a surprise to many. People had left the first day believing that everyone would opt for minimum change. Instead, most employees chose the answer that best met the customers' needs, optimized the design criteria, and truly positioned the office for the future.

The session ended with participants making plans to further involve staff at all levels in completing the detail of the answer they had chosen. The most striking implication coming out of the session was that nearly two-thirds of the management system would be gone within the next three to six months. The new organization had sixteen managers (where the old had more than sixty) and was significantly flatter. In addition, every employee was going to market and develop services that had never been considered before. The transition would be formidable.

Small-Group Activity: Bringing the Design to Life

Over the course of the next three weeks, subgroups met to work on the detail design of each of the new divisions. The objective of this "mezzo design" phase was to detail the organization to mid-level detail. During this phase the organization defined coordination and integration methods between the new units, defined the structures within each division (consistent with the design criteria used for the high-level design), and began to detail jobs and roles needed to support the new units.

Organization Design Teams Work

Draft Division-level design:
- Missions
- Boundaries
- Roles

May 1998

The end result of this activity was a much deeper understanding of how the new organization would really function and the jobs that would enable it to move forward. At the same time, groups estimated the costs of supporting the new mode. Estimates included assumptions regarding the number of staff and space requirements. At the same time, Task Teams worked on the marketing plan for customers and final proposals for senior management.

WOW IV: Transitioning Our Way into the Future

In late May 1998, the whole office met again. The purpose of this Whole-Scale meeting was to describe the transition process to the new office. The group reviewed the details of the mezzo design to ensure that everyone was still aligned and agreed with the decisions. They performed a check to make sure that all of the pieces fit together in a way that everyone felt comfortable with.

The end result of this whole system review was a shared understanding of how the new organization was unfolding and the kick-off of a new set of Task Teams designed to determine the implementation plan for "go live." Teams worked on everything from the selection process to move people to their new jobs, to the physical layout and office reconfiguration. Another team focused on the training requirements and plan for transitioning.

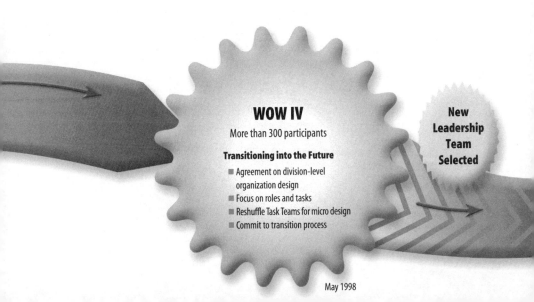

WOW IV

More than 300 participants

Transitioning into the Future

- Agreement on division-level organization design
- Focus on roles and tasks
- Reshuffle Task Teams for micro design
- Commit to transition process

New Leadership Team Selected

May 1998

Shortly after this meeting, the organization selected its new Leadership Team. The team held its first meeting. The only jobs that were not rebid at the leadership level were the Director and the Deputy Director positions. The off-site for the Leadership Team began their efforts to create Strategy and to form as the new team. As a part of their development, the entire team visited another organization (sort of a team benchmark visit). This visit served to highlight the priorities this team needed to pay attention to and to identify the most important issues they would have to address to ensure that they launched the new organization appropriately.

WOW V: Implementation Event

The move to the new organization design began in earnest during the Implementation Launch Event. At this one-day meeting attended by almost three hundred staff, the leader articulated the game plan for moving to "go live." The large group reviewed and agreed to plans for job selection. The leader introduced the new Leadership Team. He outlined the initial training plans for the start-up of the new teams, and the group agreed upon a schedule for the movement of the entire staff.

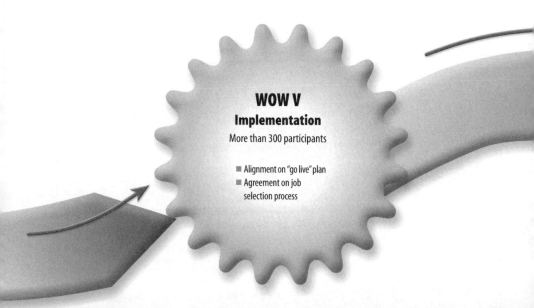

WOW V
Implementation
More than 300 participants

- Alignment on "go live" plan
- Agreement on job selection process

Micro Design: Taking Hold of the Day-to-Day

The term *micro design* means the operational-level detail of the new organization—*micro* in the sense of very detailed, down to the day-to-day work responsibilities of the entire staff. It can take place only when the new incumbents have assumed their new roles. This level of organization design activity took place in the new teams and divisions over the course of the next two months. Each division kicked off this activity with their own Launch Event. Work groups met next. Each division and work group outlined how to function day-to-day, developed process procedures for key activity within their scope of responsibility, and defined the job authority and responsibility for each position within the work group.

Templates that guided each group through the process facilitated the micro design activity. These templates, structured by the previous Task Teams, helped guide the Work Groups through the various conversations that needed to take place. In addition, the templates provided standardization across the organization. These templates could also then be posted on the internal web site, so that everyone could see the progress and the results of these conversations.

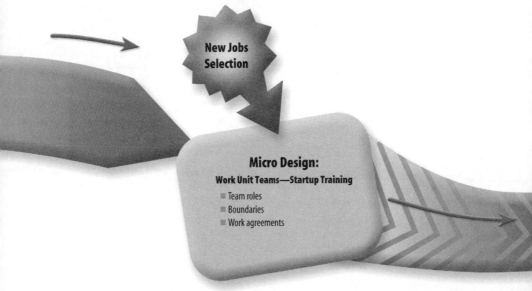

New Jobs
Selection

Micro Design:
Work Unit Teams—Startup Training
- Team roles
- Boundaries
- Work agreements

Continuation and Follow-through

As the organization moved forward, continuation work began to organize itself into several categories. Most of the sustaining work fell into the following categories: leadership, keeping purpose front and center, ongoing involvement, infrastructures for implementation, process design, and retention of disciplines.

Much of the continuation work focused on supporting the new leadership group in maintaining focus on the change throughout the organization and developing the group as the Leadership Team. This group developed workout-type sessions to address organizational policy and procedures that were now in conflict with the new culture. They began to articulate a new business strategy with key measurement indicators and continued to address the customer issues.

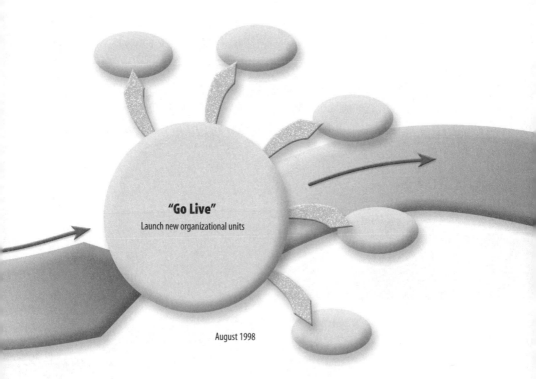

"Go Live"
Launch new organizational units

August 1998

Insights Concerning Moving Fast and Deep

Be Clear About What the Core Team's Role Is and Is Not   Some consultants believe that everyone should help design organizational change. With this belief, it feels autocratic and controlling to have a Design Group. Whole-Scale uses the Core Team to educate the system so that they make better decisions. It's not about the Core Team deciding for the participants; the decisions still lie with the organization members.

The Core Team accomplishes three things:

1. To educate the participants in the redesign effort as to what's possible

2. To be the communication link between the process and the people who can't be present

3. To do the "staff work" of fleshing out the solutions and the details that participants decide on in the large-group event

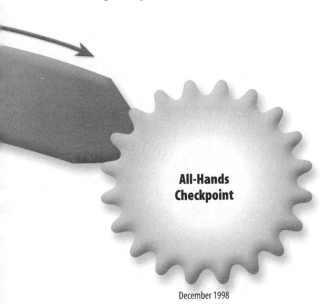

All-Hands Checkpoint

December 1998

**Get as Many People as You Can into the Launch and Implementation
Sessions**   When the entire organization is involved in creating a common
database about the business case for change, the possibilities, and first steps to
get there, people make it happen! Checkpoints keep the process moving forward
in integrated ways. If it is possible, launch and implement with the whole
organization, and engage as many people as you can in between to design for
the following reasons:

- **People can't create what they can't envision.** It's all about possibilities.
  That's the reason it works for Core Teams to bring "straw dogs" to the
  organization and for possibility panels to bring in new ideas. If this
  work can open up minds, people will make the right choices and be
  creative in the process.

- **Whole-Scale is messy and chaotic.** The process an organization goes
  through mirrors reality, and people work with it. The underlying
  beliefs are that systems are self-organizing and that the wisdom is in
  the organization.

- **It's like breathing in and breathing out.** Each piece on the Roadmap
  enables the next. Large-group work enables small-group work, which
  in turns enables the next phase of large-group work. Just as in an event,
  the process continually moves from the individual's perspective, to the
  table's perspective, to the whole room, and back to the individual.

**The Chartering Activity That Is Embedded in the Process of Getting
Started Is Critical**   The Steering Committee does the chartering by
considering boundary conditions (Givens, Constraints, Opportunities, and
Guarantees) and design criteria (what is important to the organization). Leadership alignment is also vital as is a Launch Event that sends a wake-up call to the
organization. This large-group event can be followed by small-group activity,
design events, transitioning and training work, implementation events, reunion
events, and Deep Dives to tackle and solve specific problems.

Summary

Focusing on the four points of the Star of Success that address processes, structures, resources, and information enables an organization to quickly align the whole system to support change and reward changed behaviors.

As a result of the integration of large-group processes with work design for a Whole-Scale approach, organizations have been able to reduce the cycle time on creating work design solutions by one-half to two-thirds. The cycle time from initial alignment, through design, to full implementation can, in some cases, happen in less than twelve months. An aspect of the process that has significantly helped this reduction in cycle time is the immediate implementation of new ways of working. New work processes can be implemented on a logical basis along the way to full redesign.

Whole-Scale has indeed become a process that allows the simultaneous creation and implementation of a new organization with whole system involvement.

C h a p t e r **6**

Integrating:
Mergers and Acquisitions

"How today's combination [merger] is managed shapes the
organization's operating culture, business practices, interpersonal
dynamics, and employee spirit for years to come."

> —*Joining Forces: Making One Plus One Equal Three in Mergers, Acquisitions and
> Alliances.* Marks, Mitchell Lee, and Mirvis, H. Jossey-Bass, 1998.

Introduction

Mergers and acquisitions are increasingly more common in today's rapidly changing environment. Driving forces in business, industry, government, and the nonprofit sectors are creating the need for new organizations. Statistics are plentiful about how few mergers and acquisitions fulfill the initial intention of bringing the organizations together. Many reasons have been identified for why organizations are combined, but never truly become one, such as, incompatible cultures. Often too much talent leaves in the transition to make the new organization successful, or combining the organizations takes too much time. In still other cases, combining the business processes did not result in the needed efficiencies, or the strategy for the new organization was not communicated well or committed to by enough people to carry it out.

Mergers and acquisitions developed through the Whole-Scale approach, balance all aspects of the new system:

- Driven by Purpose, Mission, and Guiding Principles

- Energized by the Strategic Goals as a Preferred Future

■ Driven by a culture that serves the Purpose, Mission, and
  Guiding Principles

■ Implemented through the actions arising from the Strategic Thrust

■ Measured by progress toward the Strategic Objectives

The creation of a new, truly integrated organization from two previously distinct
enterprises involves many complex change processes. This chapter addresses
how to use the Whole-Scale approach to successfully navigate through these
complex change processes. In the case of mergers and acquisitions, we are really
using the entire range of Whole-Scale practices. The processes we use in mergers
and acquisitions really combine both the Strategic Direction Development and
Implementation Roadmap (see chapter 4) and the Organization Design
Implementation Roadmap in chapter 5.

The Need for a Business Case

Before systems and/or organizations combine, they must be clear about the
reasons for creating a new organization in the first place. These reasons vary,
but must always exist. For example, in industry, the business case may include:
faster development of products and services, increased efficiency in production,
access to new clients or markets, or the acquisition of talent or technology that
will provide competitive advantage. As the Federal Government has downsized,
federal agencies have found themselves redefining their missions, combining
with other agencies to find efficiencies in operations, and developing new
cultures to work differently with clients.

The critical merger and acquisition decision revolves around the central
question: *Will the combination be able to create better stakeholder value than
either organization can now create?*

Whatever the business case for combining organizations or creating new ones,
the resulting new entity, driven by the reasons defined for creating the new

organization, needs to begin to build that new entity. The Whole-Scale approach offers options for building a new organization that can fulfill the promise of the business case.

Newly Formed Organizations Face Numerous Challenges

Newly formed organizations, created by either combining two organizations or the acquisition of one organization by another, face many challenges, such as:

- Formulating and implementing a short-term plan to quickly integrate the two organizations to accomplish the short-term goals of joining the two organizations

- Assembling and launching a transition team to manage the transition changes needed to integrate the two organizations

- Developing and implementing a longer-term strategy to move the new organization forward

- Beginning to define the culture of the new organization and practicing the behaviors that establish that culture

- Quickly assessing the talent of the two organizations to place people in spots that will make the new organization successful

- Examining work practices in the two organizations to look for greater effectiveness and efficiencies that the new organization can achieve by practices that support its goals

- Building relationships among the people in the two organizations to allow them to make plans and work effectively together

- Developing information flow among the people in the new organization to ensure that:
  - Everyone knows the organization's Purpose, Direction, and Progress

- Everyone knows his or her role in the new community and has the tools to fulfill that role

- Everyone receives feedback on his or her performance

Another component of the challenges to leadership in the new organization is that all of these major activities need to happen rapidly to allow the new organization to begin to function as quickly as possible. The Whole-Scale approach enables many of these major activities to occur simultaneously and in complementary ways to help speed up this change process.

The Star of Success

Using the Star of Success (see figure 6.1) as a guide, the key points the new organization initially needs to address on the Star are Strategic Direction—the Star of Success—as well as the Resources and Relationships points.

Strategic Direction: Star of Success

New organizations need to address short-term and long-term strategies simultaneously. Newly formed organizations need to plan for and produce short-term results to build experience and confidence. The organization is too tied up in its start-up activity and has too little experience to define and plan for long-term results yet.

For example, the business case for putting two organizations together often drives the short-term results. In one situation the business case called for increased savings in buying raw materials for the key product. Part of the short-term strategy was to quickly move to find the opportunities for those savings and to develop and implement a plan to realize those savings. In a large-group meeting of managers and key staff a specific, measurable objective was set, a task force was established, and work was begun to achieve the specific results.

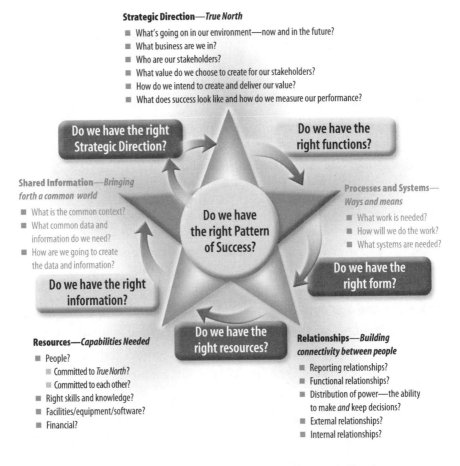

Strategic Direction—*True North*
- What's going on in our environment—now and in the future?
- What business are we in?
- Who are our stakeholders?
- What value do we choose to create for our stakeholders?
- How do we intend to create and deliver our value?
- What does success look like and how do we measure our performance?

Do we have the right Strategic Direction?

Do we have the right functions?

Shared Information—*Bringing forth a common world*
- What is the common context?
- What common data and information do we need?
- How are we going to create the data and information?

Processes and Systems—*Ways and means*
- What work is needed?
- How will we do the work?
- What systems are needed?

Do we have the right Pattern of Success?

Do we have the right information?

Do we have the right form?

Do we have the right resources?

Resources—*Capabilities Needed*
- People?
  - Committed to *True North*?
  - Committed to each other?
- Right skills and knowledge?
- Facilities/equipment/software?
- Financial?

Relationships—*Building connectivity between people*
- Reporting relationships?
- Functional relationships?
- Distribution of power—the ability to make *and* keep decisions?
- External relationships?
- Internal relationships?

Figure 6.1 Mergers and acquisitions focus on the Strategic Direction, Relationships, and Resources points of the Star of Success.

Whole-Scale provides the opportunity to involve a critical mass of the organization to develop and implement the strategy, to begin to define the culture, and to define the work the organization needs to do to produce results. For many, answering the vital few questions in the Strategic Direction Point of the Star of Success may well be their first exposure to this kind of strategic planning.

Mergers or acquisitions have the opportunity to bring together the resources from the combined organizations to produce results.

The initial long-term strategy for an acquisition is often driven by the strategy of the acquiring organization. In mergers, the long-term strategy may have to be developed from scratch or from the business case for combining the two organizations. In acquisitions, the new organization will want to examine all of the components of the True North Star but may change none.

Developing All Components of the True North Star

Because mergers create a new organization, it is necessary to develop all components of the True North Star (see Deep Dive C, figure C.3).

Processes and Systems   This point of the Star addresses the work within the organization and the systems that support that internal work. In organizations formed from other organizations, the work may be essentially the same as existed in the previous entity. More likely, however, the organization will need to develop new work or new ways of doing work. For these situations, the Whole-Scale Organization Design Implementation Roadmap is an effective methodology.

In its initial year of operation, Tower Automotive acquired three companies. A series of microcosm sessions, both large and small group, were convened to develop the new organization's Mission, Vision, Values, and Goals, as well as set and implement transition objectives. This approach to developing the strategy and integrating the three organizations was a key to defining the value-based, participative culture that makes this company unique.

One of our clients, which was acquired in this case, designed a series of Whole-Scale workshops to create new business processes, to link to the "mother ship." These new processes linked planning, materials requirement planning, sales forecasting, and other processes to the acquiring organization. Using representative microcosms from both organizations also allowed the new entity to build relationships, develop mutual understanding, and gain some of the synergies that might not have been possible otherwise.

Relationships   This point in the Star of Success offers special challenges in newly combined organizations. What reporting relationships will serve the new organization best? How "flat" does the organization need to be? Who best fits in the boxes on the organization chart? How does the new organization make and implement decisions? What external relationships does the new organization need, and how do we determine, develop, and manage these relationships?

Of particular importance in the transition is the relationship with customers. Ideally, the transition to the new organization is invisible to the customer. Often, however, either the delivery of the product or the service to the customer falls from previous standards. Short-term strategies usually include how to avoid any interruption of product or service to customers.

Employing microcosms of the new organization to address key issues in the transition and convening large-group Whole-Scale meetings that focus on potential issues helps minimize these kinds of interruptions. At United Airlines Indianapolis Maintenance Center, the organization was a merger of many maintenance operations from around the country. Over the course of the year prior to the launch and almost one year after, we convened large-groups sessions to work on various aspects of the cultural merger and the business issues confronting the new organization. Building relationships meant honoring the work practices of other locations, and integrating people in new ways. Over the two years, we used numerous microcosms (some pulled together at the very last minute) and continually expanded involvement as the facility grew.

One word of caution. Some mergers are really "phantom" mergers; that is, they look like mergers, but are actually acquisitions or takeovers. It is important at the outset to understand the true nature of the situation and design accordingly.

Resources   The organization needs to examine resources to accomplish its short-term and long-term strategies. Creating a new organization from old ones upsets the people working in the new, affects their productivity, and impacts the use of facilities and equipment as well. Employees feel off balance, uncertain about their future as a member of the new organization. Because of these uncertainties, many people in the organization often pay more attention to their own needs and survival than to their work. To address these issues, the new organization needs to offer opportunities for people to begin to build commitment to *True North*, develop relationships and commitments with others within the organization, and identify and gain the skills, knowledge, and competencies they need to help the organization achieve its goals.

At United Airlines Indianapolis Maintenance Center, each time a new group came into the fold, a series of "enculturation" sessions were held. These meetings, often with several hundred mechanics who represented new microcosms, were designed and run by "Pioneers" (employees who had been the first to arrive). These "enculturation" sessions were designed to build relationships, communicate the Vision, and consciously integrate cultures.

Shared Information   Probably the number one, most frequently mentioned issue in mergers and acquisitions is communication. In newly formed organizations, communication is even more important. As the new organization forms, people throughout the organization will need to know, and may demand to know, information such as:

- What is the added value that the organization plans to offer?

- Where is the organization going, that is, what are the short- and long-term results that it plans to achieve?

- What is the work of this organization?

- What systems, processes, and procedures will change from the ways that people are used to?

- What will my role in this new entity be? How will I know how I am doing?

- And much more!

How the organization develops this information and quickly disseminates it to all of its key stakeholders goes a long way toward defining the culture of the new organization. In organizations that want to share information freely and involve many people in making and implementing decisions, Whole-Scale meetings provide one way to disseminate information and engage a whole system.

The main purpose of communication in a new organization is to generate a common database within the organization and create excitement and enthusiasm. This shared understanding helps keep the organization whole. Seeing the "whole" system brings meaning and clarity for employees as they struggle during the stresses of transition. Whole-Scale meetings involving a critical mass of people in the organization offer a whole-system opportunity for generating and sharing information. Outside these large-group sessions, the organization needs to find many creative ways to keep the common database intact. See figure 6.1.

Roadmap for Mergers and Acquisitions

Figure 6.2 shows a Roadmap for mergers and acquisitions. This Roadmap, fashioned after the two Roadmaps for Strategic Direction Development and Implementation and for Organization Design Implementation, depicts the application of the Whole-Scale approach to change in merger and acquisition situations. It provides a framework for creating a plan to apply the Whole-Scale approach to change to a newly formed organization.

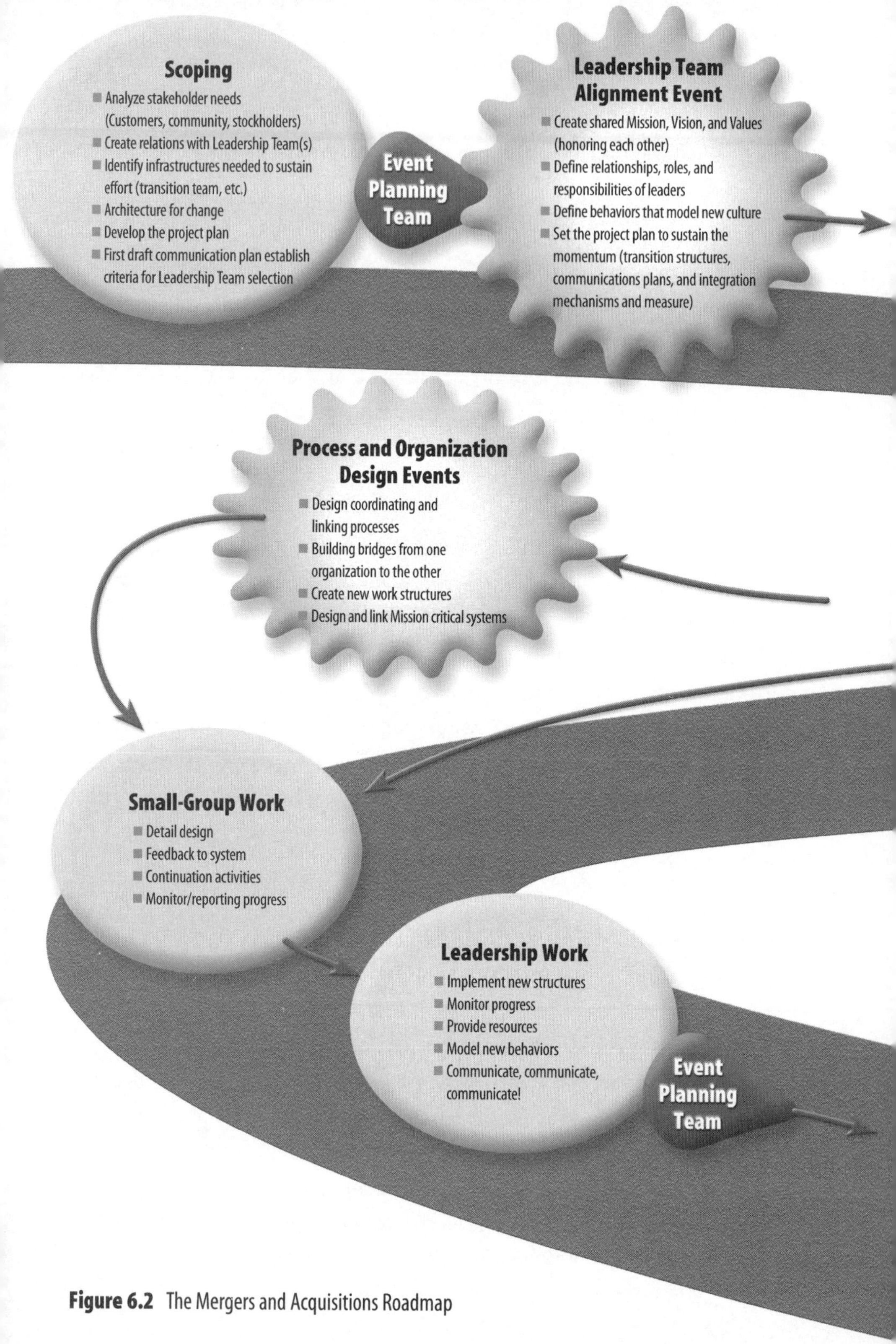

Scoping

- Analyze stakeholder needs (Customers, community, stockholders)
- Create relations with Leadership Team(s)
- Identify infrastructures needed to sustain effort (transition team, etc.)
- Architecture for change
- Develop the project plan
- First draft communication plan establish criteria for Leadership Team selection

Event Planning Team

Leadership Team Alignment Event

- Create shared Mission, Vision, and Values (honoring each other)
- Define relationships, roles, and responsibilities of leaders
- Define behaviors that model new culture
- Set the project plan to sustain the momentum (transition structures, communications plans, and integration mechanisms and measure)

Process and Organization Design Events

- Design coordinating and linking processes
- Building bridges from one organization to the other
- Create new work structures
- Design and link Mission critical systems

Small-Group Work

- Detail design
- Feedback to system
- Continuation activities
- Monitor/reporting progress

Leadership Work

- Implement new structures
- Monitor progress
- Provide resources
- Model new behaviors
- Communicate, communicate, communicate!

Event Planning Team

Figure 6.2 The Mergers and Acquisitions Roadmap

Small-Group Work

- Chartering teams
- Data gathering and analysis
- Craft draft of implementation initiatives:
  - Capacity building, customer focus
  - Communications, process understanding
  - Technology, HR assessment
  - Financial, info systems, etc.
  - Select Event Planning Team

Event Planning Team

Purpose Agenda

Small-Group Work

- Logistics planning
- Facility
- Invitations
- Speakers
- Logistics Team
- Finalize design

Organization Launch Event

- Finalizing and implementing short-term initiatives
- Crafting long-term strategy
- Beginning to develop the new culture

Reunions/Checkpoints

- Review commitments
- Assess progress
- Learn from what has happened
- Celebrate successes
- Decide what needs to happen next
- Review metrics and goals

Small-Group and Leadership Work

- Continuous monitoring, communication, and improvement

Not shown on the Roadmap are premerger activities, such as:

- Identifying the key drivers for combining the two organizations. What is the business case? What added value will the new organization bring that the current ones do not?

- What are the specific criteria for making this particular acquisition or for this merger? In the case of a business, will it bring, for example, increased market share, new products, new customers, or new geographic areas of coverage? What short-term and longer-term results are expected from the new entity?

Once the merger or acquisition has occurred, the activities shown in the Roadmap begin. As you help a company follow the Roadmap, you must remember that, as always, it will be an Action Learning journey. In fact, we have never done a merger or acquisitions process the same way twice. In some instances we have done the Launch Event and then an organization design session. In others, the process design meetings have come before the organization design work. It all depends on the situation. In one spin-off we actually conducted a Leadership Alignment Event and then a Management Alignment Event, before we held the organization launch meeting. In that instance, the client believed that having Managers onboard early was critical to the success of the organization launch meeting!

You will adapt the activities to the particular situation. No two plans will come together the same way; no two plans will be implemented the same way. In fact, you may need to change the plan several times over the life of the project. As you learn from each step, you may need to revise the next step and perhaps others as well.

Tower Automotive: Growing a Culture While Growing a Company

Tower Automotive was established in early 1993 after the purchase of the R. J. Tower Corporation by investors headed by Hidden Creek Industries. In late 1993, Dugald (Dug) Campbell became the formal leader of the "foundation" company of two locations, four hundred colleagues, producing $83 million of structural metal stampings for the automotive industry.

The strategy was to grow by balancing internal and external growth. New program awards were targeted to be between 10 to 15 percent per year, and similar growth was planned through the acquisition of other companies bringing new products, processes, or customers. After acquiring eight additional companies and forming two international partnerships, sales in 1998 were in excess of $1.8 billion, with forty locations and almost nine thousand colleagues.

Dug used the Whole-Scale process to help develop the company's Strategy and Values to align the new acquisitions around the Strategy and those Values. In 1994, Tower Automotive held four Whole-Scale events; the first was two days long and the others were each one day. The Purpose of the first event was to begin to develop the company Strategy and culture. At the end of those four events, about sixty colleagues had come to a consensus on the company Mission, Visions, Values, and three-year Goals and had developed and implemented a short-term transition plan.

Beginning in 1995 Tower Automotive held one-day Reunions about every six months. These Reunions included up to three hundred salaried and hourly colleagues from across the company. The purpose of these Reunions was to continue to strengthen the culture and to align more colleagues around the

Strategy. Each year these sessions were used to deepen the knowledge, understanding, and practice of a key part of the culture; for example, in 1995 empowerment, in 1996 leadership, and in 1997 commitment.

Many of the business units began to use Whole-Scale events as part of their leadership processes. In 1995-96, one business unit held several Whole-Scale meetings to develop its Strategy and use that Strategy to drive the annual budget. Throughout 1997 business units held one-day strategic planning sessions to set direction for their units.

Based on the belief that a key to Tower Automotive's success was its being a Values-based company, in the fall of 1997 all business unit leaders, mentors, and the Tower Automotive Leadership Team met to begin a whole-system change effort to build commitment throughout the organization to being a Values-based company. This session was followed in February 1998 by a meeting of the same Leadership Team plus all of the business unit Leadership Teams, about 225 participants. The Purpose of this session was to speed up the transition throughout the organization to moving to Values-based leadership. Participants left the session with immediate action steps and a process for speeding up the implementation of Values-based leadership.

Over this four-year period, Tower Automotive made the Whole-Scale process an integral part of its approach to leading the organization through its rapid growth. The principles of Whole-Scale are now an integral part of the mental models that guide the leadership of the company.

Summary

Whole-Scale change enables and facilitates mergers, acquisitions, and even spin-offs. Engaging microcosms of staff from the affected organizations builds powerful bridges between cultures. Honoring each person's truth as truth and building a common database allows organizations to begin creating new organizations by bringing those systems together in Whole-Scale ways.

The process of thinking whole system and acting whole system begins at due diligence. The business case and the promise of the integration guide the Whole-Scale Change process.

Whole-Scale facilitates mergers and acquisitions by:

- Giving voice to and hearing the issues, concerns, and opportunities of the other party

- Involving all levels in well-planned communication strategies and Whole-Scale events

- Enabling people to work the short-term objectives and simultaneously seeing a bigger picture and a longer view

- Engaging microcosms of staffs from both organizations

- Simultaneously working all the points of the Star of Success

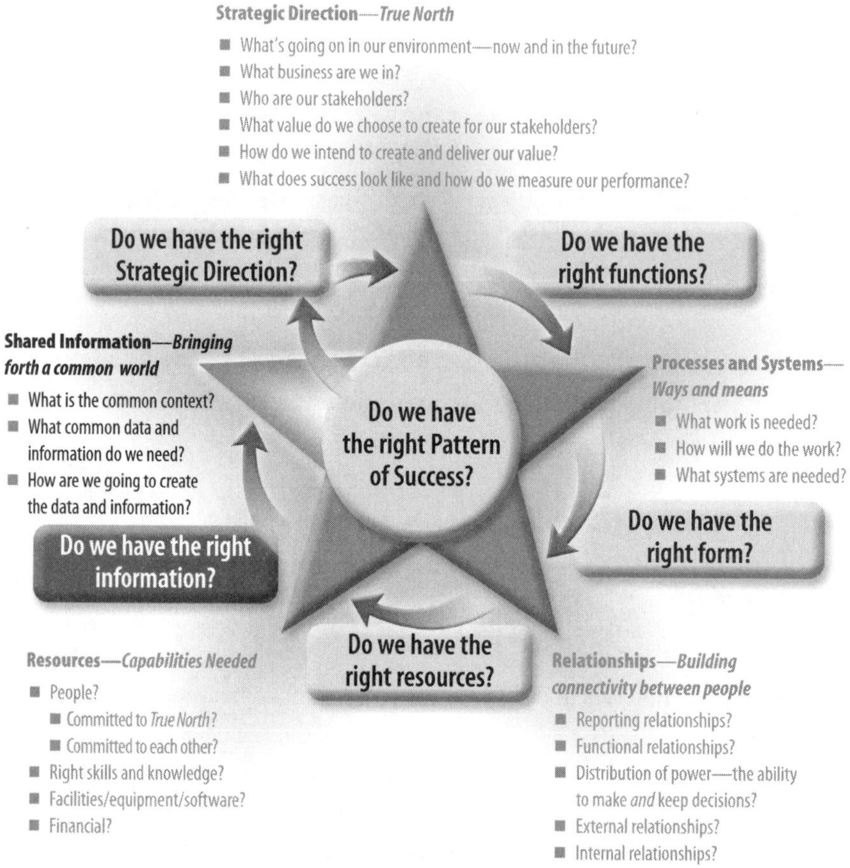

Strategic Direction—*True North*

- What's going on in our environment—now and in the future?
- What business are we in?
- Who are our stakeholders?
- What value do we choose to create for our stakeholders?
- How do we intend to create and deliver our value?
- What does success look like and how do we measure our performance?

Do we have the right Strategic Direction?

Do we have the right functions?

Shared Information—*Bringing forth a common world*

- What is the common context?
- What common data and information do we need?
- How are we going to create the data and information?

Do we have the right Pattern of Success?

Processes and Systems—*Ways and means*

- What work is needed?
- How will we do the work?
- What systems are needed?

Do we have the right information?

Do we have the right form?

Resources—*Capabilities Needed*

- People?
  - Committed to *True North*?
  - Committed to each other?
- Right skills and knowledge?
- Facilities/equipment/software?
- Financial?

Do we have the right resources?

Relationships—*Building connectivity between people*

- Reporting relationships?
- Functional relationships?
- Distribution of power—the ability to make *and* keep decisions?
- External relationships?
- Internal relationships?

Figure 7.1 The Shared Information point of the Star of Success is important to sustaining momentum for change.

Sustaining the Momentum Systemically

"The proof is always in the eating of the pudding."

The momentum of a major change effort is sustained when the organization anchors the required changes in the fiber of the organization while maintaining its ability to respond to the next set of challenges. Sustaining the momentum of change is a challenge for any organization; sustaining the momentum of change systemically is one of the important attributes of the Whole-Scale approach.

Systemic momentum is achieved through paying attention at all times to all points of the Star of Success. At times, the work of the change effort may focus more on one of the first four points, such as setting the Strategic Direction, and all points are kept in mind at all times. We have come to believe that for sustaining momentum for change, the most important point on the Star of Success is the fifth and final point, Shared Information (see figure 7.1). When an organization has been able to share information in a way that sustains a common worldview, it has achieved the ability to sustain change.

Planning for Sustaining Momentum:
"Good post-work planning begins the work."

The change Roadmaps shown in chapters 4, 5, and 6 always contain options for ways to address the efforts that need to go on before, between, or after large-group events, as well as the large-group events themselves. We can understand these charts intellectually, yet the preparation for and execution of a large-group Whole-Scale Event creates a dilemma that must be addressed if we are to sustain the momentum of the change process.

On the one hand, those involved in preparation for a whole system event believe that it will have major impact on those attending, that it will leave the participants with hope, expectation, and energy to create their own future. In addition, because so many important things need to happen to get ready for Whole-Scale Change processes, focus is often on the immediate tasks rather than on the future. The danger is that these events can become a kind of end point, rather than a step in the change journey. (One metaphor that we use to help overcome this syndrome is to think of a large Whole-Scale Event as a window to the future of the organization, not a wall that stops us from going in that direction.)

On the other hand, the exact outcomes of the event are not totally predictable, so detailed planning cannot take place until the event is over. Before an event, people are concerned with what will happen after the event is over. They have become somewhat cynical because of the many "flavor of the month" burnouts they have experienced in previous change efforts.

So the dilemma is that much of the organization's change energy focused on the event and the inability to see past the event. One of the challenges of practitioners of the Whole-Scale approach is to be able to hold this dilemma and help the client hold this dilemma as reality without losing the big picture of the change effort. Recognize the dilemma, name it as such, and then keep moving ahead.

During start-up, the discussion about sustaining momentum centers on the awareness that Whole-Scale involves more than leadership alignment and big events. Follow-through thinking begins even before activity starts. It requires sustaining the excitement and commitments so critical for long-lasting success and for anchoring the change in the bedrock of the organization. Ongoing work to implement actions that enable change gets the organization to the point where it is no longer possible for it to "snap back" to old ways.

The possibilities are endless for continuation activities that are systemic. The answers to what needs to happen to keep systemic change moving exist in the organization . . . they need only to be harvested. The people in the larger system (including and beyond those who were in the event) will have the answers if you are wise enough to ask them. Together with our clients (the whole system), we do a true brainstorm (wild and crazy) to come up with every idea anyone has about how to maintain the momentum begun in an event or in a series of Whole-Scale events. People have plenty of ideas that they don't normally get asked to throw out. You will be amazed at the wisdom you can get!

Here are some examples from one brainstorming session with a client. This is a partial list. After they brainstormed *every* idea, they *"asterisked"* the best ones that they absolutely had to put energy toward:

* Spin off teams for follow-up

* Get an "operations coordinator" to manage the excitement

* Collect and circulate on e-mail all the values and beliefs we've uncovered

* Collect stories of new behavior illustrating that we're starting to live our values

* Make it management's responsibility to solicit and communicate new stories

* Add in all kinds of "hero" stories

✽ Look broader than you might be thinking now . . . ask customers, stakeholders, and so forth

✽ Get input from front line across the whole system

✽ Get input from leaders across the whole system . . . get them to give ideas and articulate their personal yearnings. "How I wish that . . ."

✽ Close and debrief the Event Planning Team with a celebration. Give super-hero awards and recognition

✽ Actually, systemwide "thanks" would be great

✽ Set a date and advertise it for the next meeting in another part of the system

✽ Publicize office/team successes, with thanks

That was just a few, to give you the idea. There will be literally thousands, if you ask and listen. Everyone wants it to continue in the right direction!

Ideas for continuation that we have seen used successfully with our clients include, but are not limited to:

■ Initiate ongoing communication processes that enable the organization to remain "whole" about the changes taking place

■ Train people to carry out new roles and to relate with each other in new ways

■ Make systems changes, especially human resource systems changes, that build and support the new culture

■ Initiate Task Teams to plan and implement specific activities for systemwide change

■ Monitor progress, provide feedback, make midcourse corrections, change direction, and so forth

- Coach leaders and others in their roles in the change process

One of the underpinnings of the Whole-Scale approach is Action Research. Consequently, continuation thinking needs to begin at start-up. Collectively, the organization will become wiser about continuation strategies and specific actions along the way as they continually ask themselves the Action Learning questions:

- What's happening?

- What are we learning?

- What do we need to do next?

- Now what's clearer about continuation?

The reasons why this seems to be true are the following:

1. **Everyone needs to know where the organization is going.** What is its purpose? A strategic plan—including such things as Mission, Vision, Values, Guiding Principles, and Goals that people throughout the organization understand and are committed to—meets this need. The best way to get people to commit to a strategy is to have them help develop it.

2. **Everyone needs to know how the organization is going to get where it wants to go.** The action plans to carry out the strategy, linked to the budget, are generally the means to achieve the strategic plan. Cross-functional groups often develop these action plans. The danger with these groups is that they may go off on their own, form their own chimneys, and stay isolated from the rest of the organization. Communication needs to exist within these groups as well as between these groups and the whole organization.

3. **Everyone needs to know his or her role in helping the organization achieve its strategy.** In other words, each person wants to know how to be a good citizen in the organizational community. This includes regular

work roles and roles related to the activities special to carrying out the strategy, for example, being members of action teams.

4. **Everyone wants feedback on his or her performance as a citizen in the community.** This includes regular feedback from supervisors or team members and recognition from others in the organization. Rewards and recognition are included here.

5. **Each person wants to be heard in the life of the organization—in strategy development, strategy implementation, everyday work, and so on.** This means that instead of leaders always telling the employees what is going on, the employees also tell the leadership what is going on. In this case it is the job of leadership to listen.

These five needs form a framework for the issues a communication system needs to address to sustain the momentum of change. How organizations meet these needs makes the difference in their ability to sustain momentum for years on end. Certain application principles can make a tremendous difference.

Application Principles

Four principles help drive implementation of change. These are seen in Figure 7.2 Principles and Practices of Implementation:

- Keep the system whole

- Engage as many microcosms as possible

- Build critical mass for change

- Keep the flame of change burning by using the formula:
  Meaning × Hope × Power = Energy

Principles: **Microcosm Practices:**

Keep the System Whole

- Meaning/Purpose of organization
  - Whole organization
  - Department
- Staying connected as a community
- How we are doing as a community
  - Feedback to me on my performance
  - Listen to my voice

- Written
  - Report card
  - Visual display
  - Newsletter
- Face-to-face
  - Town hall/all-hands meetings

Engage as Many Microcosms as Possible in Everything We Do

- Common database and practices

Build Toward Critical Mass

- Large-group meetings
- Deep Dives
- Checkpoints
- Reunions
- Action Teams

Keep the Flame Burning:
Meaning × Hope × Power = Energy

- Meaning

  - Purpose of organization
  - Strategy: Mission, Vision, Strategic Objectives
  - Structure for change

- Hope

  - Reunions
  - Stories of success

- Power

  - Shared decision-making
  - Action Teams

Figure 7.2   Principles and Practices of Implementation

Keep the System Whole

Segmenting an organization in order to control it is the old way of doing business. Organizations are traditionally chimneyed or siloed by function, layer, region, geographics, etc. A key to the success of a Whole-Scale Change process is the organization staying whole—keeping the segments integrated. In Whole-Scale Events the group stays whole because they are all attending the same event, having the same experiences, learning much the same information, and working on the same issues. After the event, staying whole is a challenge. The environment changes, people return to their silos, new information emerges, and long-term people leave and new ones arrive.

Some of the approaches that help keep the system whole include the following:

- **Have a clear direction for the organization that people throughout the whole system have in their hearts and heads and that they understand.** This direction can take many forms, such as Mission, Vision, Values, Guiding Principles, Goals, and so forth. The key is that a critical mass of the organization has committed to the direction. All decisions individuals and groups make are thus made with the global view in mind. Each person and group acts locally while always thinking whole system.

- **Stay connected as a community.** The methods to stay connected are commonly known: face-to-face communication, written communication, meetings, the Internet, and so on. The important issue, with regard to staying whole, is knowing what the organization needs to be connected about. Staying whole includes being connected, as individuals, because all know at least the following:

  - The purpose of the organization

  - The short-term objectives or results that it has committed to

- The success the organization is having toward achieving those objectives, including who is doing what, how it is working, who is struggling, what the success stories are, and so on

- Individual performance results and how they contribute to organizational results

- **Give people a voice.** It is important that people are heard, throughout the process, as the organization develops purpose, objectives, and actions

Engage as Many Microcosms as Possible

In Whole-Scale Events, as part of a microcosm, the participants make up the whole system or a critical mass of the organization itself. Groups are like a laboratory for the duration of the event; they create and maintain an environment in which the microcosm moves together toward change. Once an event is over, the laboratory is dissembled, everyone returns to the workplace, the internal and external environments change, and people who attended the event are in a different place mentally than those who did not. Microcosms that existed in the event, such as max-mix groups and ad hoc Work Groups, are no longer intact. Thus, a key challenge is to maintain momentum against numerous forces trying to shut it down.

To sustain momentum the organization must be able to re-create key elements of the large-group meeting, day to day. As the organization moves forward, it must continue to bring together groups that represent the diversity of functions, disciplines, levels, and opinions that exist in the organization. New microcosms, such as Action Teams, Task Teams, Committees, and Implementation Teams, have to be engaged as the organization moves forward. Microcosms can also come together in the form of other large-group meetings, such as checkpoints, Deep Dives, and Reunions.

At United Airlines Indianapolis Maintenance Center, using the microcosm was critical at start-up. Often people would walk into meetings and realize that they were not the right representative group to make informed choices at the moment. People would literally halt meetings to "recruit" co-workers who brought the voices the group needed to hear into the decision-making process. As a result, two things happened: (1) they moved faster and (2) they sustained and created new change energy every step of the way.

Build Critical Mass for Change

Throughout any Whole-Scale Change process, microcosms of the organization engage in activities in a way that creates a hologram of the system working together as a part of the whole. The organization must reach out to people to *continually expand the circle of involvement.* When a critical mass of these microcosms experience a paradigm shift, the whole system can change. These constantly changing sets of microcosms carry with them the seeds of change and the energy necessary to support the effort.

Within one department of the CIA, Dannemiller Tyson Associates consultants were never able to get the whole system together. They were, however, able to involve everyone by the time the change journey was done. At each opportunity, they included new people. To maintain continuity, they were always careful to ensure that each max-mix included some individuals who had participated in previous activities as well.

Underlying the principle of the critical mass is the notion of connectivity. Recently it has been shown that you can shrink organizations by looking at the numbers of connections people have to each other. Like the movie *Six Degrees of Separation,* recent research has shown that each of us in organizations is connected to everyone else in the organization through a series of interpersonal relations (*Business Week,* June 1999). Even in the largest organizations, people who do not know each other are connected by fewer than three to five people. If the organization can bring the critical connecting conduits together by having each person engage in two to three conversations, it can very easily connect the whole—even when that whole is 20,000 or 300,000 people!

Keep the Flame of Change Burning

Two Dannemiller Tyson Associates partners spent time in India working with colleagues at Eicher Consultancy in Bombay. The question they asked most frequently was, *How do you keep the fire burning? How do you sustain the passion and energy the process creates?*

People in all organizations undergoing change are very concerned about how to keep the momentum of change going. How do organizations sustain the high level of fire and commitment that they experience during a Whole-Scale? As a result of their experience in India, they created the following formula:

$$\text{Meaning} \times \text{Hope} \times \text{Power} = \text{Energy}$$

Energy for sustaining change comes from the metaphoric multiplication of meaning, hope, and power. In a way similar to the DVF Model, if any one of these factors is lacking, the "product" will be zero and there will not be the energy for sustaining change.

Meaning comes from embracing the Purpose, direction, and plans for the organization; it is achieved when everyone in the organization (1) owns the Strategy as expressed through the components of the Strategic Planning Model, (2) understands the structure for the change process, and (3) as part of a microcosm, engages in the change work of the organization.

Hope comes from knowing that the organization is being successful in its change efforts. People can nurture hope when they (1) see the organization learn and apply its learnings as it goes forward and (2) see demonstrable results. Hope stays alive through having metrics that measure the outcomes of the change efforts, monitoring results using those metrics, and keeping the system whole. Hope grows when the organization provides clear indicators of success that all can see.

Power comes from having a critical mass of the organization actively engaged in the change efforts. Empowering more people in the organization supports the power in each individual to sustain the change process. Power comes from exercising the ability to influence. Sustaining momentum becomes easy when people feel powerful about the things that matter to them.

These elements are like logs on the fire. They are the fuel that keeps the flame burning and focuses and transforms the fire's energy into momentum and forward movement. The challenge in sustaining momentum is to strike the right balance between these very critical elements. Ensuring that people always have a sense of meaning, hope, and the ability to influence the decisions that affect them ensures that the fire never dies.

How To's for Sustaining Momentum

Questions you will often be asked as you sit and listen:

- How do you assure follow-through?

- How do you sustain the momentum?

- How do you measure the results and the impact?

The answers to questions like these actually begin to emerge in the prework with clients. Good continuation and follow-through begin at the beginning of the change effort. Waiting until after a large-group meeting is often too late and will cost precious weeks of momentum.

On the other hand, the difficulty that arises as you discuss sustaining momentum is that you cannot know precisely what it will take until after a large-group meeting is completed. If you are applying good Action Research, you will wait until you have the best available data to finalize the next steps. You will never be able to fully predict what choices the whole system will make, nor will you know what requires follow-up until the intervention phase is over. You can make great assumptions and develop high-level contingency plans, but you cannot finalize the follow-through until near the end of any phase of the effort.

What follows are outlines of five possible strategies for sustaining momentum— measurements, communications, structures, meetings, and visual displays. Each of these can work well if it fits the client and the situation.

Measurements

Clients who go through a Whole-Scale process often see dramatic results in a short time. Creating metrics that define the level of business results is an important step for continuation. Having measures is not enough, though, without good means of communicating them. If people do not see or hear the results reported, they might unfortunately believe that nothing has happened. Sustaining momentum, then, is largely keeping people connected to the data, constantly building the common database.

Companies may want to consider the communication strategies that some Dannemiller Tyson clients have used:

- The Veterans Administration/Human Resources put their metrics on their Web pages or on their intranets.

- Many have created visual displays of the measures or milestones and posted them strategically throughout the organization.

- Eicher Motors in India tracked and displayed the number of "valentines" (requests for support or action) and the response rate and completion rate for the requests.

■ Richmond Savings issued a report card for the first year after its Whole-Scale Event to communicate progress.

A number of organizations have designed metrics for teams, translating the macro measures of the business into measures for each Work Group.

Figure 7.3 is a sample monitoring chart that can be used to monitor progress on specific focus areas within strategic business units (SBUs). The following

Work Units	SBU1	SBU2	SBU3	SBU4	SBU5
Focus Area					
Customer Responsiveness	Project Status		Project Status		
Information Technology		Project Status			
Supplier Relations		Project Status			
Capability Development					

Monitoring possiblities:
By focus area: quarterly
By work unit: monthly
Whole system: semi-annually or annually

Figure 7.3   Sample Monitoring Chart

procedure is one possibility a company that has been through a Whole-Scale process may want to consider:

- Post the chart in a highly visible place

- Down the side, list the focus areas (key organizational thrusts or goals)

- Across the top, list the organizational units

- Within each box, units describe all projects and their status in support of each particular goal the unit developed during the Whole-Scale process

- For each goal, each strategic business unit develops its own actions

- Through this chart, they display those actions and their status for everyone to see

- Monthly SBUs review their overall plans and actions and quarterly champions convene Whole-Scale meetings to review the results on their focus area

- Cross-functional groups meet to review the overall actions in support of that particular initiative

Communications

One way to look at communication is to consider what the organization and the leadership need to communicate. The following practices of communications seem to apply to organizations in rapid, systemwide change. They serve as the framework for establishing a communication strategy that sustains the systemwide change effort and helps an organization stay connected as a community.

- Many times, an organization cannot physically "get everyone in the room." Because of this, they can seek creative ways to keep everyone informed and engaged in the process. An organization can use report cards, newsletters, lotus notes, information fairs, videotapes, and other methods for involving those who were unable to attend the Whole-Scale Event.

■ The organization must rely on more than one communication method, over more than one channel, in order to ensure that the messages get across. Different people listen for different things and they listen over different channels.

■ A report card may work well at first, but once the bulk of the changes are underway, there may no longer be a need for such a document.

■ Videotapes of the sessions to document what happened and to show others who was there and what these people decided are another possibility. Videos are powerful communications tools because they capture (1) the content and processes of the meeting; (2) who was there; (3) the excitement and energy of the meeting; and (4) the commitments people made. Videos are visual and visceral ways of communicating the deliberations and actions that took place throughout the process.

■ A series of town hall meetings throughout the company between the large-group meetings, to involve people who were not at the meetings, can be an effective communication tool. The inputs and commitments of those not in attendance at the sessions are very important. Town hall meetings are more than just one-way communications of the results of the larger group sessions. They are mini-replications of what occurred and was experienced by those in attendance. Town hall meetings are often much smaller group meetings, facilitated by people who attended the large-group sessions. During these meetings, the facilitator can repeat some of the Whole-Scale processes, and people have an opportunity to experience for themselves the same issues and struggles as those in attendance. The outputs of these sessions can become inputs to other large-group meetings.

- Creating chat-rooms and electronic bulletin boards to enable the conversations that need to occur across time and territory is a recent addition to an organization's communication toolbox. The tools are particularly useful in distributed organizations. They enable people to input and react to the decisions that are being made real time.

The Veterans Administration/Human Resources organization created a Web page just for the results of the strategic implementation initiatives they created. On the Web page they put results on the goals set, best practice ideas from across the system, and information about where to go to see the results of the Task Teams working on the human resource initiatives.

Structures

In many Whole-Scale processes, as part of the work, organizations create teams beyond the Core Teams, the Steering Committees, or the Event Planning Teams described previously. In some situations the Core Team or the Event Planning Team continues to exist long after an event, or even a series of events. They see their role as assuring the follow-through on the work started. Event Planning Teams may want to reconvene months after their work to check progress and coach the leadership on what they need to do to achieve sustainability.

At Ferranti Packard, Corning Revere, and Ford Milan, Event Planning Teams continued to oversee the implementation work. Their action was not planned, but it was important in each case.

Still another way to encourage continuation is to put Implementation Planning Teams, task forces, and other temporary teams and structures in place to pursue the actions and decisions coming out of the work and follow-through. Often what sustains momentum is employee involvement in the issues the event has raised. Coming out of a recent event, employees volunteered to serve on Task Teams to work on the issues they said were most critical to success. Small-group activities such as those between and after Whole-Scale sessions keep people focused and engaged.

Finally, it is possible to establish a continuous improvement process and structure to ensure that processes, procedures, and policies that needed changing are addressed. Employees, customers, and providers could each input to a Continuous Improvement Team (a microcosm of the whole system). This team can set priorities and convene max-mix teams to resolve problems, using a modified General Electric workout process (see Alban and Bunker, 1996).

What follows are several examples of structures that organizations have created to manage and oversee the continuation of their change efforts. The first (see figure 7.4) represents a generic oversight structure for continuation. In this example the Leadership Team meets quarterly; the Implementation Steering Committee meets monthly; and various task groups working on specific

Figure 7.4 Generic Possibility for Continuation Structure

implementation issues meet as needed. These various task groups work on issues such as specific goals or process improvements, or intact work groups work on specific area problems. Membership in each is overlapping to ensure connectivity.

Corning, Inc., developed the second model (see figure 7.5). This approach created max-mix groups at the plant level and the department level to oversee and monitor improvement and implementation activity. The Leadership Team focused on strategy, long-term issues, and the external environment's influence on the change process. The Steering Committee focused on tactics, objectives, and cross-departmentwide issues. Departmental teams addressed internal department issues and actions and focused on the day-to-day improvements needed to sustain the change.

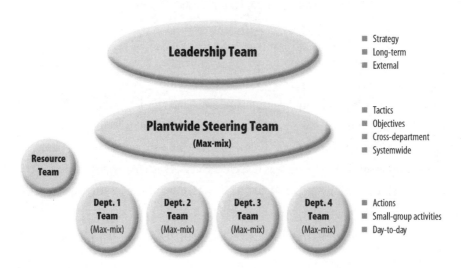

Figure 7.5 Corning's Structure for Continuation

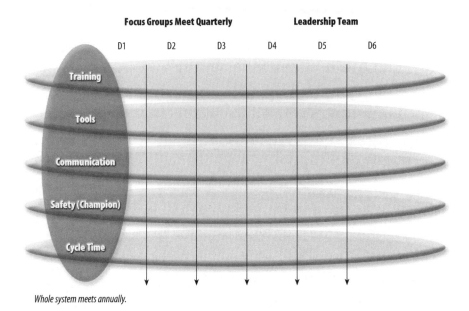

Figure 7.6 United/IMC Continuation Structure

United (IMC) Indianapolis Maintenance Center (see figure 7.6) developed a different model. United created max-mix teams of people responsible for specific issues within the organization. On a quarterly basis, all of the individuals in each area responsible for a particular focus (such as safety, training, customer satisfaction, and so on) met to review progress and set priorities for change. On an annual basis, the intent was to have the whole system review the decisions and priorities these groups had set. The system would then use this data to inform the following year's strategies and tactics.

The final structural consideration is the notion of team charters. Team charters are nothing new and the one in figure 7.7 is a good generic example a consultant can offer clients. The point is that sustaining momentum requires sustaining focus. For example, task teams may be given broad powers and, by their nature, very large problems to solve. Both the size of the issues they are addressing and the ambiguity within these issues regarding boundaries, constraints, timeframes, authority, and so forth, can cause teams to flounder and time delays in achieving

Project Team Charter

Project Title

Project Objectives/Measures of Success
1.
2.
3.

Project Rationale (Why this Project Is Important)

Team Members		**Milestone (Project Plan)**	
1.	(Leader)	Step	By When
2.		■	
3.		■	
4.		■	
5.		■	
6.		■	

Training Checklist	**Boundaries and Constraints**
Team Skills	■
	■
Problem Solving	■
	Resources Available
Other _____	■
	■
	■

Project Champion	**Expected Completion Date**

Figure 7.7 Generic Team Charter

results to occur. Simple charters can help. Charters describe the boundaries, limitations, scope of the problem the team is working on, and the basic "marching orders" for the Task Teams. These, in turn, enable teams to start up quickly and stay on task. Tackling problems that are "solvable" in ninety days also ensures that results will be visible and that the teams themselves will have enough energy to move to the next issue!

Meetings

The ability of organizations to sustain momentum is very dependent on their ability to stay focused. As soon as a Whole-Scale event is over, other day-to-day realities set in. Many organizations can maintain focus and discipline for a maximum of four to six weeks. Various types of meetings can help sustain focus. Brief descriptions of five different types of meetings show the range of possibilities:

Checkpoints These sessions sometimes involve everyone, but often bring together only a critical mass. The purpose of a checkpoint is, in the true spirit of Dr. Deming's PDCA (plan, do, check, act) cycle, to check progress toward the agreements made and to adjust the plans as required. They can occur at various times, when the system believes it should have made sufficient progress. Their purpose is both to review for progress and to spur activity. Knowing that a checkpoint is coming often spurs groups to action. It is amazing how much people can do quickly when they know they will have to share their progress with their peers!

All Hands Another form of checkpoint is an "all-hands" meeting. Organizations can simply bring people together regularly (monthly or quarterly) for two to four hours. These meetings are really status checks and refocusing tools. Unlike a traditional meeting, these short meetings are designed in advance and are interactive and apply Whole-Scale methods (such as max-mix seating). All-hands meetings can also last for a full day or more. Again, the intent is to check progress and make mid-course corrections.

Workouts In some instances the Whole-Scale work is just the beginning of the change process for an organization. Many issues/processes remain for the organization to resolve/design. A workout-type process, modeled after the GE workout, works well in this situation. Large groups of people meet for a very short period of time to work out a specific problem, process, or issue, using the skills, methods, and tools they had learned in the Whole-Scale approach.

Deep Dives   Deep Dives are one- to three-day meetings with a very specific purpose, such as to address a specific process or system issue. The name *deep dives* fits because they bring together a microcosm of people to dig deeply into the issue for the express purpose of solving the problem or designing an answer. They work well for things such as performance management systems, rewards and compensation, and hierarchical roles and responsibilities.

Reunions   Reunions, as the name implies, reconvene the initiators of the changes in a large-group meeting to celebrate the progress the organization has made and to refocus and redirect actions if needed. Reunions can last anywhere from half a day to one or two days and can occur as often as quarterly or as infrequently as once every year or so.

Visual Displays

A big part of sustaining momentum is keeping the change effort in front of people. Visual displays are very powerful ways of letting everyone know the progress and results of the efforts to date. People need to see and/or experience the changes to truly believe that things are different.

One organization created a huge tree in the middle of the office near where everyone walked. Each time they completed a project, they put a piece of fruit, with the project or the result written on it on the tree. Over the next few months, everyone watched this tree bear fruit. Each piece of fruit gave sustained meaning to the effort and convinced people that change was real and happening.

Visual displays further demonstrate that the organization is keeping its commitments. A timeline on a huge wall is another idea that organizations have used with great success. As organizations meet milestones, the timeline takes on new life. Color codes, copies of memos, and other things that communicate that the organization is meeting its obligations are displayed. People can "experience" the changes right before their eyes.

The Stakeholder Analysis and Monitoring Chart (figure 7.8) is yet another example of a visual display. The stakeholder analysis display includes information about who the key stakeholders are, where they are in support of the change initiatives, and finally, the actions the organization is taking to ensure stakeholder support.

Stakeholder	Level of Stakeholder Involvement				
	Aware	Understand	Believe	Commit to Implement	
S1					
S2					
S3					
S4					
S5					
S6					

Figure 7.8 Stakeholder Analysis and Monitoring Chart

A Story About a Community Seeking to Intervene in Escalating Violence

Situation and Convening Issue

City government officials, community organizations, and citizens had identified the need for a community-driven plan to deal with the issue of escalating violence. Based on per capita numbers, the city was listed as one of the top five cities in the United States for violent crime. Initially the mayor's office asked a number of interested individuals and organizations (neighborhood associations, civic associations, advocacy groups, and professions) to work together to generate a common purpose, outcomes, and roadmap for creating involvement and ownership of all citizens in the community in whatever it took to reduce the rate of violent crime. Aligning the various community constituents proved to be a long and difficult process. Several high-profile murders finally pushed everyone toward alignment around the need to involve everyone in creating a community of which they could be proud.

Roadmap: Event Purpose and Its Role in the Overall Process

A Microcosm Planning Team designed a Whole-Scale Launch Event where citizens, law enforcement, and government would come together to clearly identify the problem and, together, create some alternatives. The whole community was invited to the Launch Event meeting to identify a Vision and goals for a safe community and the actions and framework needed to achieve that Vision. The Purpose of the meeting was "to come together to plan and create a safe community of which we could all be proud."

Approximately three hundred and fifty people attended the Launch Event (seventy-five teenagers from the community attended). The local news media captured the outputs from that meeting and broadcast the results (goals and action plans) to the whole city on the evening news. During the meeting a continuation plan was proposed, tweaked, and agreed upon.

Interim Results

Volunteers (who came forward and signed up during the October 1998 event) met throughout 1999 and moved forward with the actions agreed upon in the Launch Event. A local grassroots organization stepped up to sponsor the continuation efforts and help move the Steering Committee forward. They (along with the mayor's office) identified the need for a Reunion meeting to take some of the lessons learned through the efforts of the volunteer action groups and use them to generate plans that would impact neighborhoods and districts.

Reunion Event and Continuation Plans

A Reunion Event was conducted in November 1999. Approximately one hundred and fifty people attended the Reunion Event, which was again open to the entire community. Action plans for specific districts and neighborhoods were detailed and shared with the whole community. The grassroots organization will continue to oversee all follow-up activities along with a local non-profit organization, which obtained a grant to connect all of the continuation activities. Throughout 1999, law enforcement and state epidemiologists have been capturing and measuring progress toward identified goals. Violent crime rates were lower in 1999. Another Reunion Event is planned for January 2001.

Summary

Four principles and practices that help continuation occur are:

1. Keeping the system whole

2. Engaging as many microcosms as possible in the change effort

3. Building critical mass for change

4. Keeping the flame of change burning by using the formula
   Meaning × Hope × Power = Energy

Five structures make the change effort much more likely to take root and grow. These are:

1. Using measurements to track results and publishing them in a variety of ways

2. Communicating messages to the organization in a variety of media

3. Putting a structure in place to support the changes the organization makes

4. Holding meetings of various kinds to rekindle energy and make course corrections

5. Using visual displays to communicate the progress of the change effort

Continuation must be a major focus of Whole-Scale efforts. The methodology is very powerful in mobilizing energy in organizations and creating a strong momentum for moving forward. Even when follow-through is lacking, the spirit of people *may* carry the day. Results of Whole-Scale work have surfaced years after the sessions, largely because of the experiences people had when they attended a large-group meeting!

Yet the key to long-lasting change is the ability to sustain that momentum and continually re-create the magic. There is no single answer to creating sustainability and certainly no one right way to help an organization maintain its focus. Despite this uncertainty, however, the Whole-Scale consultant has a responsibility to engage in the "continuation conundrum." Not to do so is to leave an important part of the work undone.

Truly Living Whole-Scale:
Principles as Foundations

Introduction

A profound belief that underlies Whole-Scale processes is that life is an Action Learning project. At every moment each of us makes decisions for next steps that are based on things we learned from the past. Failure cannot exist when a person lives an Action Learning life. Everything that happens contributes to the next learning process. Thus, Whole-Scale processes are based on the experiences its founders had, all the mentoring we received, and all the ideas we explored. The methodology continues to grow and change every time we come together as a learning community to share our knowledge and enrich our communal wisdom.

The partners of Dannemiller Tyson Associates, the founders of Whole-Scale methodology, came from a variety of individual backgrounds (socio-technical systems, community organizing, education, politics, systems engineering, labor organizing, and so forth). We brought with us diverse assumptions about how to bring about change in people and in organizations. At first, we argued about who was right and who was wrong. What we discovered out of these "uproars" with each other was that each person's truth was true and that, combined, there was more truth than any one alone had seen up to that point.

Combining multiple realities in this way gave us the wisdom to create Whole-Scale processes. From our ongoing conversations over the years have come the principles that underlie the new theory that Whole-Scale contributes to the field of organization development.

Whole-Scale Guiding Principles

Whole-Scale Guiding Principles fall into three areas: (1) principles of the Whole-Scale approach, (2) principles that guide Whole-Scale practice, and (3) principles of Whole-Scale design. Although we have sorted them into these areas, they occur simultaneously as a consultant works with clients and other consultants.

Principles of the Whole-Scale Approach

The principles that are most compelling and enduring are the following:

Tap the power of the microcosm.   Having a microcosm of the whole organization enables the organization to change in real time, both incrementally and in a major paradigm shift. If the "right" DNA is present, a critical mass of the organization creates momentum and change in the same way as having the whole system present.

Uncover the wisdom in the organization.   The wisdom is in the people, and when you connect people, they will have all the wisdom they need to find their own answers. True wisdom for the organization will emerge from its people when they share a common database and are able to see a whole picture. When the processes allow them to continue to connect around "one-brain and one-heart," they will find the best answers for their own challenges, much better answers than any outside consultants could ever come up with!

Look at the whole system. Piecework solutions cannot resolve complex systemwide problems. Real wisdom and synergy come from the inter-connectedness of relationship, identity, and information; long-term solutions require focusing on all three of these simultaneously. There is undeniable power in thinking whole system. Bringing together various microcosms of the whole organization enables the organization to see itself as a whole and therefore be able to change in real time and in the most holistic ways.

Believe that people support what they help create. Whole-Scale work includes a deep and abiding commitment to the principles of democracy. It supports empowering people to help shape the environment in which they live and work, because people are most likely to support and sustain work they help create.

Live life as an Action Learning project. Continuously re-examine results at different points throughout a change process to inform the next step. Do this for the next agenda items in a meeting, the next day of an event, and for the next step on the journey of the whole organization.

Create self-sufficiency. Clients have the ability to bring about the changes they yearn to bring about. The consultant's goal is to evoke the knowledge and skills in client systems to enable them to carry on effectively after the consultants are gone. A smarter organization has within it the knowledge and capacity to sustain change.

Plant the seeds of generativity. Generativity is a transformational action. It starts with existing perspectives and the individual truths that each person brings. What everyone knows, as a whole, becomes the organization's new truth—an image, an idea, and a concept that unites many diverse yearnings and appeals to the hearts and minds of people. This generativity forges new pathways that serve to integrate planning and action, policy and implementation.

Use reality as a key driver.   Keep a continual focus on the simultaneous and sometimes conflicting realities that exist in the internal and external environments of the organization. Let the real needs of people shape the conversations along the way. Discuss issues face-to-face rather than simulating or role-playing them.

Build and maintain a common database.   A "level playing field" of information and common understanding of the issues informs the discretion of people at all levels so that they can make wise decisions, individually and collectively. Learning to see the world through each other's eyes and thus sharing perspectives ensures that everyone in the organization gains a more complete and consistent perspective. In Whole-Scale Events, panels from stakeholders (customers, corporate leaders, and so forth) often present their views and answer table questions of understanding toward this end.

Think about the future before you plan.   The compelling nature of a Preferred Future image people have created together forms a powerful basis for action. People support what they have been part of creating and begin immediately to act in ways that ensure they will achieve it. The Preferred Future comes about as a result of "behaving our way into the future" and "beginning with the end in mind."

Have a Purpose to drive all choices.   People must agree on what must be different in the world because they did the work. It is impossible for them to plan without knowing what they wish to achieve.

Honor the past and the present as you create the future.   Organizations must acknowledge the past and the present as they move into the future. If they are not willing to learn from where they have been and where they are, it is difficult for them to move forward.

Keep the flame of change burning.   Energy fuels the flame. The formula that expresses this relationship is: Meaning × Hope × Power = Energy. When an organization has meaning and hope and power, it will be able to continue its change process.

Principles of the Whole-Scale Practice

The principles of practice represent the way in which a Whole-Scale consultant works, individually and collectively:

Never work alone.   Ron Lippitt's voice still rings in our ears, "Never work alone! You cheat the client!"

Help the client uncover the answer.   The wisdom is in people, and when you connect them, the answers are in the organization.

Stand firm for the "silver bullets."   Silver bullets are truths that you will need to be consistent in supporting—such as the effectiveness of max-mix tables and the power of the microcosm. These silver bullets are the robust bases of Whole-Scale processes, and you will know more about them than the client will know.

Honor the individual, honor the whole.   Don't do anything for the individual that hurts the whole, and don't do anything for the whole that hurts the individual (Lippitt).

Provide Quality Consulting.   A definition of quality consulting has many facets and also represents principles of practice. You would do most or all of the following things:

- Love the work more than need the money

- Not take work you believe will not make a difference

- Know that you did your absolute best

- Forgive your clients for being who they are

- Act out of your beliefs

- Know your fears and work past them

- Have the client look you in the eye and say, "Thank you"

■ Be clear about the purpose of your interventions and act to achieve that purpose

■ Admit when you are wrong and learn from your mistakes

■ Be clear about the foundations that you believe this work is based on and commit to acting out of those principles

■ Know the boundaries between you and the client

■ Know the difference between consulting and managing, and practice being a consultant

■ Commit to deepening your knowledge of content, continuing to improve your skills, and living your values

■ Perfect the craft and art of consulting

■ Believe in the process, staying optimistic about what is happening ("It ain't over 'til its over")

■ Have the client say, "We got more than I thought we ever could"

■ Know your own strengths and limitations

■ Put as much as you have, and sometimes more, into your consulting work

■ Know what matters and go to the mat on those things that do

■ Feel part of something that really matters to the client system

■ Don't let it fail

■ Grab yourself by the scruff of the neck and shake hard when you and others are going through the motions

■ Know what pushes you to your best work and push yourself there

■ Do what is right versus what feels good to you or the client

- Seek a purpose that ennobles everyone and a design and facilitation that evokes ennoblement

- Frame every activity so that every participant knows that this activity is the right thing for him or her to do at that moment

- Always be able to say why you are doing what you are doing—its purpose and the principles that guide it

(From the work of Roland Loup, Dannemiller Tyson Associates partner)

Principles of Design

- Good, tested, and robust theory needs to underlie any design work.

- Start with a good change model (such as the $D \times V \times F > R$ Model).

- Understand the dynamics of Converge and Diverge—when to go whole and when to go detailed and smaller.

- Agree on a simple Strategic Planning Model that your participants can relate to. We use the model illustrated in figures 4.2, B.4, and C.1.

- Use a systems model like our Star of Success and North Star to ensure that all of the systems issues have been addressed.

- Have an adult education model in mind, which speaks to how to help people learn the right things to achieve the right purpose. We use one called DPPE (Data Purpose Plan Evaluate) shown in figure B.7, which we learned at the National Training Labs in the 1960s.

- Have a sound, robust team building theory to shape the work of the whole systems, large and small; we use one called MCG (Membership-Control-Goals), which is shown in figure B.8 and grew out of Jack Gibb's work many years ago.

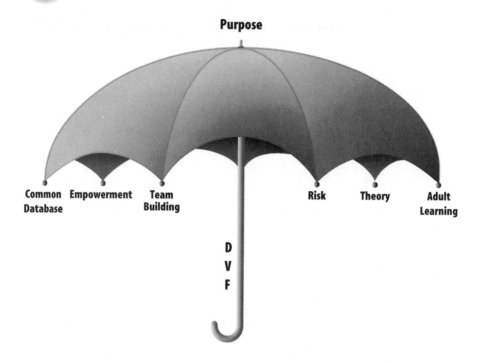

Figure 8.1 The Design Umbrella

The important message is that you use models of your own experience or borrow ours and make them your own. Don't design an intervention without good, solid theoretical underpinnings and beliefs.

The Design Umbrella shown in figure 8.1 encompasses the major tenets of Whole-Scale methodology. Without an engaging purpose to move toward, nothing else will work. The principles of DVF support the purpose. Six "spokes"—common database, empowerment, teambuilding, risk, theory, and adult learning—contribute in an aligned fashion to achieve the organization's purpose. The key to good design will be that each module you create will include a focus on each and every spoke:

Common Database   Each module needs to consciously add to the database being created in each person's mind, new data that each and every participant will add to his/her data, making it common in the room.

Empowerment   Each module has to include some elements that will empower people, making them aware of their freedom to choose steps needed and to shape their own environment. Each person needs to feel increasingly empowered because of the conversation that will take place in the particular module.

Team Building   Each module needs to improve team building in one or more configurations in the room: at a table, within a functional team, and/or in the whole room.

Risk   Each module needs to have an appropriate level of risk built into the assignment. If you make the assignment too risky, people will head for the "woodwork" and you'll have trouble getting them empowered again. If there is no risk involved in the assignment, people will get bored and won't reveal anything of worth to each other.

Theory   Each module needs to be based upon, and driven by, solid, tested organization theory. Avoid "theory of the moment," which often comes from someone's new book. Fashionable is not "solid," necessarily.

Adult Learning   Each module needs to be based upon, and driven by, principles of adult learning, which assumes knowledge on the part of a participant and all participants, and uncovers and uses that knowledge.

If a module supports one or more spokes and negates one or more other spokes, true unleashing of wisdom will not occur. Every design step must be moving us toward the purpose, as well, or why bother doing it. We often comment that there are no "throw-away lines"—there is meaning in every step the group takes together, if you remember to be conscious of impact, continuously.

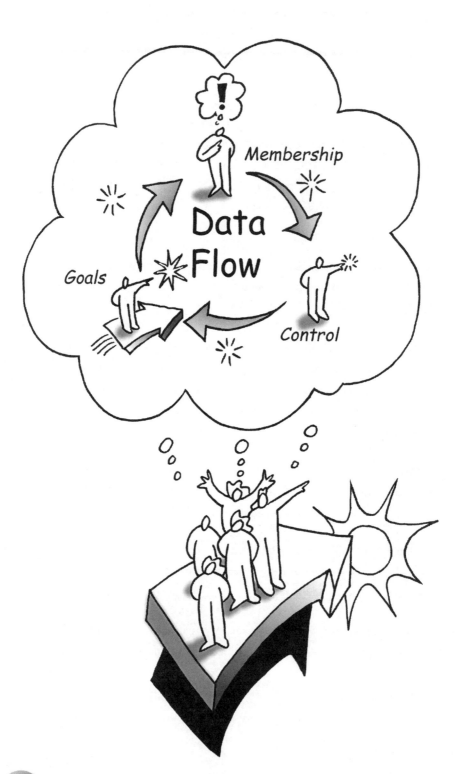

The Real Secrets
of Whole-Scale:
The Heart of Our Work

Those of you who have tried to follow someone's excellent recipe and then have had the product turn out to be something less than the chef produced will know that the missing element is usually something that is so much a part of what the chef believes that he or she doesn't even think of it. We at Dannemiller Tyson Associates want to add some important pieces before you head out to actually utilize the good tools of Whole-Scale. The real secret, which we do not want to forget to tell you, is in underlying principles and beliefs—about people, about empowerment, about integrity and trustworthiness—that shape everything we do. They are so important that the client will know, on some level, if you don't have them . . . and the recipe will produce a mediocre product. In our experience, our tools never truly fail . . . but mediocre is a failure we can't live with, and if you don't want to live with it either, compare your beliefs to the following.

We don't assume that we have a unique corner on good principles. You have plenty of your own. We do, however, know that the theories, processes, and tools of Whole-Scale will truly work only if you believe these principles . . . *truly* believe them.

First, let us describe what the outcomes of this work need to be. Barry Camson, a senior consultant trained and experienced in Gestalt therapy, process consultation, and work design (STS) processes describes it best. Barry visited us when we were working with a Ford Motor Company plastics plant some years ago. We had been doing the work for several months when he arrived, and the day of his arrival was the first day of a two-hundred-and-fifty-person, three-day Launch Event. Three Dannemiller Tyson Associates partners were facilitating the Launch. Barry watched and noted what we did and wrote up a paragraph describing the outcomes, as follows:

> This is a generative, transformative action. It is facilitated when people are fulfilling the need to have their voices heard and to belong to a community or society in which they believe. It starts with the existing perspectives and the individual truth that each person brings with them. It moves beyond that to a collective knowing— to a new ordering of old and new wisdom that comes from within and from outside the community. It expands what people know as individuals into a common database of what people know collectively. This knowing becomes the basis for their collective wisdom. What people know as a whole becomes their new truth. Generativity starts with each person's yearning and moves toward an image, an idea, a concept that serves to unite the yearnings of many diverse people and which has a universal appeal to it. Such an image appeals to the hearts as well as the minds of people. It is out of this generativity that new paths are forged which serve to integrate planning and action, policy, and implementation.

Profound thoughts Barry uncovered—the real explanation, we believe, of the magic we keep uncovering in organizations. If you truly believe in the power and integrity described in that paragraph, take another step to look at another of Barry Camson's gifts to us.

Barry took notes during the three-day Launch Event he observed and sent them to us when he returned to Boston. His notes profoundly described everything we believed and had worked out in our processes. Since that time, we have been using this brainstorm of principles as we teach people to do Whole-Scale work. They are true statements of the work we do with clients and why we do it . . . in a large meeting, in a small meeting, in any part of the relationships we build and honor with our clients.

As you read these principle statements, look for one or two that are vitally important to you in your work with clients. These are so critical that you could never forget to live them. Then watch for statements that speak to what you truly believe, but sometimes have a little trouble living. Get a colleague to read them also and identify the two types of statements. Take twenty to thirty minutes to share with each other what you have chosen and identify implications for the future:

Whole-Scale Principles

by Barry Camson, Observer and Documentor

- This work is about moving people from passivity to activity—the activity of mind, of action, of faith, of trust, of engagement of people with each other and their work.

  e.g. Representative participants are engaged in the planning and logistics process so as to move them from passivity to activity.

- Create a contactful environment. Contactfulness is built into the heart of the event. Enable people to make contact with each other. Facilitate points of contact among different views. Enable each person—leader, member, management, union to articulate what they believe. Support each person in listening to the other's truth and not arguing with it.

  - From the very beginning a different kind of listening is stressed. A neutral, non-judgmental kind of listening.

- Support people in taking in and reflecting on what others have said.

  e.g. The open forum format of:

  - what we heard others say

  - what is our reaction to it

  - what questions of understanding do we have

  e.g. Keep easels out of the way except when people are working on them so that nothing blocks contact, interaction.

  e.g. When asking questions of people up front in the open forum, put their name first.

- A different kind of speaking is also supported as an alternative in which people take time to listen to themselves before speaking.

  e.g. Facilitator suggests, "take a minute and go inside to reflect on your answers."

  Bringing the speaker's voice out into the room is also stressed.

  e.g. "Telling your stories."

- Focus on the details of empowerment.

  - Help create an environment where people are willing to push-back and have comfort around that.

    e.g. Participants are asked if they got the answer they were looking for from the speaker. "Did he get it?" "Don't just say it was answered if it wasn't."

    e.g. "Don't let us beat you down" is an occasional reinforcing comment from the facilitator.

  This also fosters a willingness, skills and a feeling of safety to speak out.

- Create mini moments of truth.

  - Ask people to speak out if their questions were not answered.

  - Intervene to push leaders to answer tough questions.

    e.g. "Will you overrule the team's decision if you feel it was wrong?"

- Intervene to facilitate people getting to and speaking out of their courageous parts.

  e.g. "Do you believe him?" (in response to a leader's answer).

- Intervene to facilitate clean interactions.

- Intervene to paraphrase to help make points clear where there may be some confusion or to show where people agree.

- Create interaction based on a perspective of multiple realities. Help create an environment where each person realizes that they bring their own truth; that when dealing with each person's own truth, there is no right or wrong way.

  - Help people become aware of how each hears the message differently. This reinforces awareness of multiple realities. It also enables people to begin to become aware of how their own filters, perspectives or need to be defensive impacts the message.

  - Help people to attain some degree of neutrality regarding other peoples' truths. Help people to listen to see the world through each others' eyes.

    e.g. Leaders set out their truth, participants set out theirs.

- Operate with a maximum mix of viewpoints. Utilize microcosms of the whole—a holographic approach in design team work, logistics team work and in some subgroupings used in the workshop.

- Create in the workshop a community operating from one brain and one heart. The community builds a common, interactive picture of their future arising from a common database which is composed of the individual pictures of each member of the community. This leads to a common sense of caring amongst the members of the community.

- Everything in the workshop, in the change work of the organization, as well as its future operation derives from the vision and values. This is the major value and core of this process. The organization and consultant always tune in to that and keep going back to it as the core of all current and future work.

■ Vision and values are powerful because they arise from full input of all members of the organization, the certainty of being heard, full opportunity for clarification, and consensus among everyone. The possibility of coercion is checked out.

■ Having a common picture in the organization of where the organization wants to be and uniting around some strategic direction becomes an important guide to the organization around choices.

■ Data is brought into the workshop forum from a variety of different sources and in a variety of different modes.

■ This work is about the assumption of responsibility by all. Participants operate in roles of facilitator, recorder, reporter. Everyone is asked to take responsibility for creative thinking.

■ Competencies are built along the way, e.g. in listening, speaking, scribing, recording and in more subtle skills such as identifying themes.

■ Use of the dynamic huddle. "Stand, pull-up a few chairs." People end up standing, talking, huddling around their work. This results in keeping the room in motion, in ongoing momentum, activity. Instead of having groups sitting and working around tables all the time, a flow in the room is maintained by having people stay active.

■ Enable the organization to diagnose itself and make meaning out of it.
  e.g. Sads, Mads and Glads look at what has worked, not worked in the organization.

  ■ Hearing from competitors and best practices from site visits enables participants to diagnose what their own organization needs and could apply in moving to a desired future state.

■ This work helps to build the organizational field. Input is continually provided from different sources. The group field continues to be enhanced through discussions in different groups. Out of each of these groups emerges key questions which have the virtue of having the support or awareness of that group behind them. These questions are asked of people up front and perhaps of each other. The answers as well as the questions then move into the organization field from which new key questions, ideas, awareness arise on a large organizational level.

e.g.   Input is brought in from a variety of outside sources using a variety of modes, e.g. customers, views of competitors, benchmarking ideas from other redesign sites through the research team.

e.g.   Creating a larger and collective group field is facilitated through the "Open Forum" which expressly looks at what people heard, what reactions and what questions of understanding they have.

■ Create contact with outside information—from customers, from competitors, from benchmarked organizations. Activities in the workshop help facilitate this contact.

e.g.   Presentations by customers followed by an open forum. Role play presentations of competitors followed by an open forum. Presentation by design team after site visits followed by an open forum. Panel of Possibilities setting out what has worked, been problematic in other sites.

   ● The implicit question is continually asked: "What is the most important thing that has stood out for us that the organization could learn from?"

■ Create the design team/research team as a facilitating and catalyzing force for larger organizational involvement. Bring new people into this configuration from the organization and enable it to be used in different ways and in different configurations.

Imagine a constantly changing, self-organizing entity moving through the heart of the larger organization, responding to different situations with different modes of self-organization as a model of the future and as a way of bringing light to and releasing energy in all different parts of the organization.

- The importance of bringing yourself fully into the process as:
  - Management leader
    - e.g.   Leader shares a very personal vision. "I walk in and I see…"
    - e.g.   Leader shares personal anecdotes of how she got where she was at the start of the work and how she moved to new places during the work.
  - Union leader
    - e.g.   Union leader sets out his high level of commitment and what the union is willing to do in the context of personal stories about himself. "My daddy once told me…"
  - Members
    - e.g.   Members are asked to tell their stories at an early part of the workshop.
    - e.g.   Volunteerism to the extent used, asks the members to take an affirmative action to bring themselves more fully into the process—their volition married with their actions.
  - Consultants
    - e.g.   The consultants constantly demonstrate and model that they are willing to be themselves and help the community gain some insight about this way of being.

- Value of transformational leadership. This is the process of speaking out, of allowing others the space for taking in what was said, the process of each enriching what the other has contributed. The act of taking in and enriching in return transforms the listener.
  - e.g.   The leader sets out his/her vision for the organization; the members take that in and enhance it with their own.

■ End the work with specific, realistic and supported action plans with commitments made to take action on them. This enables moving from the desired future and supporting values—to intentionality and volition—and then to concrete behaviors. This is crucial in order to dispel the memories of past failures, to build credibility and to enable this work to have full operational value.

■ As the consultant, be open to live your commitment to your client. Be open to that commitment engaging your heart, gut, intellect, and spirit and your values, personal vision, and enthusiasm. Be willing to be expressive about that commitment.

At the same time recognize that the client must decide to take responsibility for their individual change and for leading the organizational change. Consultant commitment to the client does not mean doing for the client.

Be prepared to live out of that commitment.

e.g. "We'll come in that day for free if it will make the difference in bringing about the changes needed."

■ The commitment of consultant to the client at its ideal is based on unilateral love by the consultant for the client in which the consultant affirms the client for who he/she is. This results in pulling forth the essence of the client and a working relationship based on trust.

　■ Create a large group, total system dialogue.

　■ Create conversations among small groups.

　■ Create conversations with sources bringing information into the room.

　■ Create conversations among teams, sub-groups.

　■ Create conversations between consultants and the client.

　■ Create conversations among and within the large group.

■ Have groups speak their commitment.

■ Build teams at different levels of the organization.

    e.g.   Design team/research team

           Logistics team

           Individual, max-mix working groups

           The overall organization

■ There is an undeniable power in having the whole organization in the room. It enables the organization to change in real time, both incrementally and in major paradigm shifts. It creates a common shared experience that the organization and all of its components can reference and operate out of in the future which will in time as it is enhanced take precedence over the old ways.

The workshop becomes a river in which the many strands of the organization are immersed, risking a complex flow of chaotic elements until the threads of the new organization begin to emerge.

■ This work is about a sincere, deep, abiding, unwavering, and non-faddish view of empowerment that runs to the core of one's being and is reflected in behaviors with other consultants, with the client and in how one works with the client. It is totally encompassing and pervasive.

■ This work is about the personal commitment to contactfulness in any personal interaction, of expressing feelings and expectations, and a willingness to do so in as close to real time as the realities of the work allows. This results in an ability and willingness to facilitate and support the client in being similarly contactful with each other. Not doing the work as a consultant can result in blind spots with the client around the same issues.

■ This work is about tradition—a knowing, deep and abiding commitment to the roots of organization development as a democratic practice, which support the empowerment of people to achieve their full potential as individuals and as groups and to live in a humane way.

■ This work is about using the different technologies to carry out the intentionalities of democratic and empowering values rather than using the technologies in a detached or value-independent mode. It is about using the technologies in ways that continually track and respect where the organization is at any given moment in their path toward their desired future.

■ This work is about freeing up the flow of valid information within a client group and supporting that flow and helping people to develop and fully use the skills that will enable them to fully make use of the information.

■ This work is about living out of your heart.

■ This work is about sharing the wealth with the abiding faith that those who receive will do the same thus creating an ongoing, positive force for change.

*   *   *

So there you have it. Pretty much everything we think we know at this moment. Let us know how it goes for you. We want to learn more!

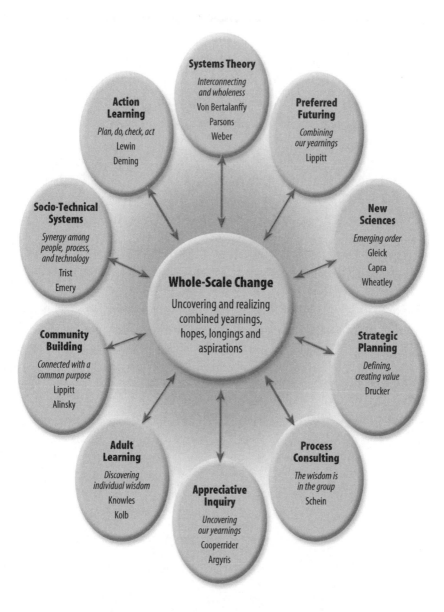

Figure A.1 Foundations of the Whole-Scale Approach

Deep Dive A:
Theory and Roots Underlying Whole-Scale

Foundations of Our Work

The purpose of this section is to go deeper into the theoretical traditions supporting Whole-Scale Change. As you do Whole-Scale, you are standing on many strong disciplines of whole system change practice. Figure A.1 illustrates the foundations from which we have derived our theoretical beliefs.

Older and Newer Wisdom

Many of you will recognize the theories and models that underpin our approach as coming from the familiar pathfinders in the fields of organization development and systems thinking. Lippitt, Trist, Schein, Beckhard, Von Bertalanffy, and Parsons are a few pathfinders whom you derive wisdom from as you practice this approach. Much of our knowledge comes from the laboratory method of learning developed by Ron Lippitt and others at the National Training Labs (NTL). Other knowledge comes from Eric Trist and his colleagues at the Tavistock Institute who pioneered the socio-technical systems approach to designing organizations.

More recently Meg Wheatley, Myron Kellner-Rogers, Fritjof Capra, and others have clarified and advanced our understanding of how chaos theory and systems thinking fit into organizational change. Rick Maurer, in his book *Beyond the*

Wall of Resistance, has reframed resistance in a way that is also very helpful. And Dick Daft and Robert Lengel, in *Fusion Leadership,* have distinguished between fusion and fission forms of organization change. Each of these has added to our understanding of why the Whole-Scale approach works instinctively. We will not cover all of these disciplines in detail in this appendix. Instead, we will describe a couple of the concepts in order to illustrate how we have assimilated the thinking behind them.

We see all of these theoretical foundations in figure A.1 interconnected. This picture emerged from asking ourselves the questions: *Where did we first learn that theory? Who was our first teacher? Where did that concept come from?* This model is the synthesis of all of our answers. In Deep Dive D you will find a list of readings that support this foundation.

Because the Whole-Scale approach to change rests on both older and newer wisdom, this next section will start with more depth about how we understood the wisdom from either its creator or trailblazer. Then each area will end with a description of how Whole-Scale made sense out of the work, then combined that value into the approach.

Socio-Technical Systems (STS)

Pathfinders' Wisdom

The STS (socio-technical systems) approach to designing work and organizational structures integrates three concepts:

- Social—people's needs, culture, rewards, training, and relationships

- Technical—tasks, activities, work processes, tools, and technology

- Systems—the relationship of all the pieces as they interact (living systems)

The foundation for the socio-technical systems approach lies in the work of Eric Trist and researchers from England's Tavistock Institute as well as Fred Emery's work in Australia. Their work in the late 1940s and 1950s demonstrated that the introduction of new technology produced dramatic results only when the design of the technical system was consistent with the organization's social systems. They also recognized the need to do their work in a context of general systems theory, which Bertalanffy was describing in biology years ago.

Trist and Emery's work pioneered specific STS design principles such as:

- Joint optimization (must maximize all of the pieces of the parts)

- Construct meaningful task patterns that lead to more holistic jobs

- Leave room for workers to set their own standards and determine their own means of production

- Ensure that jobs are worthy of respect in the community and contribute directly to the end product

- Make certain that the design of the organization fits with the goals intended and that each part of the design fits with the others

- Redundancy of functions, which is that you have to build redundancy of functions into the tasks of each team/group/unit to create self-sufficiency

What practitioners have learned over the last twenty-five years is that there is a set of characteristics that define and describe meaningful work. The seminal piece written by Hackman and Oldman *Work Design* (1980) describes the elements that define quality jobs across a wide spectrum of professional and nonprofessional work. The characteristics that they defined were:

- Job variety

- Job significance

- Feedback

- Task Identity

- Autonomy

- Continued learning

In today's environment, organization design changes must move fast and deep. Designing an organization's structures and processes includes making an important series of choices, often about work boundaries and structures. Historically in STS, a Design Team made those choices, based on benchmarking within and/or outside the organization, getting input from employees and managers to give relevance to the Design Team's beliefs. Then the Design Team had to move ahead to gain the alignment needed to implement the new design. This became the fundamental journey of most organizational design efforts of the last twenty years.

How Whole-Scale Internalized STS

The fundamental principles of STS that are also embedded in Whole-Scale Change are:

- Change is always a journey and never just "an Event"

- Any time you touch any one part of the system, you impact all of the rest

- Critical mass is required for whole system change

The Whole-Scale approach to work design moves more quickly to engage the larger microcosm of the organization in understanding its environment. Looking at possibilities and determining holistic choices about processes, jobs, supporting structures, and culture becomes the work of the larger group. The Whole-Scale processes create an environment for continuous alignment by tapping the wisdom of microcosms of the organization to uncover the choices for change in real time. As soon as the critical mass sees the answer, it can be put in place. We believe that people will implement that which they helped to create.

Whole-Scale Change as an Enabler of Process Consultation

Pathfinders' Wisdom

Following the seminal writing of Edgar Schein, we know that organizations creating their own solutions can create the most effective change. The consultant's role is to guide, coach, and teach whole system organization change skills, without being prescriptive. Process consultation results in joint diagnoses of problems, with the organizations coming to their own understandings of issues particularly relevant to them.

This approach still holds true to the underpinnings and principles of Schein's original model. The process consultant recognizes an effective role as being the expert in process. It is also necessary to help the organization come to its own understanding about the content, such as plans and actions. Although the consultant may think he has expertise that could solve the organization's problems, a consultant proficient in gaining client commitment recognizes he does not have enough grounding in the organization's past and present to implement a process to which everyone is committed. "Grounding" is meant in terms of culture, hopes, aspirations, yearnings, and longings. Thus, if the consultant were to drive solutions, they are likely to be the wrong solutions just because of the "not invented here" phenomenon. The process consultant is positioned with the client as a process expert, and also as a careful, wise content coach.

Schein believes that good process consultation results from proficient skills in:

■ Establishing helping relationships with clients

- Knowing what kinds of processes to open up between key stakeholders in organizations

- Intervening such that organizational processes are improved overall

The ultimate measure of process consulting success is when the organization acquires the ability to diagnose its own situation, develop appropriate responses, and implement such responses. Helping the organization to help itself is the objective of process consulting.

How Whole-Scale Internalized Process Consultation

What we have added to process consultation is in its application. In Whole-Scale process consulting, we seek to help the organization by jointly designing and executing processes to:

- Diagnose the organization's external and internal environments, creating shared information on important trends—what's working and what's not working

- Uncover and combine the shared hopes, aspirations, yearnings, and longings of key stakeholders

- Create shared plans to move the organization forward in pursuit of its shared hopes, aspirations, yearnings, and longings

- Execute the shared plans successfully

The essence of the Whole-Scale effort is jointly designing the right set of conversations (and silences) among the right set of stakeholders and then facilitating these conversations. One key difference you notice when doing Whole-Scale process consultation is that you see and work "whole system," rather than just solving problems and working on capabilities in subsystems.

Have the client stay in charge by making the key decisions in the change process and participating in the improvement of their own situation, thus staying true to the process consultation model. In the traditional process consultation, the consultant gathered diagnosis data and developed a diagnosis and a plan for the intervention. In Whole-Scale, the consultants work with the Microcosm Planning Team to gather data to make a joint diagnosis in the moment. The microcosm, representing all levels and areas of the organization, makes real time decisions about intervention choice points.

Whole-Scale Change as an Enabler of Strategic Planning

Pathfinders' Wisdom

Peter Drucker taught our founder, Kathie Dannemiller, to love strategic planning for its richness and wholeness. He and she taught us to identify stakeholders' hopes, longings, yearnings, and aspirations and to build those into business purpose. They taught us to identify and continually evaluate strategies to ensure that the strategies captured the hearts and minds of the stakeholders and move the whole system toward meeting the business purpose. Peter taught us to think about strategic planning as a rich, meaningful, whole system journey one takes and not just a one-time event.

Many different authors conveyed similar beliefs. In the late 1970s, Porter reminded strategic planners that this was an open system exercise. He wrote about the importance of aligning organization capabilities (internal focus) with competitive forces in the environment (external focus).

Henry Mintzberg (1987) wrote about the need for the strategic planning process to be a fluid one: "Formal planning alone is not the best way for managers to develop strategy. Facts, figures, and forecasts are necessary; but managers also need an intuitive understanding of the organization, a feel for the business not unlike a potter's feel for the clay. Strategy is not just a plan for the future but also a pattern out of the past. Strategies are not always deliberate—they also emerge over time as organizations innovate and respond to their markets. By seeing patterns take shape in their environments, the best strategists find strategies as well as create them."

How Whole-Scale Internalized Strategic Planning

Leaders around the globe are beginning to understand the ineffectiveness of the old "command and control" doctrine. They are starting to realize the need to inspire people to greater success. Most are trying to align and change the directions of large, cumbersome, hierarchical organizations quickly. With the old "command and control" doctrine, employees were expected to follow a strategic plan that they had neither seen nor contributed to. In the old way, strategic planning was often carried out by a few people at the top of the organization with the implementation controlled by these same people. Employees want more of a contribution to a strategic plan than a thirty-minute interview that was billed as "input to the plan."

In Whole-Scale, the strategic plan is initially developed by the Leadership Team or a small group within the organization with feedback from a microcosm. Everyone in the organization can influence the strategy and its implementation by their eventual involvement in the strategic planning process. Everyone participates in a meaningful way in the development of and carrying out of the actions in implementation. They are not just interviewed and thanked for their input. By having the power to help formulate the strategies and actions for implementation, everyone is aligned around the plan and its implementation throughout the organization. We believe that when people are able to see the whole diverse stakeholder value-picture, they are able to make wiser decisions about strategy than just the traditional small group of managers. This true empowerment frees all the people in the organization to contribute to the success of the whole.

Whole-Scale Change processes allow information to flow in such a way that the common database is created at a higher level of understanding than any one person could get individually. People have the opportunity to explore the past, present, and potential future of the organization together. Views come from key stakeholders such as customers, shareholders, union leaders, suppliers, employees, top management, community, and so forth. When the organization has a clear, common picture of the internal and external environment, the whole group can work together to focus on an ennobling picture of their future. They are then able to build goals, objectives, and plans based on their insights into stakeholders' needs. This leads to systemwide action planning to help people pull together various views into a coherent plan of action. As the whole organization works together over time to see and shape their future, they are free, at whatever level and whatever location in whatever part of the world, to do whatever needs to be done to achieve their purpose and create value for all key stakeholders.

The Whole-Scale Strategic Planning Model (figure 4.3 on page 68) has assimilated many different components of strategic planning from several different management thinkers. The key difference in Whole-Scale strategic planning is more than just the sum of the intellectual discoveries. It is more than how fancy the plan looks or how much intellectual or academic integrity the plan has. The real value is in the process, whereby everyone's wisdom contributes to the living product.

Whole-Scale Change as an Enabler of the Systems Theory

Pathfinders' Wisdom

Whole-Scale Change, a symbol of organizational robust growth and longevity, draws its sustenance through roots deeply planted in systems theory's fertile soil. Whole-Scale Change stands firm, rooted deeply in ground made solid by the structure created through more than 100 years of systems theory development.

Ludwig Von Bertalanffy, *General System Theory* (1956), captures the need for wholeness in the following, "The only goal of science appeared to be analytical, i.e., the splitting up of reality into ever smaller units and the isolation of individual causal trains . . . We may state as characteristic of modern science that this scheme of isolable units acting in one-way causality has proven to be insufficient. Hence, the appearance, in all fields of science, of notions like wholeness, holistic, organismic, gestalt, etc. which all signify that, in the last resort, we must think in terms of systems of elements in mutual interaction . . ." Von Bertalanffy also went on to postulate the need for general principles of systems theory to formulate a general systems theory.

Russ Ackoff is yet another source for systems thinking wisdom. His illustration (1971 unpublished speech, *The Second Industrial Revolution*) of the pragmatism of systems thinking is one of the best:

> Let me try to give you a feeling of why that [systems thinking] is so, by giving you an example rather than trying to give you a generalized proof. I would like you to go through the following thought experiment. I read in the *New York Times* the other day that there are 142 makes of automobiles available in the United States. So let's get one of each and bring them into a large garage—142 cars.

We'll hire ourselves a good group of first rate automotive engineers and first ask them to do the following: Inspect those 142 cars, test them, do any damn thing you want to, but come out and tell us which one has the best carburetor. So they run a series of tests and they come out and say the Buick has the best carburetor. So we make a note—Buick carburetor.

Then you say fine, now we would like you to do the same thing on transmissions. So they test the transmissions and they come out and say the Mercedes has the best transmission—we make a note—Mercedes transmission.

You say okay, take the distributor, and they run through and they come out and say the Dodge has got the best distributor.

Then one by one, we take every part until we have every part required for an automobile and we have identified the best parts available. Now when that is done, we tell them to take those parts off those cars and assemble them, because then we ought to get the best possible automobile.

But, do you get it? You don't even get an automobile. And for a very obvious reason.

Because it turns out that the parts don't fit, and that's what systems thinking is all about.

It says that the performance of the whole is not the addition of the performance of the parts, but it is a consequence of the relationship between the performance of the parts. It is how performance relates, not how it occurs independently of the other parts. That is what systems thinking is about.

So, synthesis is a different way of thinking and looking for explanations. It tries to find it by looking at wholes, the larger whole, of which things are a part rather than by taking things apart.

How Whole-Scale Internalized Systems Theory

The last sentence in the previous extract illustrates one of several key beliefs that Whole-Scale rests upon. You do not analyze and break down issues into smaller problems to be solved. This leads to a waste of energy, the same magnitude of which it would take a mechanic to rework the separate parts from the 142 cars and combine them into a functional automobile.

During each phase of a Whole-Scale Change process, questions are often asked of the client in order to get them to uncover possibilities and discover new wisdom about the whole organization. Questions are asked to get a subsystem to think about the implications of the larger whole.

Whole-Scale Change as an Enabler of the New Sciences

Pathfinders' Wisdom

Whole-Scale change draws on systems theory's insights of how living systems organize and operate as self-organizing systems, with new properties emerging over time in response to changes in the environment. Our knowledge is that people find meaning in the pursuit and attainment of their individual and organizational purposes. Through Whole-Scale Change, we create robustness and adaptability in our work and support our clients as they do the same in their organizations.

Four years ago, all of us at Dannemiller Tyson Associates shared the experience of Margaret Wheatley's and Myron Kellner-Roger's Sundance workshop, where we explored whole systems thinking as a community. We accepted the view of an organization as a living system represented by a collection of objects (people, equipment, software, and brick and mortar) joined together through a set of relationships to achieve some purpose and operating on system-generated information. We came to understand that in the same way we believe that "purpose drives choices," in systems thinking, "form follows function." What we learned at Sundance is that to create new form and new function requires us to balance the dynamics among: identity, information, and relationships. We validated that identity, the system's Purpose and the meaning it seeks, is the central driver of self-organization.

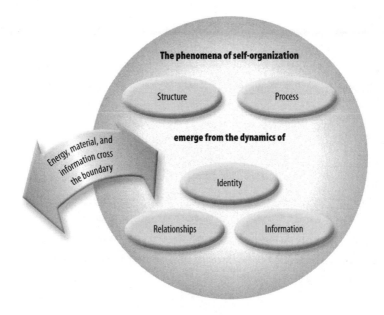

Figure A.2 Margaret Wheatley Systems Model

We also learned that organization is represented by the system's structure and processes.

Figure A.2 captures how organizations enact systems thinking. As organizations seek to create new forms and new functions, the conversations they have are mostly about structures, processes, and strategy. For us, the essence of organizations as living systems is, however, the interplay of the three bubbles in the lower half and the two bubbles in the upper half of figure A.2.

A key insight led us to understand that structure is a snapshot, an image at any given instant, of the nature of the system's objects and the relationships among them. Here's how we understand self-organization to work. As a living system self-organizes, it combines identity, its relationships, and information toward the pursuit of purpose. As the objects of the system (people) become a part of identity, relationships, and information, they produce interaction dynamics. It is these dynamics that create new structures and processes. Therefore, in Whole-

Scale, as organizations seek to create new forms and functions, everyone, as a member of the system, simultaneously experiences identity, establishes relationships, and creates shared information—resulting in a powerful shift in ways of believing and behaving.

Systems Thinking and the Role of Chaos in Change

Chaos is a form of order. The system learns from its chaos and is able to find things out and make needed changes. The system selects for itself what works and what does not work. You do not need to recognize the patterns in the chaos or study it. If you create and put in motion processes that will help the system do its own work, you will have exhibited the patience necessary to help a system work through chaos.

How Whole-Scale Internalized New Sciences

Our knowledge base was expanded and fortified by our learnings of the new sciences. Self-organizing systems theory validated Whole-Scale Change principles and approach. We are now able to frame Whole-Scale Change as a powerful way to guide the emergence of new system properties. Central to Whole-Scale is a shared Strategic Direction, which forms the system's identity and focuses and links all change efforts. Whole-Scale Change integrates the individual identity, helping to shape the organization's Strategic Direction which, in turn, reshapes the individual's identity: Action Research at work. The same is true for relationships among the people and the organization. We found the organizational equivalence of identity to be Strategic Direction.

Whole-Scale Change is working simultaneously on several dimensions of organizations: strategy, direction setting and implementation, forming the identity of the system; work and organizational design, developing and aligning resources, linking and integrating relationships, processes, and work systems, and creating shared information; and creating a supporting culture.

We believe that life itself is attracted to order, that it uses "messes" (chaos) to get to well-ordered solutions. If processes are set in motion to build toward a whole picture, the system will be intent on finding out what "works" and what's "right." Everything in the system will be involved in a constant process of discovery and creation.

We have learned that using the power of microcosms in our work allows all of the sought-after order within the chaos to uncover itself and form new paths. Whatever the size of the microcosm or how many microcosms are working simultaneously, the system will change as it recognizes its collective potential and identity. Whole-Scale processes evoke the system's wisdom without needing to direct or control the results. Thus, when the system is ready, the answer will come. The consultant's job is to help the system to become ready. The microcosm will have all of the knowledge it needs, once it has been uncovered and combined. It is possible to create identity in the moment and to form new identities, without having to define every aspect of the system or get inside each person's head.

This moment, when new identities have formed within a microcosm, is the moment we call the paradigm shift moment. People (individually and as a whole) are seeing the world differently, are seeing themselves differently, and are connected around a common picture of their future, including the actions they will need to take to get there. After the paradigm shift experience, people are able (and indeed clamoring) to flex their newly uncovered wisdom and build toward the yearnings they have uncovered together.

Whole-Scale Change as an Enabler of Appreciative Inquiry

Pathfinders' Wisdom

David Cooperrider and his associates at Case Western University in Ohio have been publishing their work for ten years about a way to help organizations change by focusing on what is great about that organization. A key principle of this process, appreciative inquiry, is that it is a generative process. This means that it is a moving target and is created and constantly re-created by the people who use it. Unlike a cookbook approach to change, appreciative inquiry is a thought process. Every participant makes a contribution. Appreciative inquiry suggests that we look for what works in an organization. The tangible result of the inquiry process is a series of statements that describe where the organization wants to be, based on the high moments of where they have been. Because the statements are grounded in real experience and history, people know how to repeat their success. The journey they take an organization on to transform it is:

1. Discovering and valuing the best of "what is"

2. Envisioning "what might be"

3. Involving many in a dialogue about "what should be"

4. Constructing the future using innovation and action for "what will be"

An assumption of appreciative inquiry is the belief that the language we use creates our reality. All words have definitions, but some words have emotional meanings as well. The emotional meaning in the words we use affects our thinking.

Appreciative inquiry rests on the assumption that problem solving is not enough to help transform an organization and that what we focus on becomes our reality. If we focus on what is wrong or what is missing, we tend to see everything through that filter or frame. The tangible result of appreciative inquiry is a series of positive statements phrased as if they were already happening. It is essential that the entire organization engage in activities that work toward a positive expectant result that is sustainable in the long term.

How Whole-Scale Resonates with Appreciative Inquiry

Whole-Scale is also built on the notion that problem solving is not enough. Engaging an entire organization's work on what's right, what might be, and how to sustain the change *may* be the right journey for an organization to embark on. "*May* be the right journey" is added because Whole-Scale is not a mandate, it is a choice. Giving a microcosm group both the process understanding they need and the power to choose the path of the journey has its roots in the process consultation section described previously. It is an addition that Whole-Scale makes beyond both appreciative inquiry and future search. Whole-Scale is both flexible in design as well as outcomes. We believe that this is unlike any other large-group methodology.

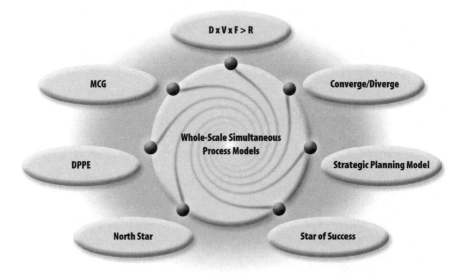

Figure B.1 The Seven Models that Guide Whole-Scale Work

Deep Dive B:
Models and Processes that Unleash the Magic

Throughout this book, various models have been described to provide a visual representation of the way Whole-Scale processes work. This section "assembles in one spot" seven models that, for us, exemplify what Whole-Scale is about and bring the work to life so you can use them to educate clients and other consultants.

Seven Models that Work Simultaneously to Guide Whole-Scale Work

Each of the following models has a role to play in unleashing the magic of an organization moving mindfully toward its Purpose and becoming what it wants to be. Individually each model is valuable, and the combination of all of them, "running" simultaneously in the mind of the change agent, allows the full potential of an organization to emerge.

Figure B.1 shows all seven models. Going clockwise around the circle starting at the top, center, the models are as follows:

- $D \times V \times F > R$—Shows the conditions necessary for a paradigm shift—a formula for change; the overarching model for Whole-Scale work

- Converge/Diverge—Demonstrates the power of Whole-Scale as it works with small groups to inform large groups, and large groups to inform other small groups in a cycle

- Strategic Planning Model—Outlines the path for seeking Strategic Direction

- Star of Success—Provides a way to frame the key questions critical to a successful whole system change journey

- North Star—Answers the questions asked in the Star of Success Model

- DPPE—Helps uncover the conversations people in organizations must have if they are to change and describes the flow of work that needs to exist in any meeting, large or small

- MCG—Articulates a model for building relationships and describes the issues teams deal with in a never-ending cycle

$D \times V \times F > R$
The Paradigm Shift Model:
Formula for Change

The DVF Formula has been and continues to be a cornerstone of Whole-Scale work. This concept is based on the work of Richard Beckhard at the National Training Laboratories. It explains what it takes to bring about real change in an organization or in an individual. Everyone must be able to see and understand the sometimes opposing views that others hold, and to understand that "each person's truth is truth." People in an organization need to see and value others' views and combine those with their own views to create a common database from which the entire organization can move forward.

Each individual and the organization as a whole need to share a common database of dissatisfaction (D) with things as they are right now. They also need a common vision (V) of what they all yearn to be in the future; and they need agreement on significant systemwide first steps (F) that could begin to move them in that direction. If any of these three elements is zero, the drive for change cannot overcome the natural forces of resistance (R).

The $D \times V \times F > R$ Model, figure B.2, is a great deal more than simply a model for change. It is an important model for enabling a paradigm shift to occur. When D, V, and F are all combined, when each person in the room sees the multiple realities that connect them, the system as a whole, and they as individuals shift. When they see the world differently, it causes them to act differently in the future. When that shift occurs, you can feel it in terms of higher excitement and energy. The paradigm shift lasts beyond the initial euphoria. Once an organization has made a real shift, it is literally impossible to go back to seeing the world in the old ways.

Figure B.2 The DVF Formula: A Model that Describes Conditions Necessary to Get a Real Paradigm Shift

$$D \times V \times F > R$$

| **Dissatisfaction** | **Vision** | **First steps** | **Resistance** |
| with the current situation | of a positive possibility, more than the absence of pain in the present situation | in the direction of the vision | to change |

When all of the elements (**D** and **V** and **F**) are in place, in the individual and/or in the organization, the paradigm will have shifted and changes will be a given.

Applications of the DxVxF>R Model

The Consultant's Initial Interview   To use DVF at the start of a change effort, spend time listening to the client to hear his/her "truth" of the situation. Don't be in a hurry to evaluate or diagnose. Take in the data. Immerse yourself in it. Discover and help the client discover their D, the reasons for the change. When the time is right, ask something like, "What would it be like if things were really going well around here?" or "What would your job be like if things were going the way you would like them to be?" Listen again to hear a vision, longings for the future. When you have a clear picture of D and V, you are ready to start talking about next steps, the possibilities for the project plan. If you do not hear the compelling reasons for the changes or a clear direction for the organization, you may have identified where to begin! If all three conditions are not present, the time may not be right to initiate a change effort.

Designing Event Flow   In Whole-Scale events that may involve hundreds of people, you can use DVF to guide the flow of activities. Broadly speaking, people need to build a common information base, to understand first the reasons for change, and to express their own opinions of the current situation. With the information that comes from each other, their leaders, customers, and stakeholders comes the understanding of why things must change. Only then can you discuss the future direction of the organization.

Finally, Vision must be clear before you can determine the actions that would be appropriate to close the gaps between it and current reality. How much time you must spend on each of these in a Whole-Scale meeting will determine the length of the meeting itself. A review of any design for a Whole-Scale meeting will show the following pattern:

- Beginning—Building a case for change

- Middle—Creating Vision or direction

- End—Planning next steps that will sustain the efforts coming out of the work

The Converge/Diverge Model

The Converge/Diverge Model, figure B.3, shows the ways in which an organization moves, over time, through a series of activities that create and sustain change in the organization. It represents a connected flow that integrates the work of individual, small microcosms and the work of whole system groups that key stakeholders go through to expand their database (diverge), combine their multiple realities (converge), explore possibilities (diverge), and make systemwide decisions (converge). The large ovals depict opportunities for a critical-mass microcosm to "get whole" (converge). In the flow of converge/diverge, large-group events accelerate the change journey. They bring together a critical mass that combines everything people have been learning from their individual and small-group efforts into a whole picture. In the larger group, they will make the decisions that will move them forward faster and deeper. The wisdom is in knowing when to "go whole" and when to "go deep."

One process for thinking about when to "go whole" comes from the work of Lawrence & Lorsch, in their book *Organization and Environment* (*Organization and Environment: Managing Differentiation and Integration* by Paul R. Lawrence and J. W. Lorsch). In this book the authors talk about the need for an organization to have both differentiation and integration. They define differentiation as "differences in attitudes and behaviors among functional

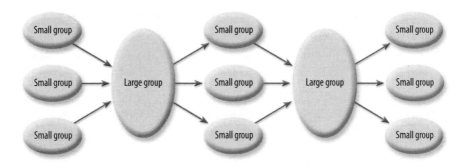

Figure B.3　The Converge/Diverge Model

organizations resulting from organizational segmentation with consequent development of specialized knowledge and mental processes." They see integration as "the quality of the state of collaboration that exists among departments that are required to achieve unity of effort by the demands of the environment." They also use the term *integration* as a process of achieving a state of integration.

In the Whole-Scale approach, the Converge/Diverge Model depicts how you can seek to help an organization unleash and combine its wisdom and magic by ensuring that productive differentiation is brought "whole" by productive integration. The moment to "get whole" is the moment of maximum differentiation. It is the moment at which to diverge one more inch would pull the organization apart or cause people to disconnect from each other.

Setting Strategic Direction Within Organizations: The Strategic Planning Model

Having a common sense model of strategic planning is essential to getting people to think and act strategically. Strategic planning often seems to be a complex, technical process that only "experts" can create or understand. The Whole-Scale Strategic Planning Model, figure B.4, takes the mystery out of the planning process and allows people to make the connection between strategy and the work they do every day. It represents the process for taking the framing questions from the Star of Success and providing the answers for the content of the North Star. The Strategic Planning Model is an application of the DPPE Model.

The model describes the process of developing, implementing, and evaluating a plan using simple terms with very specific meanings. You can use the model in several ways. The first is in thinking about building the case for change. The model provides a framework for helping identify whom the organization needs to hear from in order to understand its past, present, and future. Views come

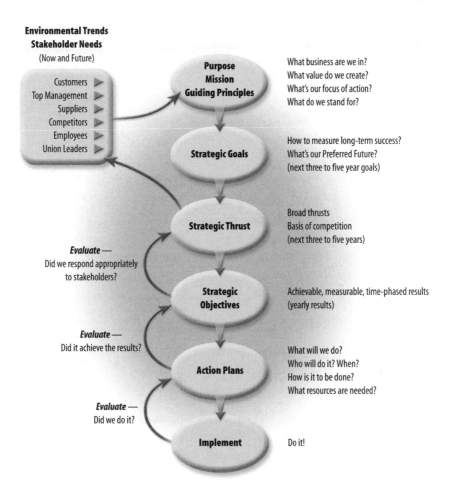

Figure B.4 The Strategic Planning Model

from many sources: customers, shareholders, union leaders, suppliers, employees, top management, and leading thinkers and doers. The framework of the model enables the organization to fully understand the case for change. The second way to use the Strategic Planning Model is contextually for action planning. The process of having good, clear, impactful action plans is anchored in clarity of Purpose, Mission, Guiding Principles, Strategic Goals, Strategic Thrust, and Strategic Objectives.

Purpose   What business is the organization in? What are the boundaries of its activities? What are the hopes, aspirations, and yearnings of the stakeholders? What do we mean by value—the deeply seated reactions and responses to our activities? What possibilities can be envisioned for creating stakeholder value? What is the fundamental reason for the organization to exist—expressed in terms of value to be created for each set of key stakeholders?

Mission   What is the focus of all value creating action? What is the short, clear, compelling statement that captures everyone's hearts and mind, serving to focus everyone's daily activities on actions that achieve the Purpose?

Guiding Principles   What are the vital few rules and tenets that govern behavior when "the going gets tough"? What are the core values that define what we stand for? What really defines us behaviorally? What are our sacred core beliefs about behavior—if we violate them, are we not suitable to belong?

Strategic Goals   What will success look like for this organization at the end of the planning period? What does the organization aspire to become? What is its Preferred Future? What are the broad focus areas that the organization needs to address? What is the desired end state in the next three to five years?

Strategic Thrust   What is the basis of competition (the strategy) for capturing stakeholder time, energy, and money? How will value be created? What are the threats and opportunities? Who are the target customers? What products and services will be offered? What are the focusing guidelines for developing work processes and systems, organizational relationships, external relationships, resources and capabilities, and sharing information needed to achieve the Purpose?

Strategic Objectives   What are the time-phased results of our Strategic Thrust? What specific results by year will the organization accomplish over the planning period? What are the milestones that will tell us we are making progress on our Goals as we head toward the organization's Preferred Future? How will we measure success along the path to our Preferred Future?

Applications of the Strategic Planning Model

Depending on the nature of the work, the Strategic Planning Model adapted from Peter Drucker works well in several ways.

Thinking About Building the Case for Change First, the model provides a framework for understanding who the organization needs to hear from in order to understand the past, present, and future. Views come from different stakeholders such as: customers, shareholders, union leaders, suppliers, employees, top management, and so forth. The model leads people to understand the voices everyone needs to hear in order to create direction wisely.

Building Organization Alignment Second, Whole-Scale events that launch a change effort often have as their center piece a turnaround on Strategy. Someone, usually a Leadership Team, presents a draft strategy to a microcosm group of the whole system (or the whole system in some cases) after everyone in the room has a rich information base upon which to evaluate it. Participants provide feedback on improving the Strategy at the end of one day, and the leaders return the next morning with a revised strategy to present to the group. Participating together in crafting Strategic Direction is a powerful way to align and focus a group. And the revised strategy is *always* richer and better than what the leaders came up with alone.

Providing a Context for Action Planning Third, the process of having good, clear action plans that will make a difference is anchored in clarity of Mission, Vision, Values, and then Goals and objectives. The journey of a large-group meeting is to provide the outside data (stakeholder views) first, and then to enable people to build goals, objectives, and plans based on their insights into those stakeholders' needs. Building that common database provides people with a systemic view of reality. From this systemic view, people are able to create a coherent plan that represents value added for all the various stakeholders.

The Star of Success and the North Star

See chapters 2, 4, 5, 6, and 7, as well as Deep Dive C, for a complete understanding of these models. They are reproduced in a reduced form below.

Figure B.5 The Star of Success

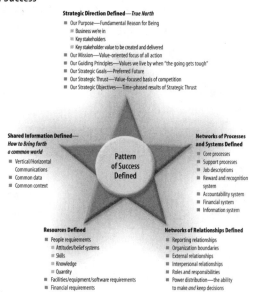

Figure B.6 The North Star

DPPE (Data, Purpose, Plan, Evaluate)

DPPE—Data, Purpose, Plan (or agenda flow), and Evaluation (see figure B.7) is a model for uncovering the conversations that people in organizations must have if they are to change. It describes the flow of work for any meeting, large or small. The agenda for planning a meeting is a journey through these four elements.

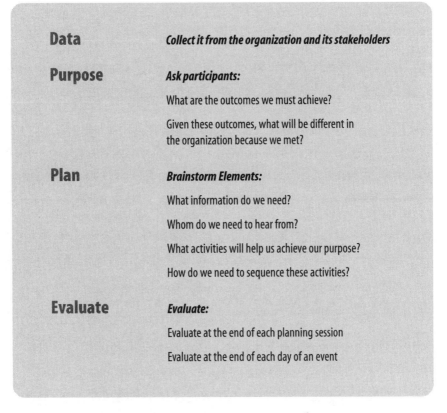

Data *Collect it from the organization and its stakeholders*

Purpose *Ask participants:*

What are the outcomes we must achieve?

Given these outcomes, what will be different in the organization because we met?

Plan *Brainstorm Elements:*

What information do we need?

Whom do we need to hear from?

What activities will help us achieve our purpose?

How do we need to sequence these activities?

Evaluate *Evaluate:*

Evaluate at the end of each planning session

Evaluate at the end of each day of an event

Figure B.7 The DPPE (Data, Purpose, Plan, Evaluate) Model

Data

First, gather contextual data from the Event Planning Team, individually and in the whole team, about the organization, their assessment of the current situation, and their yearnings for their organization. Spend as long as it takes to develop alignment on the Purpose (and outcomes) that speaks to how the organization will be different at the conclusion of this meeting or event? *What will be different in our work lives because we have been together?* is the question to ask.

Purpose and Plan

Develop a common database among the planners, reach consensus on the Purpose (the *True North* that guides the organization), and only then get into the planning of the meeting itself. Figure B.5 provides questions to answer as you move through the process of designing a meeting. With the answer to each of these questions, return to the purpose and ask *Will this activity move us toward our purpose?* If the answer is no, then rethink that particular idea for a design element!

We have three key questions that Ron Lippitt taught us to be sure to ask continually of Event Planning Teams; they are central to our Whole-Scale work:

- Who needs to be in this meeting if we are actually going to be able to achieve our Purpose?

- Whose voices need to be heard if we are to achieve the best possible common database?

- What conversations need to take place in order to achieve the Purpose?"

If the Event Planning Team answers differently at this point than the Leadership Team, the Team will be able to explain their reasoning to the leadership and can convince them of the wisdom of the change. The Event Planning Team will be amazed at how much power leaders, who are beginning to understand what a resource this Team can be, will give them.

Evaluate

End both the planning meeting and each day of an event with an evaluation. With the evaluation data, look back to determine if the agenda for the next day will accomplish the Purpose and deliver the desired outcomes. In an actual event, at the end of each day, ask everyone in the room to evaluate, anonymously, how the day went. Have them say what needs to change to make tomorrow a better day. The Leadership Team, the Event Planning Team, and the consultants will read these individual evaluations together and learn where the group is in its "one-brain and one-heart" development. Then they can answer the questions, *What does that tell us about what we have planned for tomorrow? Are we on track? Do we need to make changes?*

Finally, describe the evaluation feedback to the group the next morning. When you collect feedback, you set up an expectation that you will do something with what people tell you. The feedback the next morning lets the group know what they said as a whole community and what, if anything, has changed as a result.

Applications of DPPE

Planning Projects   At the highest level, DPPE can be an excellent framework for planning a change project (or any kind of project for that matter). In particular, creating a focus on data and Purpose *before* planning action can lead to a better plan and a more aligned task group implementing the plan.

Planning Nonprofit Strategic Planning Retreats   Whole-Scale processes work well to help nonprofit boards develop organizational strategic plans. Using DPPE to plan a board retreat will often uncover outcomes in addition to creating a strategic plan, such as addressing roles and responsibilities of board members, a short-term funding crisis, or conflict between the board and staff. With clarity about the intended outcomes, it is possible to define the real Purpose and create a larger and more relevant conversation than board members originally contemplated.

Planning Large-Group Events   The DPPE Model defines the typical agenda for an Event Planning Team meeting used to prepare a design for a large-group Whole-Scale meeting. Using a max-mix microcosm group to plan provides an effective way to get to the purpose and an event design that will work for the large group.

MCG: Membership-Control-Goals

There are numerous team development models in use today. The Whole-Scale Membership-Control-Goals Model is adapted from the thinking of Jack Gibb many years ago (figure B.8). It shows that when a group gets together, they will need to deal with three basic issues as a group—Membership concerns, Control concerns, and Goal formation concerns (MCG).

Stage One: Membership

When a group meets for the first time, the presenting issues will be questions such as:

- Who's in this group?

- Why was I chosen?

- Why were they chosen?

- Do I have values and beliefs that are the same as the others or different?

- Will the others accept me if they really know me?

- Will I want to be in this group if I really know them?

People need to address these questions in some fashion before they will do any real work as a group. One way of helping a new microcosm group get answers to these first-stage questions is to begin with some type of "Telling Our Stories" or "Getting Connected" activity, where each person answers questions and the

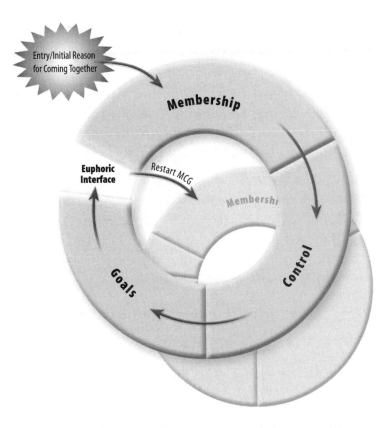

Figure B.8 The MCG (Membership-Control-Goals) Model

rest of their group listens to see the world through that person's eyes. Planners will decide ahead of time the actual questions similar to the ones following:

- Who are you? How long have you been in this organization? What has your role been along the way and what is it now?

- Why have you stayed here?

- As you look back over the past year, what have you been able to accomplish in this organization that makes you proud? What have you seen the organization accomplish that makes you proud?

- What has been going on—in your own work and in the work of the organization—that makes you nervous or frustrates you?

■ What do you need to get out of this session to make it worthwhile for you? What will convince you that we can change?

In a large-group meeting, the room is set up in Table Teams of eight. Often these Table Team participants do not know each other and have little experience working together. It is important to build membership first. People need to feel comfortable in these Table Teams, and they need to feel membership in the larger community in the room. Throughout the meeting or event, participants will be making decisions as a group about what they believe. It is essential that they become a real group in order to "act" as one group. The underlying principles are:

■ Connect before you get to content

■ People are not truly in a meeting until their voices are heard

A STORY FROM RON LIPPITT

This story describes the importance of paying attention to membership. The story goes like this: Ron came into a room where Fritz Reidl (a child psychiatrist) was holding a child firmly on his lap. The kid was struggling and yelling. Ron said, "Having trouble with your client?" Fritz replied, "No, I don't have a client until I help him develop his ego and center it."

The moral of the story: You don't have a group until they have developed a group ego or group identity. You can't expect them to make wise decisions as a group until that moment arrives. Some activity, such as "Telling Our Stories" to connect people to each other and to the work, is essential. As each person listens to see the world through their table group's diverse eyes, they expand their own database and gain a wider system view of the organization's multiple realities. Each person's truth depends on where that person sits in the organization and how far he or she can see out into the larger organization or world.

Data around Membership issues has to flow in order to be ready to move to the next stage of development.

Stage Two: Control

Once the group has connected around beliefs and values (M), they will need to answer questions about control (C):

- Who's in charge here?

- Do I have any influence?

- Do I have too much influence?

- Will decisions of this group matter at all in the future?

Action Research, evaluations, and feedback on evaluations focus on answering these questions. Control is the ability for people to know their voice is being heard and acted on. When a participant hears someone in the front of the meeting repeat back his or her words in an evaluation and then show that they have made changes based on that voice, the participant feels heard and learns to trust just a little bit more than before.

With the powerlessness that people describe that exists in organizations today, there are two significant types of response. One is that people feel unvalued and separate from the group or organization rather than part of it. If a person feels powerless, he or she will likely withdraw completely, psychologically unwilling to risk being involved in any way ("It doesn't matter what I think.").

Another type of response to the feelings of powerlessness is to become the rebel, the cynic, or the fighter. "Nothing you do can convince me to get involved," this person might say. Anything we can do as part of the Whole-Scale processes to move people out of their feelings of powerlessness and passivity will bring great benefit to people themselves as well as to the organization/system as a whole.

Data around control issues (which may indeed need to include some feedback) must have flowed enough to move the group to the next stage.

Stage Three: Goal Development

When the group has developed a sense of membership and has addressed control issues, they need to work together to ask the question: "What do we need to/want to accomplish by working together?" The group will need to get data moving in their conversations about what each person yearns to accomplish, and then they will be able to come up with goals that are richer and more vital than those that any one person might have.

In Whole-Scale sessions, you can explore the concept of Preferred Futuring (see Ron Lippitt's Preferred Futuring article in "Deep Dive D: Resources"). Lippitt's first test of the power of people connecting around a future they all prefer occurred when he first came to the University of Michigan in the 1950s. He pulled together Leadership Teams from companies and/or nonprofit organizations and gave them the following assignment:

- First brainstorm everything any one of you sees as inhibiting movement toward success in the organization.

- Second, agree on the key inhibitors, then using any problem-solving model of your choosing, analyze those inhibitors and agree on action plans to address them and bring about change.

The students who were watching and documenting these meetings identified three common things with each Leadership Team:

- The longer the group worked together, the less energy they maintained in the group.

- The longer they worked together, the more they blamed others for the problems—"It's not me," "It's not my job," were common refrains.

- The actions they came up with tended to be "reduction of pain" solutions—"stop the bleeding" solutions. The students thought of these solutions as tourniquet or band-aid solutions.

Then Lippitt gathered together a new set of Leadership Teams and gave these groups the following assignment:

- Brainstorm together your answers to the following question:
  It is three years from today. You are looking down from a balloon in the sky at your own organization. You are pleased and proud of how effective the organization has become. What do you see happening? What do you see people saying? What do you see people doing? What makes you proud?

- When they had created this list as a freewheeling brainstorm, he would invite them to vote for the absolutely vital things identified on the list . . . from their own perspective.

- Then, using the results of that voting, what do we need to commit to do differently right now in order to begin to close the gap between where we are right now and where we yearn to be in the future?

When these groups reported, students found the following commonalties:

- The longer they worked together as a group, the more energy they had, as individuals and as a group.

- The longer they worked together, the more they each took responsibility for things not working.

- The solutions they reported tended to be innovative ideas, things they had never thought of before this time.

At some point in a Whole-Scale process, you can tell this story and turn a group loose to unite around common yearnings and insights.

This approach almost never fails . . . which makes it even more astonishing that many consultants still do problem-solving interventions. **People are capable of remarkable innovation if they are a connected team and feel valued by the system and by their peers.**

All people want clarity of Purpose—a clear picture of why they're here and what they can accomplish that will make a difference. They yearn to be able to shape their work to achieve that worthwhile picture of success. All that they ask is to know what's happening and have people ask them to become involved, give them a voice in setting goals, and set them free to be part of creating action plans to get there. Based on this kind of involvement, the organization can count on people to be committed.

The Euphoric Interface

When a group has moved through all three phases of MCG successfully, they will enter into a state Jack Gibb used to call the "euphoric interface"—a warm glow of identity and pride: "Boy, are we a good group!" they will say. The minute the group gets there, they will enter the three stages again at a deeper level.

If they don't address Membership, Control, and Goals at a deeper level, they will not stay where they were. They will begin reversing the model, asking questions, such as: "Are these goals worth it?" "Who's running this show, anyway?" and "Do I really want to be connected with this group?" With no need to stay connected, to move further ahead, the group can disintegrate in the blink of an eye. If you want a group to continue working together, some communication on Membership, Control, and Goals at a deeper, riskier (more personal, open) level will keep it going.

Applications of MCG

Open Forums   You can use MCG in a number of ways. Apply it with teams at all levels in the organization. Fundamentally, all groups of people who come together for a stated purpose go through these three stages. Design activities to consciously address each. An open forum question-and-answer process, for example, allows people to control the meeting, until their questions are answered. In the give and take of these dialogues, tables learn that they truly control the meeting, while at the same time taking responsibility to get their questions answered.

Microcosm Groups   There are many kinds of microcosm groups used in the Whole-Scale approach. Tables of eight in a large-group meeting are carefully designed to make the table look as much like the whole room as possible with people from all parts of the organization represented. Each of these tables becomes a team for the duration of the meeting in order to do the work that will accomplish the purpose of the meeting. MCG guides the meeting design (in much the same way that DVF guides the content decisions, MCG guides the process decisions) and, in particular, how activities are sequenced and designed to move the tables through the team model while also doing the work of the meeting. One of the "value added" benefits for participants is that they experience team building without ever talking about it expressly.

Task Teams   In the work of planning or implementing change, it is often necessary to establish short-term Task Teams to accomplish specific purposes. Following the MCG Model along with a clear charter of purpose, authority, outcomes, and timeframe helps assure that these teams form quickly and work effectively.

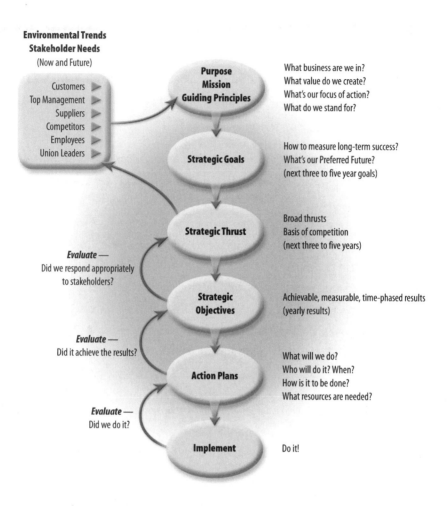

Figure C.1 The Whole-Scale Strategic Planning Model

Deep Dive C:
Strategic Planning Models and Tools

The Whole-Scale
Strategic Planning Model

Strategic Terms and the Questions They Evoke

Stakeholders Who are the people who are counting on the organization? Who can influence and impact the direction of the business? Who has important interests in the business and the efforts of the organization? Who has the power of the "no," meaning their voices could derail the effort? Who has the power of "yes," meaning their voices are needed to ensure success?

Purpose What business is the organization in? What are the boundaries of its activities? What are the hopes, aspirations, and yearnings of the stakeholders? What do we mean by value—the deeply seated reactions and responses to our activities? What possibilities can be envisioned for creating stakeholder value? What is the fundamental reason for the organization to exist—expressed in terms of value to be created for each set of key stakeholders?

Mission   What is the focus of all value creating action? What is the short, clear, compelling statement that captures everyone's hearts and mind, serving to focus everyone's daily activities on actions that achieve the Purpose?

Guiding Principles   What are the vital few rules and tenets that govern behavior when "the going gets tough"? What are the core values that define what we stand for? What really defines us behaviorally? What are our sacred core beliefs about behavior—if we violate them, are we not suitable to belong?

Strategic Goals   What will success look like for this organization at the end of the planning period? What does the organization aspire to become? What is its Preferred Future? What are the broad focus areas that the organization needs to address? What is the desired end state in the next three to five years?

Strategic Thrust   What is the basis of competition (the strategy) for capturing stakeholder time, energy, and money? How will value be created? What are the threats and opportunities? Who are the target customers? What products and services will be offered? What are the focusing guidelines for developing work processes and systems, organizational relationships, external relationships, resources and capabilities, and sharing information needed to achieve the Purpose?

Strategic Objectives   What are the time-phased results of our Strategic Thrust? What specific results by year will the organization accomplish over the planning period? What are the milestones that will tell us we are making progress on our Goals as we head toward the organization's Preferred Future? How will we measure success along the path to our Preferred Future?

What Is Strategic Direction? Why Is It So Important?

Definitions from several sources combine to give a multifaceted look at what Strategic Direction is:

From the dictionary:

- The science and art of using all of the forces and minds of an organization to define and execute actions toward a common goal(s) that will effectively ensure victory.

- The science and art of command leadership as applied to the overall planning and conduct of large-scale successful movement in concert toward the common goal(s).

- A whole system plan of action intended to accomplish specific goals.

From Kathie Dannemiller:

- A one-brain and one-heart plan of actions that enables an organization to be successful now and in the future, as a whole entity and as individuals within that organization. Being as good as it can be.

From the nature of organizational reality:

- Organizations are successful only to the degree they create and deliver value for key stakeholders.

- Every organization—for example, charities, for-profit businesses, government agencies, not-for-profit businesses, Boy Scouts, Girls Scouts, and churches—must compete for key stakeholder time, energy, and money.

- Strategic Direction defines the master pattern of success that creates and delivers value to key stakeholders.

A History of Creating Strategic Direction

Strategy has been part of management thinking since the early days of developing a body of management knowledge that began after World War II. The questions leaders needed to answer even then were:

- What does the organization need to accomplish in order to be winners in the race it has chosen to enter?

- What behavior is required so that the organization positions itself for success in its environment?

In the days after the war, business leaders still believed it was the role of the hierarchical leadership to decide on Strategic Direction for the future. They believed that top leaders were the only level of the organization that needed to understand external environment changes. As a result, leaders would make decisions and tell everyone else what to do. If I worked for you, and I thought that the direction, or my assignment, was wrong, I would be expected to obey anyway. If I questioned the direction, or my assignment, I was often labeled as insubordinate. If I questioned too much, I could be fired for insubordination.

So, the answer to the question *What is Strategic Direction?* is *It provides guidance and points the way for everything the organization does.* Strategic Direction defines the master pattern of success that creates and delivers key stakeholder value. The answer to the question *Why is it so important?* is *It helps the organization create and deliver value for key stakeholder, without which the organization will not survive.* Again two truths apply:

- Organizations exist only to create value for key stakeholders. Value is difficult to measure and articulate because it is a stakeholder's emotional response to actions organizations take or don't take. Value exists in the eyes of key stakeholders who may not be able to articulate it. But they know it when they see it and experience it.

■ Organizations must compete for key stakeholder time, energy, and money. Therefore they must create more value for stakeholders than their competitors do.

Creating Strategic Direction:
The Star of Success and the North Star

The Star of Success (figure C.2) Strategic Direction point asks the framing questions for Whole-Scale Change. Its companion star, the North Star, shown in figure C.3, answers the framing questions posed by the Star of Success and then operationalizes the answers. It provides a clear outline of the content for Strategic Direction.

Strategic Direction addresses four key questions:

■ What business are we in?

■ What value do we intend to provide for our key stakeholders?

■ How will we create this value?

■ How will we know when value is created?

The elements of Strategic Direction provide answers to these four questions.

Strategic Direction articulates the fundamental purpose for the organization and illuminates the pathway to follow. When it articulates a shared, compelling Purpose—The Fundamental Reason for Being—that "speaks to" the hopes, aspirations, and longings of key stakeholders, it creates energy—the potential for action that creates Value. When it illuminates an exciting, achievable pathway to pursue Purpose, it defines a course to unleash and direct that value-creating action.

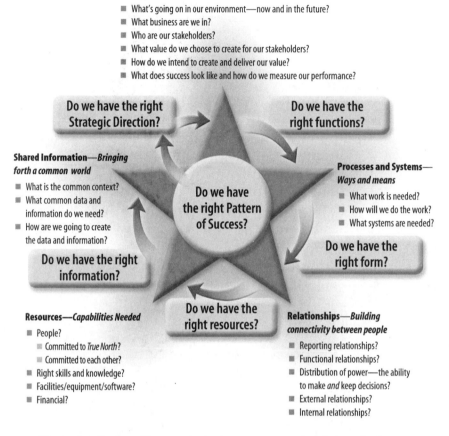

Figure C.2 The Star of Success asks the framing questions for Whole-Scale Change.

A brief explanation of the Strategic Direction elements shown in figure C.1:

■ **Purpose**—*the fundamental reason for being*—articulates the organization's Purpose in terms of key stakeholders' hopes, aspirations, and longings, and explains how the organization intends to create value for them. The organization has created Value when key stakeholders see that the organization's Purpose and intent has the potential for creating results meaningful to them.

   ▢ Shareholders might see the potential for financial security through stock price growth, assured income, or income growth.

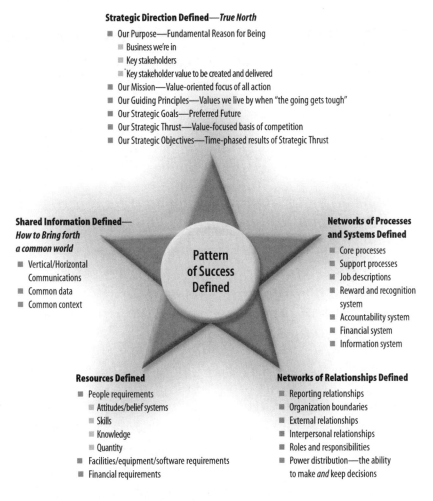

Strategic Direction Defined—*True North*
- Our Purpose—Fundamental Reason for Being
  - Business we're in
  - Key stakeholders
  - Key stakeholder value to be created and delivered
- Our Mission—Value-oriented focus of all action
- Our Guiding Principles—Values we live by when "the going gets tough"
- Our Strategic Goals—Preferred Future
- Our Strategic Thrust—Value-focused basis of competition
- Our Strategic Objectives—Time-phased results of Strategic Thrust

Shared Information Defined—
*How to Bring forth
a common world*
- Vertical/Horizontal
  Communications
- Common data
- Common context

**Pattern
of Success
Defined**

**Networks of Processes
and Systems Defined**
- Core processes
- Support processes
- Job descriptions
- Reward and recognition
  system
- Accountability system
- Financial system
- Information system

Resources Defined
- People requirements
  - Attitudes/belief systems
  - Skills
  - Knowledge
  - Quantity
- Facilities/equipment/software requirements
- Financial requirements

Networks of Relationships Defined
- Reporting relationships
- Organization boundaries
- External relationships
- Interpersonal relationships
- Roles and responsibilities
- Power distribution—the ability
  to make *and* keep decisions

Figure C.3 The North Star answers the questions posed by the Star of Success.

- Organizational management might see the potential for job satisfaction and wealth creation through leadership and management of an organization, which makes useful contributions to society while returning excellent financial results to shareholders.

- Organizational members might see the potential for quality of life and work, financial well-being, and personal/professional growth by making useful contributions to society and their professions while being well compensated.

- Suppliers might see the potential for job satisfaction and financial stability by supplying products and services which make useful contributions to society and are valued by the organization as their customer.

- Communities might see the potential for tax base security or growth, environmental security, and community stature because the organization will contribute usefully to society and behave with environmental responsibility.

Note: Purpose might be one-half to one page in length.

- **Mission** is the succinct, compelling summary of Fundamental Reason for Being that provides a focus for action. Fundamental Reason for Being creates the organization's potential energy. Mission is the short, clear, and compelling statement that guides and focuses the energy and brings the Fundamental Reason for Being to life!

Note: Mission might be one-half dozen words in length.

- **Guiding Principles** articulate the vital few rules guiding behavior and action, particularly "when the going gets tough." They state the nature of desired relationships and behaviors that shape and form the core around which people relate to each other as they execute the Mission. The acid test comes when the going gets tough. At these times, people under stress can internalize and bring to bear on their behavior only a few Guiding Principles. It is these fundamental rules—guidelines for which actions are acceptable in the pursuit of mission and which are not—that the organization needs to articulate.

Note: Guiding Principles might be one-half page in length.

- **Strategic Goals** are the articulation of the organization's Preferred Future, or vision of success, in the three- to five-year timeframe.

Strategic Goals articulate the key, major (strategic) observable results that will indicate success in the pursuit of Mission and achievement of the organization's Fundamental Reason for Being. The Strategic Goals are a compelling statement of the desired strategic results, which, if achieved, will meet stakeholder hopes, aspirations, and longings: The organization will have created Value.

Note: Strategic Goals might be one-half page in length.

■ **Strategic Thrust** (sometimes called Strategy) is the articulation of the basis of competition—"the way." Every organization competes for key stakeholder time, energy, and resources. Because stakeholders must choose among ways to spend their time, energy, and money, organizations creating more value than competing organizations can create will be more successful. Strategic Thrust defines the following:

■ The target markets to serve

■ Key stakeholders and the products and services to provide for them

■ The nature of the relationships to establish with these key stakeholders

■ Guidelines for the processes and systems to use to provide products and services and to sustain the desired relationships

■ Guidelines for creating shared information that helps the organization to operate optimally

The Strategic Thrust must provide these definitions and guidelines in ways that direct and guide (focus) action, and in ways that provide extraordinary value. Strategic Thrust defines how the organization will create and deliver value better than competing alternatives for key stakeholder choices on how to spend time, energy, and money.

Note: Strategic Thrust might be eight to ten pages in length.

■ **Strategic Objectives** define the time-phased, measurable results the organization intends to achieve with its Strategic Thrust. The time horizon is one to two years. They are milestones along the path to Strategic Goals.

Whole-Scale change offers a way of doing business that engages the hearts as well as the minds of all of the organization's stakeholders.

Note: Strategic Objectives might be one-half page in length.

Strategic Direction *must* be driven by data. Environmental scanning is a process for collecting data, then interpreting it in the context of *Purpose*. Critical environmental scanning questions are:

- What are the technological, legal, social, and political trends in our world, and what are the driving forces behind these trends?

- How are our key stakeholders responding to, or are likely to respond to, these trends and driving forces?

- Who are the leaders or likely leaders in our business and how could they be successful in our business?

- What are the possibilities for us to create and deliver value to our key stakeholders?

See figure C.4. It is a sample one-page draft strategy that a Leadership Team prepared for "the turnaround" at their Organizational Alignment Event (an IT organization, with a one-year focus to regain internal customer satisfaction and business in a time of off-the-shelf products).

Draft Strategy

Mission Statement

Provide quality communications and processing systems in partnership with COMPANY'S workforce.

Guiding Business Principles (fundamental values, everyday behavior, stands up to adversity)

- Focus on customers and clients as partners
- Apply creative learning to dilemmas
- Pursue technical excellence
- Act with integrity
- Timely collaborative win/win decisions
- Take calculated risks

Strategic Goals

- Clients are satisfied, complimentary, and use more IT products/services
- All systems availability greater than 98 percent
- People feel good about themselves and their Work Teams
- Projects are on budget, on schedule, meeting technical, and business requirements
- Right data is at the right place at the right time >98 percent of the time
- We will facilitate the quickest, the highest quality, and the most cost-effective method of exchanging information to the people who need it, regardless of where it resides

Strategic Objectives

- Develop a unified, homogeneous, reliable WAN/AN that will meet the COMPANY'S business needs by *month*
- Deploy the customer/client partnership, attitude, and process as measured by the customer satisfaction index (CSI) improvement of 15 percent by *month*
- Implement a fully operational data administration function to provide simplified access to corporate data (business and technical) by *month*
- Transfer application development and maintenance to client groups. Provide consulting/technical support to clients by *month*
- Highly qualified COMPANY people perform critical functions. Change the mix of involvement

Figure C.4 Sample One-Page Draft Strategy

The Breakpoint Model

The Breakpoint Model, figure C.5, illustrates the nature of organizational reality (Land and Jarman). The portion of the breakpoint curve labeled "Invent master pattern" represents the organization's start-up. Experimentation is the norm, as the organization searches for the master pattern of

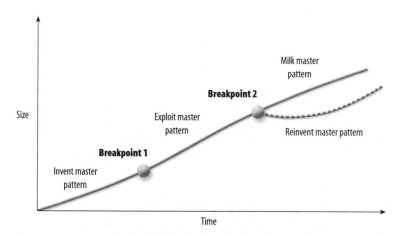

Key Insights

Organizations:
- Are successful to the degree they create key stakeholder value.
- Must compete for key stakeholder time, energy, and money.

Key stakeholders: People who have a vested interest in the organization's success.

Value:
- Value is created by the degree to which key stakeholders' hopes, aspirations, yearnings, and longings are met by the organization.
- The pattern of success; the repeatable ways of doing business; organizing, developing, and deploying resources; sharing information and implementing strategy; defines the value-creating mechanism.

Breakpoints: Points in time where the rules change 180 degrees:
- Breakpoint 1—Pattern of success has emerged, stability is required.
- Breakpoint 2—Pattern of success is not creating value, renovation, and update is required.

Figure C.5 The Breakpoint Model

success that creates value. At breakpoint 1, the rules change 180 degrees because the master pattern of success has emerged. The task now is to exploit the master pattern of success. At breakpoint 2, the key stakeholder values have changed sufficiently that a new pattern of success is required; the rules again change 180 degrees. The organization must once again experiment *while simultaneously* milking the current master pattern of success.

Combining this definition with a strong grounding in living systems theory means that the organization can equate its Strategic Direction with its *True North*. The Strategic Direction point of the Star of Success is the same as the Strategic Direction Defined point of the North Star. Heading for *True North* provides the compelling, driving force for change.

Leaders must agree on the organization's Strategic Direction. Two truths apply:

1. If an organization doesn't know where it's going, any road will get it there.

2. If an organization keeps doing the same things it has always done, it might get the results it has always gotten, if the environment remains the same. Or, the organization might even get worse results.

Doing the Strategic Gap Analysis Homework: Finding the Strategic Drivers

One of the major tasks in Strategic Direction development is performing a gap analysis. At this getting-started point in the process, there may not be a clear understanding of the convening issues. Therefore, one leadership (and consulting) challenge is to reveal the gaps between current reality and the preferred reality—to identify gaps as a basis for planning and implementing strategic change. The Star of Success and the North Star provide a way to illuminate the gaps and help to define a Roadmap for the Whole-Scale Strategy development effort. Because the two Stars portray the whole system, using them as aids in determining current reality and framing the desired reality keeps a whole system frame for the Strategy development Roadmap. Because the organization is a system, however, a change to one part may cause serious unintended consequences in other parts. As Russel Ackoff stated in his paper, "The Second Industrial Revolution," there are two critical system thinking corollaries:

- If a system is operating optimally, then, no subsystem can be operating optimally.

- If a subsystem is operating optimally, then, the system cannot be operating optimally.

Because Strategic Direction illuminates the path to *True North,* all other dimensions of the system must be linked and integrated and aligned to *True North.*

Whole-Scale starts with a whole system assessment. Initially, you can do the assessment from "high altitude." As you collect more data and derive more and greater insights, you can make more detailed assessments.

Figure C.6, the Whole-Scale Strategic Gap Analyzer, illustrates a gap analysis framework that can be the basis for developing a Roadmap to guide a whole system going forward. The analyzer derives from the Star of Success, and thus it provides a whole system assessment framework.

Initially, the gap analyzer's dimensions can use the top level Star of Success questions. As more data is collected, the gap analyzer can be expanded to include the subquestions of each Star point. This increases the number of assessment dimensions so more detail is available to develop the Strategic Direction.

The performance level descriptors are generic. They serve to help you get started, but the organization needs to reformulate them in order to provide framing based on the organization's current reality.

Figure C.6 Generic Whole-Scale Strategic Gap Analyzer: A Six-Key Assessment Framework

Performance Level	Strategic Direction	Processes and Systems	Relationships	Resources	Shared Information
Performance Level 5— *Currently Invincible*	Compellingly defined. Extraordinary stakeholder value creation is a consuming focus.	All processes and systems are flow and pull based with perfection as the standard.	Relationships are superbly defined and working.	Superb facilities and equipment. People have unexcelled passion for *True North* and unsurpassed skills and knowledge.	Superb communication processes and superb data commonality. Truly a common world.
Performance Level 4— *World Class*	Well defined. Stakeholder value creation is a key focus.	Core processes and systems are flow and pull based with perfection as a goal.	Relationships are excellently defined and working.	Excellent facilities and equipment. People have passion for *True North* with excellent skills and knowledge.	Excellent communication processes and excellent data commonality. A high degree of a common world.
Performance Level 3— *Competitive with the Pack*	Defined. Stakeholder value creation is important.	Some core processes and systems are flow and pull based with quality being important.	Relationships are well defined and working.	Good facilities and equipment. People are committed to *True North* with adequate skills and knowledge.	Good communication processes and good data commonality. Good degree of a common world.
Performance Level 2— *Beginning to Improve*	Defined. The importance of stakeholder value creation is recognized.	Some core processes and systems are becoming flow and pull based with quality becoming important.	Relationships are defined and beginning to work well.	Mostly adequate facilities and equipment. People understand *True North* with mostly adequate skills and knowledge.	Improving communication processes and improving data commonality. Beginnings of a truly common world.
Performance Level 1— *Just Getting Along*	Poorly defined. No concept of Purpose—The Fundamental Reason for Being.	Processes and systems are traditional batch and queue with marginal quality.	Relationships are unclear and/or not working well.	Marginal facilities and equipment. People are not committed to *True North*. Marginal skills and knowledge.	Marginal communication processes and little data commonality. Small degree of a common world.

One way to get started is for the Leadership Team to use the generic analyzer to assess the *current* performance level for each of the five Star points to establish the *current* reality. It can then establish the *preferred* performance level for each of the five Star points to establish the *preferred* reality. The current reality is represented by the sum of all the performance levels, with 25 points as the maximum. Similarly, the preferred reality is measured by the sum of the preferred reality performance levels, with 25 points as the maximum. The difference between the preferred and current realities forms a gap, the basis for the whole system strategy development. Movements of more than one performance level per Star point per year are unrealistic. Therefore, a Strategy Roadmap that intends to cause shifts of more than 5 points per year are unrealistic.

Once the gaps show up, they form the basis for determining the focus of the whole system strategy development. It is likely that some gaps are more urgent and important than others, so the strategy will likely focus on only two to three Star points. Following the initial assessment, the Leadership Team can do a more detailed gap analysis, going into a higher level of detail. The results of the more detailed assessment drive the Strategic Direction development. A Core Team frequently does the more detailed assessment as a critical element of its homework. Finally, see figure C.7 to see the results of such an analysis.

Figure C.7 Vision Systems Company: Whole-Scale Strategic Gap Analysis Results

Performance Level	Strategic Direction	Processes and Systems	Relationships	Resources	Shared Information
Performance Level 5— *Currently Invincible*	Compellingly defined. Extraordinary stakeholder value creation is a consuming focus.	All processes and systems are flow and pull based with perfection as the standard.	Relationships are superbly defined and working.	Superb facilities and equipment. People have unexcelled passion for *True North* and unsurpassed skills and knowledge.	Superb communication processes and superb data commonality. Truly a common world.
Performance Level 4— *World Class*	Well defined. Stakeholder value creation is a key focus. **To Be** (2 years)	Core processes and systems are flow and pull based with perfection as a goal. **To Be** (2 years)	Relationships are excellently defined and working. **To Be** (2 years)	Excellent facilities and equipment. People have passion for *True North* with excellent skills and knowledge. **To Be** (2 years)	Excellent communication processes and excellent data commonality. A high degree of a common world. **To Be** (2 years)
Performance Level 3— *Competitive with the Pack*	Defined. Stakeholder value creation is important.	Some core processes and systems are flow and pull based with quality being important.	Relationships are well defined and working. **As Was**	Good facilities and equipment. People are committed to *True North* with adequate skills and knowledge.	Good communication processes and good data commonality. Good degree of a common world.
Performance Level 2— *Beginning to Improve*	Defined. The importance of stakeholder value creation is recognized.	Some core processes and systems are becoming flow and pull based with quality becoming important.	Relationships are defined and beginning to work well.	Mostly adequate facilities and equipment. People understand *True North* with mostly adequate skills and knowledge. **As Was**	Improving communication processes and improving data commonality. Beginnings of a truly common world. **As Was**
Performance Level 1— *Just Getting Along*	Poorly defined. No concept of Purpose—The Fundamental Reason for Being. **As Was**	Processes and systems are traditional batch and queue with marginal quality. **As Was**	Relationships are unclear and/or not working well.	Marginal facilities and equipment. People are not committed to *True North*. Marginal skills and knowledge.	Marginal communication processes and little data commonality. Small degree of a common world.

Deep Dive D:
Resources

This section is divided into several groups of resources related to the development and practice of the Whole-Scale Approach:

General Readings   These books and articles have been helpful to us in our thinking about the development of the Whole-Scale Approach.

Roots and Theories: Selected Readings   These readings are specific to those areas that form the roots of the Whole-Scale Approach. This list reflects those writers and teachers who have impacted us and is not intended as an exhaustive list of resources.

Readings About Whole-Scale   These are articles and books that have been written about the Whole-Scale Approach.

World Wide Web Links   The Dannemiller Tyson Associates home page, links to further readings about Whole-Scale, and links to a calendar of upcoming events.

"Future Before You Plan"   This is an article written by Ron Lippitt that we have not been able to find in published form, so we have included the text here. The idea of a Preferred Futuring, invented by Ron Lippitt, is one of the keys to the success of the Whole-Scale Approach.

General Readings

Axelrod, D. "Getting Everyone Involved: How One Organization Involved Its Employees, Supervisors, and Managers in Redesigning the Organization." *The Journal of Applied Behavioral Science,* vol. 28, no. 4, 499-509 (December 1992).

———. *Terms of Engagement,* San Francisco: Berrett-Koehler, 2000.

Beckhard, R., and W. Pritchard. *Changing the Essence: The Art of Creating and Leading Fundamental Change in Organizations.* San Francisco: Jossey-Bass, 1992.

Block, P. *Flawless Consulting.* Austin, TX: Learning Concepts, 1999.

———. *The Empowered Manager.* San Francisco: Jossey-Bass, 1987.

Feldman, M., and M. Spratt. *Five Frogs on a Log: A CEO's Guide to Accelerating the Transition in Mergers, Acquisitions, and Gut Wrenching Change.* New York: Harper Business, 1999.

Gibb, J. *The Basic Reader: Reading in Laboratory Training.* Detroit, MI: Province V, The Episcopal Church, 1970.

Hackman, R., and G. R. Oldham. *Work Design.* Reading, MA: Addison-Wesley Publishing Company, 1980.

Hamel, G., and C. K. Prahalad. *Competing for the Future.* Boston: Harvard Business School Press, 1994.

Hanna, D. P. *Designing Organizations for High Performance.* Addison-Wesley, 1988.

Holman, P., and T. Devane, eds. *The Change Handbook.* San Francisco: Berrett-Koehler, 1999.

Keidel, R. W. *The Triangular Organization.* San Francisco: Berrett-Koehler, 1995.

Lippitt, R., and E. Schindler-Rainman. *Taking Your Meetings Out of the Doldrums.* San Diego: University Associates, 1963.

Lytle, W. O. *Socio-Technical Systems Analysis & Design Guide (for Linear Work, for Non-Linear Work).* New Jersey: Block-Petrella-Weisbord, Inc., 1991.

Marks, M., and P. Mirvis. *Joining Forces: Making One Plus One Equal Three in Mergers, Acquisitions, and Alliances.* San Francisco: Jossey-Bass, 1998.

Mohrman, S. A., S. G. Cohen, and A. M. Mohrman Jr. *Designing Team-Based Organizations.* San Francisco: Jossey-Bass, 1995.

Nadler, A., and M. Tushman. *Competing by Design: The Power of Organizational Architecture.* New York: Oxford University Press, 1997.

Nadler, D. *Feedback and Organization Development: Using Data-Based Methods.* Reading, MA: Addison-Wesley, 1977.

Nadler, D., M. Gerstein, and R. Shaw. *Organizational Architecture: Designs for Change Organizations.* San Francisco: Jossey-Bass, 1992.

Owen, H. *Open Space Technology: A User's Guide.* Potomac, MD: Abbott, 1992.

Pascarella, P., and M. A. Frohman. *The Purpose Driven Organization: Unleashing the Power of Direction and Commitment.* San Francisco: Jossey-Bass, 1990.

Pasmore, W. A. *Creating Strategic Change: Designing the Flexible, High Performing Organization.* New York: Wiley, 1994.

Schindler-Rainman, E., and R. Lippitt. *Building the Collaborative Community: Mobilizing Citizens for Action.* Riverside, CA: University of California Extension, 1980.

Schein, E. H. *Process Consultation: Its Role in Organizational Development.* Volumes 1 & 2 (2nd Edition). Reading, MA: Addison-Wesley, 1988.

Seiling, J. G. *The Membership Organization: Achieving Top Performance Through the New Workplace Community.* Palo Alto, CA: Davies-Black Publishing, 1997.

Taylor, F. W. *The Principles of Scientific Management.* New York: Harper & Row, 1915.

Weber, M. *The Theory of Social and Economic Organizations.* A. M. Henderson and T. Parsons, trans.; T. Parsons, ed. New York: Free Press, 1947.

Weisbord, M. R., *Productive Workplaces.* San Francisco: Jossey-Bass, 1987.

———. *Discovering Common Ground.* San Francisco: Berrett-Koehler, 1993.

Weisbord, M. R., and S. Janoff. *Future Search.* San Francisco: Berrett-Koehler, 1995.

Wheatley, M. *A Simpler Way.* San Francisco: Berrett-Koehler, 1996.

Zell, D. *Changing by Design: Organization Innovation at Hewlett-Packard.* Ithaca: Cornell University Press, 1997.

Roots and Theories: Selected Readings

Adult Learning

Knowles, M. *The Modern Practice of Adult Education*. New York: Cambridge, The Adult Education Company, 1980.

Knowles, M., E. Holton, and R. Swanson. *The Adult Learner: The Definitive Classic in Adult Education and Human Resource Development*. 5th Edition. Houston: Gulf Publishing Company, 1998.

Kolb, D. *Experiential Learning: Experience as the Source of Learning and Development*. Old Tappen, N.J.: Prentice-Hall, 1984.

Appreciative Inquiry

Argyris, C., and D. Schon. *Organizational Learning: A Theory of Action Perspective*. Reading, MA: Addision-Wesley, 1978.

Cooperrider, D., and C. Pratt. *Appreciative Inquiry*. Weatherhead School of Management, Case Western Reserve University, 1997.

Community Building

Lippitt, G., and R. Lippitt. *The Consulting Process in Action*. San Diego: University Associates, 1978.

Socio-Technical Systems

Emery, M., ed. *Participative Design for Participative Democracy*. Canberra, Australia: Center for Continuing Education, The Australian National University, 1993.

Trist, E. "The Evolution of Socio-Technical Systems." In *Perspectives on Organizational Design and Behaviour* by Andy Van de Ven and William Joyce. Wiley Interscience, 1981.

Chaos Field Theory

Gleick, J. *Chaos: Making a New Science.* New York: Penguin, 1987.

Sanders, T. *Strategic Thinking and the New Science: Planning in the Midst of Chaos, Complexity, and Change.* New York: Free Press, 1998.

Wheatley, M. *Leadership and the New Science.* San Francisco: Berrett-Koehler, 1992.

Zohar, D. *Rewiring the Corporate Brain: Using the New Science to Rethink How We Structure and Lead Organizations.* San Francisco: Berrett-Koehler, 1997.

Systems Thinking

Deming, W. *Out of the Crisis.* Cambridge, MA: Massachusetts Institute of Technology, Center for Advanced Engineering Study, 1986.

Action Research

Frohman, M., M. Sashkin, and M. Kavanagh. "Action Research as Applied to Organization Development." In *Organization and Administrative Sciences,* vol. 7, nos. 1, 2, 129–42 (1976).

Preferred Futuring

Leider, R. J. *The Power of Purpose.* San Francisco: Berrett-Koehler Publishers, Inc, 1997.

Lindaman, E., and R. Lippitt. *Choosing the Future You Prefer.* Washington, D.C.: Development Publications, 1979.

Lippitt, L. *Preferred Futuring: Envision the Future You Want and Unleash the Energy to Get There.* San Francisco: Berrett-Koehler, 1998.

Lippitt, R. "Future Before You Plan." In *The NTL Manager's Handbook.* Arlington, VA: NTL Institute, 1983.

Beckhard, R., and R. Harris. *Organizational Transitions: Managing Complex Change.* Reading, MA: Addison-Wesley, 1987.

Readings About Whole-Scale

Blixt, A. "Launching a Team-Based Renewal Effort Using Whole-Scale Methodology—The Ferranti-Packard Story." For the International Conference on Work Teams, 1997.

Block, P. "Consulting that Unleashes the Spirit" in *The Flawless Consulting Fieldbook and Companion.* San Francisco: Jossey-Bass, 2000.

Breisch, R. "A Conversation with Kathleen Dannemiller." *Entre Nous,* vol. 2, no. 1. The Midwest Organizational Learning Network, 1998.

Bunker, B., and B. Alban, eds. "Large Group Interventions." *Journal of Applied Behavioral Science,* vol. 28, no. 4 (December 1992). Newbury Park, CA: Sage Press.

———. *Large Group Interventions: Engaging the Whole System for Rapid Change.* San Francisco: Jossey-Bass, 1997.

Chase, T., ed. *Large Group Interventions for Organizational Change: Concepts, Methods, and Cases.* Readings for the OD Network Conference, March 19–22, 1995. Call Conference Support Systems (603) 942-8189. Tapes available from Audio Cassette Taping Service (800) 642-2287.

———. *Large Group Interventions for Organizational Change: Concepts, Methods, and Cases.* Readings for the OD Network Conference, March 17–20, 1996. Call Conference Support Systems (603) 942-8189. Tapes available from Audio Cassette Taping Service (800) 642-2287.

Cook, J. "Tackling Large-Scale Change." *Human Resource Executive,* 44–46 (May 1997).

Daft, R., and R. H. Lengel. *Fusion Leadership.* Publishers Group, 1998.

Dannemiller, K. "Team Building at a Macro Level, or 'Ben Gay' for Arthritic Organizations." In *Team Building: Blueprints for Productivity and Satisfaction.* W. B. Reddy and K. Jamison, eds. Alexandria, VA: NTL Institute, 1988.

Dannemiller, K. D., et al. *Whole-Scale Change Toolkit,* San Fransisco: Berrett-Koehler, 2000.

Dannemiller, K., and R. Jacobs. "Changing the Way Organizations Change: A Revolution of Common Sense." *Journal of Applied Behavioral Science,* vol. 28, no. 4, 480–498 (December 1992).

———. "Large Scale Organizational Change: A Conversation with Kathie Dannemiller and Robert Jacobs." Audio tape. Ann Arbor, MI: Dannemiller Tyson Associates.

Dannemiller, K., and M. Eggers. "One Brain and One Heart: Unleashing the Magic in Organizations." *CBODN Channelmarker* (May 1999).

Filipczak, B. "Critical Mass: Putting Whole-Systems Thinking into Practice." *Training* (September 1995). Minneapolis: Lakewood Publications.

Fox, J. "Going Into Circles." *Amtrak Express,* 8–10 (1995).

Jacobs, R. W. *Real Time Strategic Change: How to Involve an Entire Organization in Fast and Far-Reaching Change.* San Francisco: Berrett-Koehler, 1994.

Kaschub, W. "PECO Energy Redesigns HR." *HRFocus* (March 1997). American Management Association.

———. "Employees Redesign HR." *Human Resource Professional* (July/August 1997). Horsham, PA: LRP Publications.

Litsikas, M. "Clorox Benefits from New Culture." *Quality* (June 1995). Chilton Publications.

Loup, R. "Real-Time Strategic Change Technology: Speeding Up System-Wide Change." In *Practicing Organization Development.* W. J. Rothwell, R. Sullivan, and G. McLean, eds. San Diego, CA: Pfeiffer and Company. appendix IV, 595–607, 1995.

Maurer, R. *Beyond the Wall of Resistance: Unconventional Strategies that Build Support for Change.* Austin: Bard Press, 1996.

McCallum, T. "Vision 2000: Staying Ahead of the Competition." *Human Resources Professional* (1996). Horsham, PA: LRP Publications.

Modic, L. "Changing the Process, Improving the Productivity." *Engineer's Digest* (April 1995).

Nicholas, G. "Vision Quest." *Credit Union Management* (July 1995). Credit Union Executives Society.

Pasmore, W., and P. D. Tolchinsky. "Doing It Right from the Start." *The Journal for Quality and Participation* (December 1989). Association for Quality and Participation.

"Richmond Savings Follows Unified Vision." *Credit Union News* (June 1995).

Shadovitz, D. "Power in Numbers." *Human Resource Executive* (May 1995).

Tolchinsky, P. "Flying Solo: Consultants' Process Has Become a Way of Life at United." Ann Arbor, MI: Dannemiller Tyson Association.

———. "Still on a Winning Streak." *Workforce* (September 1997).

———. "Working From the Bottom Up at Clorox and Corning Plants." *AIPE Facilities* (July/August 1995).

Tolchinsky, P., and M. Johnson. "A Redesign in the Central Intelligence Agency," *The Journal for Quality and Participation* (March/April 1999). Association for Quality and Participation: 31–35.

World Wide Web Links

Dannemiller Tyson Associates home page:

http://www.dannemillertyson.com

Further readings about Whole-Scale:

http://www.dannemillertyson.com/wholescale.html

Find out what is coming up on our calendar that can help you:

http://www.dannemillertyson.com/upcoming.html

Not finding what you need? Please let us know what you'd like to see:

http://www.dannemillertyson.com/feedback.html

Future Before You Plan

by Ronald Lippitt, Professor Emeritus, University of Michigan
(with the assistance of Edward Lindaman)

Note from the author: My colleague, Ed Lindaman, died in China in August 1982. As a full-time futurist he was my mentor and inspiration. The presentation in this chapter is derived from a book in progress, which we were co-authoring. As published in Interactive Strategic Planning *by Dannemiller Tyson Associates.*

For the past five years I have been discovering how important and different an activity futuring is as a prelude and adjunct to strategic planning or MBO or other approaches to long- and short-range goal setting. I'd like to report some of my discoveries and the designs which have emerged as organization development strategies.

Images of Potential versus a Problem-Pain Focus

Twelve years ago a team of graduate students, in a social research methods course, made a study of about twenty-five problem-solving planning and goal-setting groups, such as agency boards and staff goal-setting sessions. The sessions were tape recorded. The analysis indicated that such groups usually began with some type of inventory of problems, sometimes called a problem census. The coding of the tapes from these sessions revealed an increase of depression in voices from one fifteen-minute interval to the next.

A second finding was an increase in the frequency of statements of attribution of the causation of problems to sources outside the control of the group, which was interpreted as mobilizing a rationale for rejecting problem-solving responsibility. A third finding was an increase in the frequency of words and phrases indicating feelings of impotence, futility, and frustration. When the decisions, goals, and plans of the groups were assessed, they seemed to indicate short-term, symptom-oriented goals aimed at getting away from pain rather than moving toward positive future-oriented goals.

These findings led three of us (1) to begin experimenting with what we called "image of potentiality" exercises. To quote from our work at that time, "The motivations and perspectives generated by getting away from pain are not likely to contain the creativity or to generate the energy that derives from aspirations generated by images of concrete feasible steps toward desirable goals. Images of potential are not only strong initial sources of direction and motivation, but they also provide the basis for continuous feedback, motivation, and renewal. The excitement and rationality of taking initiative toward the future must replace the anxiety associated with reactive coping with confrontation." (1, p. 4)

Working with many clients—school boards, agency staffs, company management, families, and individuals—I affirmed many times the validity of this observation. But I had a growing concern about the quality of the imagination revealed in some of the imagery. Then I met the futurists.

The Development of Futurism

Three years ago I found myself on the long-range planning task force of the National Council of the YMCA. It was chaired by a full-time professional futurist, Edward Lindaman. Twenty years earlier he had joined the new offbeat World Future Society. He was soon to become director of planning of the Apollo mission to the moon. Let me quote a brief historical statement from Ed Lindaman. (2, pp. 3, 4)

Thinking about the future is increasing rapidly. This is a hopeful sign. The membership of the World Future Society, for example, has grown from a few thousand persons in the late sixties to well over 20,000 persons worldwide. The National Conference of State Legislatures recently held a major conference under the theme "Foresight Activities in State Legislatures." They defined legislative foresight as the function "by which the legislative process anticipates and deals with approaching problems, issues, needs, and opportunities, and by which the potential future impacts of pending or proposed legislation are determined, analyzed, and assessed."

In 1972 Congress established the Office of Technology Assessment to provide early indications of the probable beneficial and adverse impacts of the application of technology, and to develop other coordinate information which may assist Congress. They have already done future-impact studies in the fields of energy, the ocean, health, transportation, and world trade.

In 1976 a group of eleven members of Congress created an organization entitled "The Congressional Clearing House on the Future." Now more than two hundred congressmen and their staff members meet monthly to discuss issues that affect the future. The organization is for the purpose of assisting members of Congress to become more aware of the ways in which the future is affected by today's decisions.

Many states have futures programs, including: Hawaii 2000, Goals for Georgia, Idaho Tomorrow, Alternatives for Washington 1985, California Tomorrow, and many others. Major universities now offer extensive courses, even degrees, in futuring. The World Future Society recently published a book entitled *The Future: A Guide to Information Sources.* It has 600 pages!

On the way to the moon the Apollo astronauts made tiny "mid-course corrections" that enabled them to land at an exact predetermined spot on the moon. The corrections were small, but because the moon was far away they made a big difference. It is like that with us. Some of the changes we make in society, in our lives, or in our organizations seem insignificant, but over the years they can have a major impact.

Where We Get Our Data from to Think About the Future

1. In our culture we tend to avoid or neglect reflecting on our past (as a country, community, organization, or self) as a source of perspective in thinking about the future. With many clients we have found a Decades Exercise (1, p. 11) very revealing. The group brainstorms the memory of themes and events of the past by decades, and reflects on the meaning of

those themes—as achievements, mistakes, important values, successful copings, and so forth.

2. A second neglected source of data for future planning is a review of policies and priority goals we have set and have not yet fully actualized.

3. A third more familiar source is input from our assessments and surveys of the needs, expectations, and desires of those we serve as clients, consumers, and markets.

4. A fourth source of data is the review of our own current operations and achievements. Unfortunately, we tend to focus on the problem-pains instead of including the accomplishments we are proud of. To balance this we use a prouds and sorries exercise (1, p. 17) with our clients.

5. A fifth source of data is the policies and goals set by those above us in our systems. These must be related to as we do our own goal setting.

6. A sixth very familiar source is the extrapolations and trend analyses and predictions about the future made by "the extrapolators."

7. A seventh source of input to help us think creatively in the future tense is a scan of the goals and successes of others which we see as comparable or relevant to our situations.

All of these are triggers for our own imagination in projecting our scenarios for the future.

Preferring versus Predicting

In a presentation to the NTL Laboratory on futuring at Bethel in July 1982, Edward Lindaman remarked, "If we could only have used a small proportion of the millions of hours humankind has devoted to trying to predict the future in imagining preferred future options, we would be living in a different world today." Efforts at predicting have been of little value, and lead to a reactive psychology of adapting or fitting in rather than a pro-active posture of "what do we want." In his remarks Lindaman quoted a leading futurist, John McHale, "The question is no longer can we change the world, but rather the question now is, 'What kind of world do we want?'"

In his newsletter, *Future Tense* (3) Lindaman quotes Professor Magoroh Maruyma of Portland State University:

> We are now entering an era of transition of a different nature. It is a transition from a chain of stationary patterns—which the population accepted *as given*— *to a duration of perpetually transforming patterns which depend upon people's will and choice.* It is a transition between types of transitions. This can be called a meta-transition.

Lindaman goes on to say that Professor Maruyma "suggests that this cultural symbiosis (the accelerating interaction of what are sometimes severe opposites—for mutual benefit) demands a totally different educational philosophy."

The Pulitzer Prize–winning biologist, Rene Dubois, who died in February 1982, said in his last essay, "A Celebration of Life":

> Human beings inevitably alter the course of events and make mockery of any attempt to predict the future from an extrapolation of existing trends. In human affairs, the logical future, determined by past and present conditions, is less important than the *willed future,* which is largely brought about by deliberate choices—made by human free will. Our societies have a good chance of remaining prosperous because they are learning to anticipate, long in advance, the shortages and dangers they might experience in the future if they do not take technologically sound preventative measures.

Many have challenged our enthusiasm about future tense thinking. Their personal experiences have caused them to question "whether there is much point in trying to think about the future or plan for the future." They feel, "It just leads to disappointment because things are so unpredictable," or "Forces outside of our control are really calling the shots."

Our experiences with ourselves and with many persons, groups, organizations, and communities confirm the insights of the poet, Bradford Shank, when he observes: (4, p. 30)

> The sleeping person (or group)
> Resembles a Brownian particle
> Tossed about in a meaningless
> And endless dance.
> But the awakened person (or group)
> Like Maxwell's demon
> Chooses among the influences
> Emanating from their environment—
> Admitting those which favor their purposes
> Avoiding those which hinder—
> Thus steering an increasingly
> Self-determined course
> Toward inwardly chosen goals

And later he adds: (p. 41)

> The future holds unpatterned potentialities
> Which are molded into a unified whole
> By all nature.
> The bolder strokes of creation
> Involving vast and enduring masses
> Are fixed for you and me
> But the finer details of the pattern
> Lie within our creative influence.
> And the amplification
> Of small but consistent choices
> Confers the geometrically mounting
> Power of time
> Upon the enlightened choosers.

So the job of Preferred Futuring requires that we examine the data of the past, the present, and the events, trends, and developments (EDTs) going on around in our world, community, organization, and personal lives. Then we use these data to imagine and envision images of the future that we prefer, not limited by presently perceived frontiers, yet triggered by the realities of the present and emerging human technological situation.

Then we take that commitment to preferred and prioritized images and move toward intentional action by preparing a goal-and-action implementation plan that will make optimal use of the human and technical resources of the organization.

Differentiating Futuring and Planning

As we have worked with organization leaders, top managements, and planning teams on the futuring and planning process, we have been impressed with the different psychological postures, group climates, and types of activity designs involved in the freedom of futuring and the discipline of planning. We have asked quite a few groups that have been through the flow of work to list some of the distinctions they can make, from their own experience. Here is an incomplete list of the distinctions they have proposed.

Futuring	Planning	Futuring	Planning
Right brain	Left brain	Images	Goals
Day dream	Decision	Scenarios	Objectives
Predicting	Intending	Expansive	Limited
Wide-angle	Zoom	Prefer	Commit
Prefer	Design	Searching	Defining
Creative	Methodical	Hypothesis	Conclusion
Fluid	Disciplined	Surveying	Mapping
Free-wheeling	Focused	Abstract	Concrete
Visionary	Structured	Sensing	Risking
Unstructured	Structured	Mind	Brain
Field oriented	Linear	Mystic	Engineer
Conjecturing	Deriving	Spontaneity	Discipline
Guessing	Concluding	Explore	Map
Ambiguous	Certain	Direction	Path
Open	Committed	Stretching	Condensing
Non-judgmental	Evaluative	Inclusive	Selective
Qualitative	Quantitative	Forecast	Decide
Comprehensive	Bottom-line	Possible	Feasible
Rainbow	Black-white-gray	Alternatives	Consequence analysis
Intuitive	Systematic		

A Case Example of the Flow of Work from Futuring to Planning

In order to be concrete in the presentation of the model, I have chosen a decentralized human service system. The flow of the process, with small adaptations, is comparable to that which we have utilized in private sector production systems, higher education, communities, local, state, and federal government units, professional associations, and action "cause" groups. Available reports are listed at the end of the case.

Creating a leadership nucleus   A group of key persons ("listened to," "able to get things done") from the horizontal and vertical structure of the system were nominated and invited to participate in a three-hour "What it might be like if" session to explore the model of futuring and planning. The nominators had considered age, sex, and racial mix as well as location in the system and evidence of leadership initiative and respect.

The three-hour session included experiences in retrieving the past; prioritizing "prouds and sorries" about present operations; and a review of a sample of events, trends, and developments in society and in their organization.

Then the group, in heterogeneous tables of six, took a future trip five years ahead. They made observations of things that pleased them (behaviors, policies, attitudes, structures, and so forth), which were results of their five years of work. These observations were in the form of brainstorm callouts, in the present tense, of all the preferred images anyone could imagine and call out. They had to be concrete. They were not predictions or fantasies, but desired possible scenarios.

The thirty persons at five tables created ninety-five images of desired futures. Energy and excitement were high. The newsprint sheets from each table were posted for reading, and each person had ten votes to cast on their top priority images.

The process was then halted. The possibility of using this procedure to involve the units of the organization in futuring was presented and ways were discussed in which this nucleus leadership group could guide the process. This involved plans to generate task forces to work on steps of action toward priority images.

Design for organization futuring   At this first session the nucleus group broke into volunteer task forces to:

- Develop the materials for futuring sessions of organizational units

- Retrieve, edit, prepare the events, developments, and trend materials needed as stimulus for futuring

- Prepare a "where we have come from" and "what we are proud of" statement from interviews with the historians and leaders of the organization

- Train pairs of persons, including nucleus group members, to lead and document the organization futuring sessions

Future kits were prepared and sessions were conducted with organization staff units throughout the geographically decentralized system. The board and top corporate staff were involved in futuring sessions.

Creating integrated scenarios of Preferred Futures   The nucleus group created a special team of five, and two editorial staff writers to read the input of prioritized future images from the forty Future Shop sessions, representing input from more than 1,500 persons. There were many items of agreement in the data from the different sessions. The twenty-five top priority images were selected and one-page scenarios were written of what that image might look like, concretely, if it were achieved or in the process of being achieved.

These scenarios went to the planning staff, executive council, and board to begin work on goal formation, feasibility analysis, priority sequencing, and potential implementation responsibilities.

Decisions on major goal thrusts   A board-staff, two-day workshop worked in small team task forces on converting the Preferred Future scenarios into detailed goal statements, with measurable criteria of achievement and identification of the units in the system that would need to have responsibility for setting and implementing operational goals and designing the steps of action and budget proposals.

The work of the task forces was presented to the total board as five-year goal and budget recommendations: recommendations of procedures for assignment of implementation planning responsibility and for feedback on this reality testing phase, which it was recognized could influence some reformulation of the goal statements.

Operational goal setting and implementation designing   The key point is that all the staff units now involved in making implementation designs and commitments had been involved in futuring sessions, preceded by event-development-trend analysis, including trends in their own part of the system, and review of their own prouds and sorries.

There was no sense that goals were imposed from on high; there was a sense that they had contributed imaginative input based on materials and activities that helped them to be, as Lindaman would say, "at least 10 percent futurists."

The continuous process of progress measurement, scanning, and refuturing   The planning staff of the organization worked on a pilot basis with several units to develop a feasible, doable procedure of stepwise progress analysis and reporting that would help each unit to define its own progress toward achievement of the organization goals. National goal monitors were selected for each goal, to receive, review, and report on progress and to identify outstanding progress to be recognized and celebrated.

An EDT scanning task force had the job of identifying new important trends in the environment or in the organization that should be used as a basis for generating new images of potential and ideas of refuturing.

Some Traps in the Futuring-Planning Process

1. The most serious trap is the limiting of the process to a small team who attempt to "do the planning" for the organization. Not only does this greatly limit the resources of experience and imagination mobilized for future imagery, but it tremendously reduces the level of commitment and motivated energy available to implement the goals.

2. Another trap is to limit the efforts to scan the environment of trends and activities that have major implications for possible futures. The futurist literature is exploding, and the information revolution is generating, for most of us, an overload of data. We must organize our retrieval and analysis efforts and teams.

3. A third trap is to confuse predicting and preferring. Clarification of preferences involves clarification of our values, which often involves confrontation and revision of our organization Mission statements.

4. A fourth trap is to short-circuit the process of priority analysis of preferred images, and the converting of images of potential into concrete well-formulated goal statements.

5. Another trap is to limit right brain creativity during the disciplined process of implementation planning. The diagnostic analysis of alternative ways of achieving the accepted goals often is a rather constricted process of considering "how we have done it." Real mind-stretching brainstorms of alternative action ideas can free up the implementation planning to a productive and creative process.

6. The sixth, very frequent trap, when good action plans have been made, is to neglect the crucial step of rehearsal before planning for keeps in the risky world of action. In our work on "connecting images to action" (1, p. 71; 2, p. 35), we have tried to look at the big gap between goal plans and skillful action.

Summary

I hope this has provided the reader with an orientation and design that complements and supplements the more familiar orientations of strategic and long-range planning. From my experience with clients, these activities are a very motivating and insight-producing intervention. And a whole new world of reading has become part of my personal professional growth program.

References on Futuring to Planning Process

Lindaman, Edward and Ronald Lippitt. *Choosing the Future You Prefer.* Development Publications, 1979.

Schindler-Rainman, Eva and Ronald Lippitt. *Building the Collaborative Community.* Development Publications, 5605 Lamar Road, Washington, D.C. 20016, 1980.

Ypsilanti Area Futures, Inc. *Building Together for the Ypsilanti Area's Future,* part 1 and 2 documentary, Ypsilanti Area Futures, Inc., 11 N. Adams Street, Ypsilanti, MI 48197, 1980.

Text References

1. Fox, Robert, Ronald Lippitt, Eva Schindler-Rainman. *The Humanized Future: Some New Images,* University Associates, Inc. (out of print), 1973.

2. Lindaman, Edward, and Ronald Lippitt. *Choosing the Future You Prefer,* Development Publications, 1979.

3. Lindaman, Edward. *Future Tense* (No. 4), 15822 Pineview Circle, Spokane, WA 99208, Summer 1982.

4. Shank, Bradford. *Fragments—Chrystallized Reflections on the Meaning of Life,* Prentice-Hall (out of print), 1952.

Glossary

Action Learning How we at Dannemiller Tyson Associates view the Action Research approach, wherein organizations and communities continually look at their experiences—What did we said we'd do? What did we actually do? What did we learn from all that?—in order to agree on what we need to do next.

Action Research Both a model and a process. As a process, Action Research is a cycle in which research is followed by change activities, the results (learnings) of which are fed into further research (*Practicing Organization Development*, p. 52, Rothwell, Sullivan, McLean).

Appreciative Inquiry An OD process that grows out of the social constructionist thought and its applications to management and organization transformation. An alternative method to traditional problem solving geared to affirm by asking powerful, positive questions, a thought process where every participant makes a contribution to identify what works and how to do more of what works. Focuses on successes rather than failures (David Cooperrider of Case Western Reserve University).

Breakpoint Points in time in an organization where the rules to be successful change 180 degrees (Land and Jarman).

Chaos Theory Dynamical systems theory or nonlinear or chaos theory is a new mathematical approach that allows scientists to study the behavior of nonlinear systems—systems that, like the weather, move, grow, or change" (*Strategic Thinking and the New Science*, p. 65, Sanders). Explains new understandings of change and disorder, the relationship between order and chaos. These two forces are now understood as mirror images, one containing the other, a continual process where a system can leap into chaos and unpredictability, yet within that state be held within parameters that are well-ordered and predictable (*Leadership and the New Science*, p. 11, Meg Wheatley).

Command and Control   A management style with its roots in military, autocratic beliefs of one person having the wisdom to lead others, "to command" and then "control" the activities to get desired results.

Consultant Team   In this book, usually we are referring to a team of process consultants, at least two in number but may be more, helping the organization to uncover and achieve its aspirations, yearnings, and longings.

Converge/Diverge   The process of moving from small group to large (whole) group in answer to the question *Who should be together in a room in order to successfully move to the next change step?* Based on seminal theory from Lawrence and Lorsch in the Addison Wesley organization development series, the ideas describe a change journey over time that integrates the individual, small groups, and whole system wisdom to appropriately expand the database (diverge) and combine their multiple realities (converge) as fuel for the change journey.

Core Team   A microcosm of people representing every part of the organization, which does homework, as well as develops options and choices to support strategic planning and organizational design for decision making by leadership and critical mass. Does benchmarking and discovery work and brings that knowledge to the critical mass system for their consideration.

Critical Mass   The set of key decision makers and decision influencers necessary for success. The sufficient group necessary to effect change.

Empowerment   To invest with power and authority (dictionary). "The belief that we have some control over our destiny...within each of us is the ability to create an organization of our own choosing" (*The Empowered Manager,* Peter Block).

Event Planning Team   A microcosm of event participants charged with planning Whole-Scale events. (New membership for each event.) Throughout the event they are participants, work with facilitators on emergent design decisions, and stay each evening to read evaluations from the day and review agenda for the next day. They may stay on after the event to help with continuation.

Future Search   A search strategy for whole systems improvement, a method for getting whole systems in one room and focusing on the future. (*Productive Workplaces,* pp. 281–295, Marvin Weisbord, describes the evolution to Conference Model). The Future Search conference is a group method to "evolve a common ground future for an organization or community and develop self-managed plans to move toward it" created by Marvin Weisbord and Sandra Janoff in the early '80s.

Generativity   Having the ability to originate, produce, or procreate *(American Heritage Dictionary)*. Generative relationships are created when two or more people or groups of people with diverse objectives and independent and autonomous responsibilities work together on a common project to improve the performance of all the participants involved (Open Boundaries Sherman & Schultz).

Gestalt   A physical, biological, psychological, or symbolic configuration or pattern of elements so unified as a whole that its properties cannot be derived from a simple summation of its parts.
Gestalt psychology holds that psychological, physiological, and behavioral phenomena are irreducible experiential configurations not derivable from a simple summation of perceptual elements such as sensation and response (dictionary).

Holistic Jobs   Emphasizes the importance of designing wholeness (task, person) into work and the interdependency with others' work.

Large-Scale Interactive Change, Large-Scale Interventions   Refers to large systems, large-group change methodologies that are participative.

Living Systems Theory   *See* Open Systems.

Logistics Team   The group of people responsible for all the behind-the-scenes support that makes each Whole-Scale event a seamless experience for participants.

Max-Mix   A maximum mixture of any group. A way to seat, or cluster, participants in a meeting where each grouping is a maximum mixture (a microcosm) of the whole group.

Microcosm   The dictionary defines *microcosm* as the small representative system having analogies to a larger system in constitution, configuration, or development. In Whole-Scale we see microcosm as the DNA of a system, with all its "voices," attitudes, levels, areas (functions as well as geographies), etc.

New Sciences   New ways of thinking and seeing that are emerging from the scientific communities in the 1990s explorations to understand chaos, complexity, and change. For scientists, the new science describes the orderly yet complicated and unpredictable behavior of nonlinear systems, like the ones in which we live and work. At the heart of the new sciences is the discovery that beneath what appears to be disorder there is order—a type of self-organizing pattern, shape, or structure that emerges . . . (*Strategic Thinking and the New Science,* Sanders).

Open Human Systems: Open Systems, Living Systems   An open system is an arrangement of interrelated parts interacting with its environment. The basic premise of Open Systems Theory is that organizations have common characteristics with all other living systems; from microscopic organisms, to plants, to animals, to humans. All living systems are also classified as open systems. Von Bertalanffy (Austrian biologist) worked in the 1950s about expanding approaches that focused on individual pieces to focus on the relationship of all the pieces as they interact together, became known as General Systems Theory. It led to the classification of different types of systems from mechanical and static systems to living systems. Open Systems Theory is the framework that emerged from General Systems Theory (*Designing Organizations for High Performance,* Hanna).

Organization   In this book when we refer to "organization" we mean all those systems where people come together in communities (at work or at home) to accomplish something meaningful (like helping the community or producing a product).

Organization Design   The set of activities necessary to determine the strategic direction and implementation needed to assure the organization's fundamental Purpose, Mission, Guiding Principles, Vision of Success, Strategic Objectives, and Strategic Thrust; and includes process and work design.

Paradigm Shift   Changing the way of thinking, perceiving, and understanding the world in such a way that we can't go back to our original view.

Pathfinders   Pioneers in change, whose explorations later become "change theories and methodologies."

Pattern of Success   The repeatable ways of doing business, organizing, developing and deploying resources, sharing information, and implementing strategy to create value.

Process Consultation Model   The ability of an organization to diagnose its own situation and develop appropriate responses to implement. Helping the organization help itself is the objective of the process consultant.

Process Design   The set of activities necessary to determine and plan the network of processes, process action steps, and systems to achieve the organization's goals.

Reengineering   The methodology for creating the organization's business processes. Historically has not included work design and/or socio-technical systems (STS).

Silver Bullets   Rare opportunities. A metaphor for a tool, technique, or practice that produces predictable and 100 percent successful results.

Steering Committee   The set of people charged with oversight of the change effort. May be synonymous with the Leadership Team, involving management and union. The Steering Committee sanctions, resources, guides, and oversees the effort. They see what needs to be different, tied to strategy, so the change is concrete and measurable.

STS (Socio-Technical Systems)   A methodology for work design. Traditionally, STS uses a Design Team to make organizational design decisions. It is derived from the early 1950s' work to study how business results were influenced by both social factors (interaction, support, supervision, etc.) and technical factors (equipment, materials, etc.). This methodology was developed at London's Tavistock Institute of Human Relations, headed by Fred Emery and Eric Trist.

Whole-Scale Change   The process of uncovering and achieving the organization's aspirations, yearnings, and longings using the principles of whole system thinking and execution by involving and engaging a critical mass, if not the entire organization.

Work Design   The process by which we determine work boundaries (individual job and team), organizational structure, role definitions, relationships, and distribution of power.

Index

About
Dannemiller Tyson
Associates

For twenty years Dannemiller Tyson Associates (DTA) has pioneered large-group processes that unleash true empowerment within organizations and communities, resulting in rapid, significant, and lasting organizational change. We are passionate advocates for whole system. We, ourselves, are a virtual company, operating around the globe with one-brain and one-heart to help our clients be successful in their environments. Together with our clients, we focus on expanding the boundaries of whole system approaches to change.

Our passion is to share with others the work we have created and what we continue to learn on our journey. In this book we cover what we are learning about whole systems change; describe the underlying theory, foundations, and history of Whole-Scale Change; and take you on the adventures we have shared with organizations and communities around the world. In the companion book, *Whole-Scale Change Toolkit*, we look at the way we make the change journey happen and give you tips on how to design Whole-Scale events as accelerators in that journey.

You can reach us, Dannemiller Tyson Associates, at

www.dannemillertyson.com

About the Authors

Jeff Belanger is an organization development practitioner. At the core of his work is attention to the system as a whole while focusing on specific organizational challenges. He specializes in coaching leadership teams for alignment and large-scale event design and facilitation.

Albert B. Blixt came to whole system change work in the mid-1990s after multiple careers as a professor, attorney, art gallery owner, and co-founder of a successful advertising agency. His practice focuses primarily on leadership development, strategic planning, culture change, and team-based work redesign for business, government, and nonprofit clients. He enjoys the challenge of pushing the boundaries of the Whole-Scale approach to find new ways of engaging people in the change process. Al is the author of numerous articles on organizational change and other business subjects. He is the co-author of the 1996 book *Navigating in a Sea of Change* and a frequent public speaker. He holds a Juris Doctor degree from the University of Michigan.

Kathryn Church designs and facilitates group processes, including real time strategic change, strategic planning, team building, multiple-party disputes, and workplace conflict. She is particularly interested in dispute systems design and is currently working with an organization of 850,000 employees, facilitating their dispute system design. Kathy also conducts on-site interventions to assist management, employees, and dislocated employees deal with the trauma of involuntary reduction-in-force (RIF), reorganizations, and workplace conflict. She is qualified in the Myers-Briggs Type Indicator and often uses "type" to enhance team performance or resolve workgroup conflicts.

Kathleen D. Dannemiller is the founding partner in Dannemiller Tyson Associates and co-inventor of the Real Time Strategic Change and Real Time Work Design (now called Whole-Scale). Kathie has been a passionate advocate of empowerment, systems theory, and whole system change for more than thirty years. She has been a consultant, coach, and mentor to countless leaders, consultants, and organizations as they build a better future. Kathie is recognized worldwide for her ability to move entire organizations forward with speed, depth, and spirit. She believes that there is no conversation that is above or beneath anyone and that everyone needs to have a voice, a real voice, in shaping their future. She has been a political organizer at the national, state, and local levels as well as a community organizer. She is a member of the National Training Laboratory and the National Organization Development Network.

Mary Eggers is a designer/facilitator of the Whole-Scale Change process and of Developing Whole-Scale Change Competencies workshops. What excites her most is the opportunity to work in partnership to tap the spirit of individuals and organizations. This happens by involving everyone, empowering them to participate in meaningful ways and giving them a voice in creating and implementing their organizations' Preferred Future. Mary has been in the field of organization development since 1985 and has experience in health care, education, government, information technology, not-for-profits, and manufacturing. She has an M.S. degree in organization development from the American University/National Training Laboratories. She is a member of the National Organization Development Network; the Chesapeake Bay Organization Development Network; Women in Technology; and the Strategic Leadership Forum, Washington, D.C., chapter.

Allen B. Gates has extensive history as an executive leading and managing organizations using Whole-Scale Change. He was a Ford Aerospace executive in the early 1980s, when large-scale, interactive change, the progenitor of

Whole-Scale, was invented by DTA. During the next fifteen years, he led various change efforts, accomplishing dramatic and rapid results. He spent part of 1995 and 1996 as a DTA partner before returning to an executive role; he rejoined DTA as a partner in late 1998. Allen worked for the U.S. Navy at China Lake, California, as an engineer, line manager, and program manager. After leaving China Lake, he worked in senior executive positions at Ford Aerospace, Computing Devices International, and General Dynamics Information Systems, and was president of Kaiser Electronics. He holds B.S.M.E. and M.S.M.E. degrees from the University of Nevada, Reno; a Ph.D. degree in systems engineering from Case-Western Reserve University (Navy Fellow); and an S.M. in Mgt. degree from MIT (Sloan Fellow).

Leigh M. Hennen is a seasoned professional with twenty-eight years of broad experience in all aspects of human resource management and leadership, organization development, strategic planning, whole systems change, and employee and marketing communications. The first twenty-six years of Leigh's experience included management and executive roles in the disk drive design and manufacturing industry; the aerospace electronics design, manufacturing, and systems integration industry; and the information services industry. Leigh also had two years of experience as an independent organization development and change management consultant prior to joining DTA as a partner. International experience includes a three-year expatriate assignment in the United Kingdom and a one-year assignment in Canada. Leigh's practice has primarily involved integration of mergers and acquisitions, strategic planning, organizational alignment, and culture change. Leigh is a member of the National Organization Development Network, the Society for Human Resource Management, the International Society for Human Resource Management, and the American Compensation Association.

Sylvia James has worked as an internal and external consultant for twenty-five years, pioneering Whole-Scale processes in aerospace in the early 1980s. She works with communities and organizations to bring about a variety of whole system change efforts in high-tech, service, manufacturing, government, and education systems in North America and globally. She has extensive experience designing and facilitating large-group interactive meetings involving more than a thousand participants for strategy, mergers, culture change, and organizational design. She has presented at conferences and led workshops on Whole-Scale processes in North America, Europe, the United Kingdom, and Australia. Since the mid-1990s, she has specialized her practice in applying the Whole-Scale approach to organizational and work design, helping organizations make rapid, sustained change in up to eleven core processes simultaneously, while creating a culture and structure that enable results and agility. Sylvia's recent focus is on creating one-brain, one-heart in virtual environments.

Henry Johnson has been involved directly and indirectly with OD technology for more than twenty-five years, most recently focusing primarily on Whole-Scale Change. He has spent the majority of his adult life in organizations that make a difference and sees his work with DTA as an extension of those efforts. His strengths are in Whole-Scale Change technology related to organizational alignment, strategic planning, diversity training, and culture change. He has a special interest in working with educational systems and transformation initiatives in urban areas. He retired from the University of Michigan as vice president emeritus for student affairs and community relations and has served as trustee of the Ann Arbor Public Schools. Henry is a graduate of Morehouse College and Atlanta University. He holds certificates of postgraduate study from the Menninger Clinic in Topeka, Kansas, and from the Institute for Educational Management at Harvard University.

Lorri E. Johnson has experience in the application of Whole-Scale methodology that includes strategic planning, work redesign, and culture change. She has consulted in a wide range of industries, such as automotive, manufacturing, health care, and information technology. Her interests include the use of Whole-Scale in government, community transformation, and the not-for-profit sector. In addition to the design and facilitation of large-scale interactive processes, her practice includes all phases of Whole-Scale, from leadership alignment through implementation. She is a faculty member of the Association for Quality and Participation at the School for Managing and

Leading Change. Lorri's background includes fourteen years' experience with Xerox Corporation and Bell & Howell in the areas of human resources, sales, and marketing.

Stas' Kazmierski spent fifteen years as an internal consultant at Ford Motor Company, creating high-performing teams, training and coaching team leaders, engineering program managers, and redesigning Ford's product engineering process. He led the design of cross-functional, co-located vehicle platform teams for vehicle engineering and development. In the past nine years, as an external consultant, he has consulted in health care, manufacturing, mining and petroleum, energy, scientific research, universities, retail food, government, and not-for-profit organizations. He holds B.S. and M.A. degrees in education and has done graduate work in chemistry and physics. His current interest is in creating strategically based, rapid, sustainable change in large organizations and helping create organizational and process designs that support humane workplaces.

Ron Koller is an organization consultant, trainer, and coach working to unlock human potential in the workplace. He specializes in working with frontline employees and middle managers as they participate in whole system change. Ron's consulting clients range from small business, construction, automotive, and organized labor to high tech, aerospace, and chemical. His future work will take him to the sports and entertainment industries.

Roland Loup has been a consultant since 1986, using Whole-Scale Change in high-tech companies, health care, manufacturing, the service industry, government, and academia. He also designs and leads courses in Whole-Scale Change. Through his efforts in international training, consulting, and coaching, he is working to ensure that the Whole-Scale approach is used throughout the world. His consulting and courses have benefited organizations in the United States, Canada, Europe, India, and Australia. As a Whole-Scale practitioner, he specializes in the architecture of systemwide change efforts, coaching individual leaders and leadership teams, and the design and facilitation of large-group events. Over the past few years, he has begun applying the Whole-Scale approach to mergers and acquisitions. Roland is co-author of *Real Time Strategic Change: A Consultant Guide to Large-Scale Meetings.*

Jim McNeil is a nationally recognized labor leader, who brings a unique perspective and passion to the work of developing and improving labor/ management relations. As a consultant and trainer, he specializes in organizational change. His background and hands-on experience with workplace change efforts and study of organization development theory and practice provide a unique grasp of the issues that confront today's workers and employers. Jim is a retired three-term president of one of America's largest local unions. He has successfully negotiated numerous collective bargaining agreements with dozens of employers and was chairman of United Auto Worker's national negotiating committee at Ford in 1993 and 1996, where industrywide patterns were developed.

Paul D. Tolchinsky has been consulting with major companies in North America for the past twenty-five years. He has extensive experience in managing and facilitating large-system change efforts, designing new plants and start-ups, and redesigning existing manufacturing facilities, particularly where unions are involved. He has also led numerous study missions to Japan. Paul's particular expertise is in the design of organizations, applying socio-technical principles and Whole-Scale approaches to the process. He is internationally known as a pioneer in the development of Whole-Scale (whole system) approaches to change. The author of numerous articles, his work is featured in *Large Group Interventions* (Bunker and Alban, 1997) and *Fusion Leadership* (Daft and Lengel, 1998). He is listed in *Who's Who in Science and Technology* and *Who's Who in the Midwest.* Dr. Tolchinsky received a B.A. degree in business administration from Bowling Green State University and a Ph.D. in organization behavior and design from Purdue University.